An Alliance Against Babylon

An Alliance Against Babylon
The U.S., Israel, and Iraq

John K. Cooley

Pluto Press
London • Ann Arbor, MI

First published 2005 by Pluto Press
345 Archway Road, London N6 5AA
and 839 Greene Street, Ann Arbor, MI 48106

www.plutobooks.com

British Library Cataloguing in Publication Data
A catalogue record for this book is available from the British Library

ISBN 0 7453 2282 4 hardback

Library of Congress Cataloging-in-Publication Data applied for

10 9 8 7 6 5 4 3 2 1

Designed and produced for Pluto Press by
Curran Publishing Services, Norwich
Printed and bound in Canada by Transcontinental

To Vania Katelani Cooley and Dr. Alexander Cooley

Contents

Foreword

John K. Cooley is a newspaperman's newspaperman. He is the sort of person newcomers always seek out when they arrive for the first time in the Middle East to cover some major story. He has been there, seen that, knows who did what to whom, when, and how. And he has been doing these things since the 1950s. His 40-plus years in the Middle East and North Africa is almost unique among American journalists. And he has dealt with issues, in dispatches and broadcasts without number, and in acclaimed books from Morocco to Afghanistan. The range of his books is quite remarkable and each one singled out a major topic for treatment.

He began with *Baal, Christ and Mohammed: Religion and Revolution in North Africa*. His eye moved south to recount the rise of Chinese influence in Black Africa in *East Wind Over Africa: Red China's African Offensive*. In *Green March, Black September: The Story of the Palestinian Arabs* he came to grips with the history, culture, and plight of the Palestinian Arabs and explained why they felt they had to turn to "the weapon of the weak," terrorism. Back to the Mediterranean and Africa, he sought to comprehend the most enigmatic of all the Middle Eastern leaders, Muammar Qaddafi, in *Libyan Sandstorm: The Complete Account of Qaddafi's Revolution*.

Dealing with terrorism took him to the Afghan story, the fight of that colorful mountain people against the Russians, then against themselves and finally against the Americans. Their involvement with guerrilla warfare, heavily subsidized by the United States as a part of its strategy during the Cold War, led the Islamic militants among them to associate themselves with Osama bin Laden. This is the subject of Mr. Cooley's *Unholy Wars: Afghanistan, America and International Terrorism*, now in three editions and eight languages. The final edition is a revision published after the 9/11 terrorist attacks on the United States.

Publishing the results of his intensive (and often intrusive) research has not always been easy. One of his most fascinating accounts, a study of the international market in counterfeit American hundred dollar bills and a history of currency counterfeiting as a political weapon since ancient times seems to have been too sensitive for the public to read. Mr. Cooley never let such issues guide his reporting: he went "where the story was," and reported it as fairly and intelligently as he knew how.

I first met Mr. Cooley when he became a fellow of the Council on Foreign Relations in 1964–65. He had just returned to his native New York from a hitch in North Africa, where he wrote his book on why Christianity failed there and was superseded by Islam because Christianity was seen as associated with European colonialism. He and I both participated in one of the Council's study groups to which he was introduced as a sort of "pioneer" for what became the prestigious Edward R. Murrow foreign correspondent fellowships. I had recently left the government where I had been in charge of planning American policy in the Middle East and I had spent a troubling period as head of the "task force" on the Algerian war of national independence so I found his observations of particular interest.

I was then deeply involved with establishing the Middle Eastern Studies Center at the University of Chicago and creating the Adlai Stevenson Institute of International Affairs, I did not see him again for several years. Meanwhile, he had begun the study that would take him deep into the Palestinian uprising and on to Libyan affairs. But our paths again crossed in Lebanon where he was the Middle East correspondent for the *Christian Science Monitor*. Again we parted, he to become an ABC News correspondent out of London and I to live in Egypt. We met again over in Iraq where in 1987, we met a number of Ba'ath party officials and got an early view of the events he describes in this book.

This account of the tragic events and historical background of the Iraq war is his latest foray into the psychological and political minefield of the Middle East. There is much to be learned in it. Even more, to be savored and reflected upon. As will immediately become evident, it is a close-up view, derived from personal observation, lengthy interviews and much wise reflection. I hope it finds a wide audience.

William R. Polk

(Dr. William Roe Polk taught Arab history and Middle East affairs at Harvard University and the University of Chicago. He advised Presidents John F. Kennedy and Lyndon B. Johnson on Middle East affairs. In 2004 he became senior director of the Carey Foundation, funding educational and developmental projects in various parts of the world. His latest book, *Understanding Iraq*, is being published by Harper-Collins in 2005.)

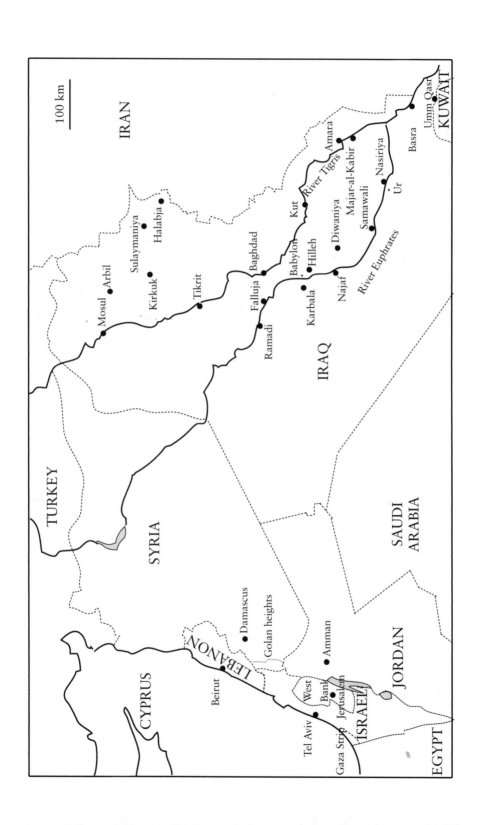

In the winter [416–15 BC] the Athenians resolved to set sail again against Sicily with larger forces…. They were for the most part ignorant of the size of the island and its inhabitants, both Hellenic and native, and they did not realize that they were taking on a war of almost the same magnitude as their war against the Peleponnesians…. Nicias had not wanted to be chosen for the command; his view was that the city was making a mistake, and on a slight pretext which looked reasonable, was in fact intending to conquer the whole of Sicily—a very considerable undertaking. So he came forward to speak, hoping to make the Athenians change their minds: "…I think that we ought not to give such hasty consideration to so important a matter and on the credit of foreigners get drawn into a war that does not concern us. … [T]his is the wrong time for such adventures and the objects of your ambition [gold, treasure and military bases] are not to be gained easily. …"

"[E]ven if we did conquer the Sicilians, there are so many of them and they live so far off that it would be very difficult to govern them…. The right thing is that we should spend our new gains at home and on ourselves instead of on these exiles who are begging for assistance and whose interest it is to tell lies and make us believe them … who leave all the dangers to others and, if they are successful, will not be properly grateful, while if they fail in any way they will involved their friends in their own ruin. …" When the news reached Athens [of defeat], for a long time people would not believe it. … And when they did recognize the facts, they turned against the public speakers who had favored the expedition … and also became angry with the prophets and soothsayers and all who had, by various methods of divination, encouraged them to believe that they would conquer Sicily.

Thucydides, ***The Peloponnesian War, Books VII and VIII***

Introduction

The living, thinking, research, and finally the writing processes that produce a book are not unlike the natural processes involved in the growth and the flowering of a tree. After more than 40 years of covering the daily life, the dramas, and the wars and revolutions of North Africa and the Middle East, it seems to me that the seeds and certainly the roots that sprang from them, finally grew this book.

In retrospect, it was fortune and chance, rather than plans or intentions, that in the 1950s, following U.S. military and government service in Europe after World War II, first set me down in part of the Arab world, North Africa during the dying years of French colonialism there. Seeking a complete change from a junior State Department job in the Vienna of Graham Greene's and Carol Reed's *The Third Man,* in 1953 still a city divided like Berlin between four "liberating" powers, the United States, the USSR, Britain, and France, I migrated during the Korean War to a job with a construction company, building U.S. strategic air bases in Morocco to "deter" the Soviet Union. Soon the French protectorate in Morocco was engulfed in an Arab nationalist struggle for independence. It spread through Algeria and Tunisia and became a major, eight-year guerrilla and terrorist war, ultimately successful, for Algerian independence.

My first personal experience of terrorism was seeing French and Moroccan Christian, Jewish, and Muslim friends blown up in a Casablanca neighborhood café. I settled into freelance journalism and wrote and broadcast for six years about the quixotic struggle of the French settlers in Algeria to hold on to their century-long domination (and to overthrow or murder the French World War II hero, President Charles de Gaulle, in the process). This struggle paralleled the French army's efforts to recover from their humiliating defeat at Dien Bien Phu and their ensuing retreat from Indo-China in 1954—the year the bloody insurrection in Algeria began. During the years that followed, most of my friends and colleagues were reporting either the long-drawn-out American debacle in Vietnam which followed the French retreat, or the last throes of Belgian, French, and well-meaning but inept UN

1

colonialism in the Congo and neighboring regions of Black Africa. Unlike those colleagues, I stayed on to witness and cover the last convulsions of the Algerian drama and its aftermath in North Africa and Europe.

While in New York as a fellow with the Council On Foreign Relations in 1964–65, writing my first books, I began to understand how any important event occurring in the space from Morocco's Atlantic coast eastward to the deserts and mountains of Afghanistan reverberates and affects the whole region and often beyond.

The large and ancient Jewish communities in Tunisia, Algeria, the former Italian colony of Libya, and especially in Morocco were profoundly affected by the North African wars for independence, and by the creation of the new state of Israel in the formerly Ottoman and British-ruled territory of Palestine in 1948. One consequence was a gradual Jewish exodus from North Africa. However, only in Libya did the Jews, along with the more recent Italian settlers implanted there by Mussolini's conquering armies, suffer major forced dispossession and displacement, and then only after Muammar Qaddafi's overthrow of the Senoussi monarchy in 1969.

By the time I took up my first major newspaper staff job as the *Christian Science Monitor* Middle East correspondent in Beirut in 1965, Egypt's military leader since 1952, President Gamal Abdel Nasser, had fired the imaginations and aspirations of most of the Arabs, from Morocco to Iraq. The reverberation of the tough but ultimately successful Algerian war for independence profoundly influenced and motivated Yassir Arafat and his generation of Palestinians, determined to recover the homeland they deemed lost in what the Arab world still calls *an-naqba*, or The Disaster: their flight and displacement at the hands of the victorious new state of Israel in 1948–49. During the period from 1967 to the 1980s, I met and interviewed Arafat (and many of his companions) numerous times, and so was a witness to his war-making, his peace-making, and his eventual decline. A book I published in 1973, *Green March, Black September,* was one of the first in the West to record many facets of the Palestinian people, their aspirations, and their woes.

From my Beirut base in 1965–78 (punctuated by a strategic retreat to Athens with my Greek wife in 1976–78, occasioned by the fratricidal and most uncivil Lebanese conflict, when our neighborhood and our four-year-old son's nursery school came literally under fire), I traveled and reported throughout the Arab world, from Morocco to Yemen and sometimes to Iran, Turkey, and Pakistan. It was clear to me then, as it had been during my early years in North Africa, that the Palestine–Israel conflict was central in the minds, the hopes and the aspirations, both noble and ignoble, of Muslims (and the native Arab Christians) everywhere. In my trips to the Persian Gulf area, Iran, and the Iraq of both the Saddam Hussein era and earlier, it became growingly apparent that Palestine–Israel was *the* problem that most obsessed the locals. I joined ABC News in 1981, and during the 1980s and 1990s I worked as an investigative and radio correspondent for ABC in the area. I found always the same obsession with Israel and Palestine that I had observed earlier in the Maghreb countries. There was an important Palestinian backdrop to the 1991 U.S.-led Allied war to expel Iraqi dictator Saddam Hussein from his seizure of Kuwait's oil, as the present book will show.

The American invasion and occupation of Iraq that began in March of 2003 was the stimulus to the final flowering, if I can revert to the tree analogy, of this book, with its roots in the past. Following the relatively easy military conquest of the U.S.-led coalition in Iraq in 2003, the ill-planned occupation went tragically wrong. The sullying of America's often self-righteous claims to be a world-class defender of human rights, in the scandalous photographic revelations of abuse, torture, and even murder of Iraqi prisoners and detainees by U.S. troops in Iraq, provided the worst possible prologue to the putative transfer of "sovereignty" on July 1, 2004, to an Iraq facing potentially fatal political, economic, and social divisions.

From the beginning of the ill-starred U.S. adventure in Iraq, it was clear that the war was launched and continued (and later prolonged as a classic colonial-type struggle against guerrilla resistance) for the wrong reasons. They were chiefly the presumptions, based on incomplete, false, or even fabricated intelligence about evidently non-existent (or no longer existent) weapons of mass destruction, and the Bush administration's conflation (deliberately confusing American public opinion) of Saddam Hussein's Iraq and Osama bin Laden's Al-Qaeda network, the origins of which I explained in three successive editions of my earlier book, *Unholy Wars: Afghanistan, America and International Terrorism* (1999–2002). The chimerical dream of Bush's neoconservative advisors of deconstructing and then reconstructing not only Iraq but also its major Arab neighbors, as "democracies" that would normalize relations both with the far-flung new American empire and with Israel, has dissolved in the fog of war and insurrection in contemporary Iraq.

Most contemporary examinations of the historical background to the two conflicts the United States and its allies, willing or reluctant, have fought against Iraq since 1991, ignore an important factor. This is the role played by Israel, and the relationships, antagonistic and otherwise, of the Jewish people with the people and states of former Mesopotamia, now Iraq, from Old Testament Bible times until now.

Depicting this role is one purpose of this book. Prime Minister Ariel Sharon's government of today's Israel did not, of course, induce its American ally to attack and overthrow Saddam Hussein and occupy his country, nor did he draw America's best ally, Iraq's former colonizer Britain, into the fray. The war was decided solely in Washington, DC, by President George W. Bush and his advisers, well before the catastrophic assaults of September 11, 2001 on the United States by bin Laden's suicide attackers. It was seconded and supported by Prime Minister Tony Blair and his New Labour government in London. However, many friends and partisans of Israel, especially the large Christian Evangelical and fundamentalist movement in the United States, and a small clique of advisers inside Washington's power structure, unquestionably helped to inspire the idea of "regime change" in Iraq, and the other, even more dubious projects for refashioning the Arab and Muslim regions in the future.

Since the twentieth century's two World Wars fundamentally changed the Middle East, composed mostly of post-colonial Arab states and non-Arab Muslim ones like Turkey and Iran, and the one post-colonial Jewish state of Israel, the U.S. role in the region has also drastically changed. In 1948 President Harry S. Truman (like Soviet dictator Joseph Stalin, but for totally different reasons) hastened to recognize the newborn Israeli state. However, today's U.S.–Israeli alliance, which in the backwash of Iraq and the failed Israeli–Palestinian peace efforts of the 1990s is antagonizing the entire Muslim world, was slow to develop.

A purpose of this book is to show how U.S. and Israeli interests (such as oil and regional security) in post-colonial Iraq seemed conflicting at first, and how later their gradual convergence did much to cement the U.S.–Israeli alliance of today. This alliance has solidified around two closely related issues: 40 years of Israeli occupation and settlement of Palestinian territory and rule over Palestinian Arabs, and what by the time this book sees print will be nearly three years of military presence in Iraq by the U.S., Britain, and some junior and token partners. A few of these partners, such as Spain and small Hispanic states of Central America, have defected from what the Bush and Blair governments persist in calling the "coalition."

To begin the story of the interaction of postcolonial Western, American, Arab, and Israeli involvements in Iraq's history, Chapter 1 reviews the Biblical and historical story of the Jews' Babylonian Captivity and the cultural heritage of those generations and centuries.

Chapter 2 describes how the Muslims, Jews, and other peoples in the three Turkish provinces of Mesopotamia fared as the old Ottoman Empire was partitioned after World War I, and how they morphed into today's Iraq.

How the founders of the fledgling state of Israel and the earlier Jewish soldiers and intelligence operatives, even before the British abandoned Palestine in 1948, managed to bring out the hundreds of thousands of Iraqi Jews and integrate them in the new state follows in Chapter 3. Mixed feelings of antagonism and affinity that this exodus helped to generate, as well as the pan-Arab sentiments in the Iraqi monarchy, helped to produce Baghdad's first military expedition to join Egypt, Syria, Jordan, and Lebanon in their failed enterprise of 1948–49 to destroy the new Jewish state, are dealt with in Chapter 4.

Chapter 5 treats the motives and modes of the early and persistent Israeli alliance with northern Iraq's Kurds. This saw the growing involvement in the area of the United States, along with another, more temporary ally of the Kurds, Iran's Shah Muhammed Reza Pahlevi, from the 1950s until the mid-1970s. In 1973 Iraq mounted its most ambitious and effective military expedition in the October war with Israel. During the same period, as Chapter 6 relates, Saddam Hussein used the nascent Ba'ath Arab Socialist Party and assistance from the American CIA to fulfill his ambition to become Iraq's absolute dictator.

The attraction of Iraq's huge and growing oil wealth and a consequential major market for investment and sales of consumer goods and arms for U.S. and other Western business interests, and parallel developments in the ruinous Iraq–Iran war of 1980–88, are described in Chapters 7 and 8.

By 1990, an overconfident and bellicose Saddam Hussein felt sufficiently strong to gamble on invading and looting his wealthy neighbor Kuwait, and by so doing to seize a larger share of the world's oil resources. Israel, as described in Chapters 8 and 9, had already used covert warfare to halt Saddam's development of armaments, including his nuclear program. However, without Israeli aid, U.S. President George Herbert Walker Bush in 1990 and 1991 rallied a huge, UN-supported war coalition that forcibly expelled Iraqi forces from Kuwait, but then failed to pursue and destroy them, or to topple Saddam.

Chapters 10 and 11 describe how the U.S. and Israel drew their sinews tighter around Saddam, even as their alliance grew closer. Without having to participate directly in the March 2003 invasion of Iraq, planned even before the 9/11 attacks on the United States and prepared after them, Israelis regarded the war and its aftermath with mixed emotions. Their strategic enemy, Iraq's armed forces, no longer threatened Israel as they had since 1948. However, the dreams of some Israeli leaders of obtaining cheap oil from Iraq had quickly dissolved. The disorder, terrorism, and sociopolitical upheavals generated or exacerbated by the war from Palestine to Pakistan were just as bad news for Jerusalem as for Washington and other world capitals. The re-election of President George W. Bush in November 2004 for another four-year term heightened the foreboding of many critics around the world of the Iraq war and Bush's wider Middle East policies.

It is my hope that this narrative, drawn from my 40-year career covering the Middle East and South Asia, researched from many published and unpublished sources, and helped by journalistic colleagues and my personal encounters with many principal players, such as David Ben-Gurion, the Shah of Iran, Gamal Abdel Nasser, Hafez al-Assad, King Hussein of Jordan and Saddam Hussein, to name a few, may illuminate this large swathe of history.

My gratitude goes to hundreds of publications and people, mostly named in the text and notes; they are far too numerous to list here. I owe much to many; perhaps most of all to my patient companion, colleague, and wife, Vania Katelani Cooley; to our son Alexander, a political scientist at Columbia University; and my daughter, Katherine Anne Cooley, now a news anchorwoman on one of France's premier cable TV channels. Any errors of research or appreciation are, of course, my own.

John K. Cooley
Athens, November 2004

1
The Babylonian Heritage

We were out a little north of Shatrah and we saw some ruins in the desert. The place was pretty much looted, huge holes everywhere. I found a conical stone with inscriptions all around it and that tablet, which was partially buried. The translator told us later it was from around 2000 BC and it was part of a King's temple. I'm pretty ignorant of archaeology. I'm just infantry. All I knew was that it was probably old. It was kind of a big deal that we found these artifacts, but at the same time I was a little ticked off—we were still in Iraq.
(Lance Cpl. Troy Merril, 15th U.S. Marines, Iraq, June 2003)
(New York Times, June 16, 2003)

As a small boy growing up in the 1930s in Mount Vernon, N.Y., a near suburb of the Bronx, Bible stories, including those about Jews and their Middle Eastern adversaries, were not my greatest interest. Both my parents were journalists. They were glued to radio news. We were mesmerized by the gathering storm in Europe. Adolf Hitler had begun to swallow Germany's neighbors, one by one. He was progressively driving Germany's and Europe's Jews toward the climactic Holocaust. My parents ordained weekly Sunday-school sessions until I was almost twelve. The Bible lore ingested at these sessions rarely stayed with me. But the music and the Biblical lyrics of the Paul Robeson vocals my father played on our phonograph did, especially one beginning:

There were three children from the land of Israel
Shadrak, Meshak, Abednego.

In the song, Nebuchadnezzar, the evil king of Babylon, holding the elite of Judah's Jewish population captive in his capital, builds a golden idol and orders the "children" (actually young Judaean princes):

You must fall down and worship the idol
Shadrak, Meshak, Abednego.

When they refused, the Old Testament Book of Daniel tells us, the three were "Cast into the midst of a burning fiery furnace." They were preserved, as any believing Christian or Jew, might tell you, by the divine protection of Jahweh, the one God and their Lord. They emerged without even the smell of fire upon them (3 Daniel:11–25).

In college freshman English, before doing my post-war military service in occupied Europe in 1946–47, I was assigned to study "The Bible as living literature."

ANCESTRAL MEMORIES

The Old Testament glories and iniquities of Assyria and Babylon, and the captivity of the Jews of ancient Israel and Judah, are living history to Jewish and Christian evangelist and fundamentalist scholars and advocates, who play such an important part in Israel's vast ideological and sentimental support structure in the United States. For every hundred American GIs fighting in Iraq since 2003, there have probably been an equal number or more of Zionist-inclined Christian evangelists like Pat Robertson, U.S. congressmen like Republican Tom Delay of Texas, and, yes, President George W. Bush. He saw his global "war on terror" in the Manichean terms of a crusade; a war between Good and Evil.

For anyone trying to make sense out of the modern Middle East, it is always a grave error to ignore ancient history. Reasons why Israel's staunchest supporters in the United States, including some of George Bush's closest advisers, are enthusiastic allies of the rightist and religious politicians and generals in today's Israel are to be found in these ancestral memories. They arise from the mists of ancient Biblical, archaeological and legendary lore—especially the dramas of the ancient Israelites and the Oriental emperors, from King Hammurabi of Babylon to Alexander the Great, who conquered the known world, then died in Babylon in 323 BC. That was two centuries after many of the children of Israel had survived their Babylonian captivity and returned to Palestine under the leadership of their prophets, Ezra and Nehemiah.

Some Israeli supporters and Iraqi-born Israelis have raised astronomical claims for the despoiled property of emigrant Iraqi Jews in modern Iraq. These claims date to the years of Saddam Hussein's despotic rule, but also back to previous Iraqi rulers, since before Israel's creation in 1948. The reviving study of Iraq, of Babylon and Baghdad in ancient history, and especially of Jewish history, helps both to explain and to complicate further the boiling nexus of conflict over Iraq's future.

Ancient Mesopotamia—its name derived from the Greek, "land of the two rivers" (Tigris and Euphrates)—appears in the often surprisingly parallel accounts in the Bible and by historians from Herodotus until today as a "cradle" of our civilization. From the earliest times, whether you accept the theories of orthodox historical evolution, or of the "creationism" that some fundamentalist Christian zealots have revived, Mesopotamia has been closely involved with the Jews and Judaism. According to Genesis, the first book of the Old Testament, the Garden of Eden was located near the torrent that separates to become the Tigris and Euphrates rivers.

The ancient Sumerians, notably in their *Epic of Gilgamesh*, generated their own creationist theories. They told of a great flood, comparable with the Genesis narratives of the Biblical flood, Noah and his ark. That Sumerian creation legend represents natural happenings as resulting not from Divine order, but from strife among the gods. Sumer's Noah, called Utnappishtim, is rescued from the Great Flood through his own physical prowess, rather than because of the moral qualities the Bible attributes to Noah.[1]

The conflicts between the Jews and their adversaries begin in Bible history. Armies of the redoubtable Assyrian empire challenge the power of the Syrians by marching out of Mesopotamia toward Palestine. Since about 950 BC, the Syrians of that epoch had been moving into Assyrian territory in the east, while to the south and west they were fighting the kingdom of Israel. Syria and Israel put aside their quarrel to confront the Assyrian threat. Together they faced the Assyrians and defeated them in a major battle at Qarqar in Syria. Soon the temporary allies, Syria and Israel, were fighting each other again.

CAPTIVES OF BABYLON

In 841 BC the Assyrians went back on the warpath. This time, Israel's King Jehu chose submission rather than alliance with Syria, which withstood the Assyrian attackers for four years. Then a new Assyrian warrior-king, Tiglath-Pileser III (c. 752–742 BC) launched war against King Menahem of Israel. The Syrians vainly tried to renew the old alliance with Israel. Instead, King Ahaz of the other Jewish kingdom, Judah (c. 732–716 BC), called for Assyrian help. Tiglath-Pileser responded by attacking the Syrians and besieging Damascus, already their capital, and capturing it in 732 BC. He then turned on Israel, blocking further aid to the Syrians, and taking the Israelite tribes of Gad and Reuben and the clan of Manssaeh as captives to Mesopotamia (2 Kings 15: 29). When Tiglath-Pileser died, the Jews stopped paying tribute to the Assyrians and struck a secret alliance with Egypt. Assyria reacted by besieging and, after a long siege, capturing Samaria. The remaining ten northern tribes of Israel were taken captive and their kingdom collapsed. The Hebrew prophets called this God's punishment for Israel's idolatry and rejection of covenants with Yahweh (Amos 5: 1–15). History does not record that the ten "lost tribes" of Israel ever returned home.

The aggressive and militaristic Assyrian rulers warred to erase Egyptian influence from Syria and Palestine. King Hezekiah of Judah (about 716–686 BC) played off Egypt and Syria, already adversaries, against one another, making Judah independent of both.

In 701 BC an Assyrian army under King Sennacherib, another notorious Mesopotamian potentate, nearly conquered Jerusalem. Assyria's military hegemony began to crumble, however. Babylon won its freedom from the Assyrian yoke, and from 626 BC a newly independent Babylon began battles that resulted in complete collapse of the once-proud Assyrian empire.

At this point Necho, an Egyptian Pharaoh, enters the scene, attempting to protect his conquests by allying himself temporarily with the remnants of the Assyrian armies. This drew the attention of the Babylonians, who defeated the Egyptians at Carchemish in 605 BC. Judah was temporarily subjugated and had to pay tribute, but its king, Jehoiakim, later rebelled. In 597 BC, strong Babylonian and Chaldean armies overpowered the defenders of Jerusalem and took "3,023 Jews" captive with them back to Mesopotamia. This was the first of three mass deportations of the Jews; the second (587 BC) and third (581 BC) apparently involved 832 and 745 captives, respectively (Jeremiah 52: 29–30). Such was the presumed end of the kingdom of Judah.[2]

One point that present-day scholars of ancient history, whatever their faith, seem to agree upon, is the great power and opulence of King Nebuchadnezzar II 604–562 BC). He kept the Jews captive, using his hostages to aggrandize and enlarge Babylon's size and opulence for most of their 70-year bondage.

About 80 years before Saddam Hussein ordered Nebuchadnezzar's palace in Babylon to be rebuilt as a temple to his own vast ego, the Hollywood impresario of silent films, D. W. Griffith, in 1916 implanted Babylon's image as a center of sinful splendor in American minds with his extravagant classic, *Intolerance*. Featuring a vast and costly reconstruction of Babylon, the spectacle ran for 178 minutes in its most widely seen version. It was shown throughout America and the world in several different prints, some with a running time of 208 minutes. Lillian

Gish, Robert Harron, Mae Marsh and a panoply of stars of the silent silver screen played out four interwoven stories of prejudice and inhumanity (themes already developed to some extent by Griffith in 1915 in his racist Civil War epic, *The Birth of A Nation*). The stories extended from the Babylonian era until the time of World War I.

BABYLON REBUILT?

One of Saddam Hussein's twisted, grandiose visions, during his quarter-century of tyrannical rule, was the rebirth of Babylon, as the high point in 2,500 years of Mesopotamian history. Saddam's vision probably resembled some of Griffith's Hollywood images. What Saddam had in mind was most probably not the ancient Babylon of Hammurabi (circa 1792–1750 BC), who promulgated a detailed legal code. It was rather that of Nebuchadnezzar II. His kingdom extended the Babylonian Empire over most of Western Asia. It survived for only 40 years, during the 70 years prophesied by Isaiah when Babylon held the Jews from Palestine captive. Nebuchadnezzar used their brains and brawn to build and enhance Babylon's temples, ziggurats, and other facets of the city's grandeur. This was the final flowering of Mesopotamian high culture. It was ended by Emperor Cyrus of Persia in 539 BC. The Persian occupation continued during another Persian dynasty, the Achaemenids, until Alexander the Great captured the city in 331 BC.

One day in our own mid-1980s Donny George, the assistant curator of the Baghdad archaeological museum (later looted of many of its priceless treasures shortly after the U.S. Army entered Baghdad in April 2003), was ordered to stand by at the site of ancient Babylon for a visit by the current reigning despot. Saddam Hussein and his security entourage swept into the ruins and confronted him. Saddam ordered George to rebuild one of Nebuchadnezzar's three palaces in time for the first Babylon Arts Festival in 1987.

Probably trembling inwardly, if not outwardly, George gave the dictator a guided tour of what was then left of the ruins. Saddam asked George how the curators knew when the original of the palaces had been built. George showed him an original brick. It was stamped with the name of Nebuchadnezzar II and with the construction date in cuneiform script; about 605 BC. (Such bricks were found by the occupying American and British armies in AD 2003 and by many explorers and archaeologists before them, wherever Nebuchadnezzar's palaces and temples to the supreme Babylonian god, Marduk, had once stood.)

In rebuilding Nebuchadnezzar's palace, Saddam told Donny George, "The name of Saddam Hussein and the date should appear in a similar inscription on the new bricks." It could be dangerous, even mortal, to offer any objection to Saddam, as George reminded his anxious staff. But many archaeologists outside Iraq strongly objected to what they viewed as "Disney for a Despot," in the phrase of Neil MacFarquhar of *The New York Times*. Saddam's proposal violated a sacred principle of scholarship: not to recreate but to preserve ancient monuments.

Publicity for the project resounded throughout Iraq and other parts of the Arab world, especially in newspapers and other media outlets that were getting regular payoffs from Saddam's coffers. The publicity barrage glorified Saddam's orders to revive in contemporary Iraq the splendors of the ancient Babylonian and Assyrian empires. Construction crews worked round the clock in three eight-hour shifts to build the replica to Saddam's designs at lightning speed and a cost of at least $5 million. If you visited Babylon before the 2003 war and looked carefully at the bricks in the wall, you read on many of them the stamped words:

> In the reign of the victorious Saddam Hussein, the President of the Republic, may God keep him, the guardian of the great Iraq and the renovator of its renaissance and the builder of its great civilization, the rebuilding of the great city of Babylon was done in 1987.

Below, lest there could be any mistake, appears the name of Nebuchadnezzar, linking the two (or so probably thought Saddam in his incorrigible egoism) for all time.

The palace was still under construction on a hot and windy, dusty day in 1987 when this author bussed down from a Baghdad under occasional Iranian air attack. (The eight-year Iran–Iraq war, which Saddam had begun by invading the Ayatollah Khomeini's Iran, ended only in 1988.)

Approaching on the main road from Baghdad, I saw only bare mounds of earth. Under a blazing sun, excavation prior to reconstruction was under way. I came suddenly upon a partly hidden, deep-dug Babylonian roadway, Procession Street, where all of the main public buildings were situated in ancient times. The museum on the site shows that the walls on either side were high and beautifully decorated. At the main entrance, there appeared a miniature reconstruction of the original Ishtar Gate, covered with glazed bricks ornamented with figures in relief of bulls and lions. (German archaeologists carted many of the original pieces off to Berlin after 1914; you'd have to make a visit to

Berlin's Pergamon Museum to see them today.) The bulls and lions are replacements for lions and dragon-like monsters on the original façade.

Excavations by Germany's Deutsche Orient Gesellschaft from 1899 to 1917 disclosed on the 2,100-acre site of the ancient city many remains of the late (neo-Babylonian) period. Besides the Ishtar Gate, the Germans dug up Babylonian temples, including Esagila or the temple of Marduk, the supreme god of the period, with its ziggurat, which some scholars believe was the Biblical Tower of Babel. The excavations also unearthed remains of private houses. In northeastern Babylon they found a theater, probably built in the time of Alexander the Great and restored by the later Persian Seleucid kings. Saddam Hussein's antiquities department also restored or recreated, along with Nebuchadnezzar's palace, substantial portions of these sites.

Since the war and occupation of the spring and summer of 2003, the only pieces left in the museum at the site of Babylon are two big chunks of what are apparently the original walls. Donny George's staff, faced with the looting of the Baghdad Museum, shipped ancient clay tablets off to safes and strong rooms in Baghdad to keep them away from looters. Through the centuries, thieves have often operated from the neighboring town of Hillal, built originally from bricks looted from the ruins of Babylon in medieval times.[3] From summer 2003 onward, it was the scene of lethal ambushes of American troops.

THE MOTHER OF ALL HARLOTS

Both Biblical and secular historians have provided ample fuel for the polemics of American and other evangelists—"born-again" Christians, like President George Bush—about Saddam Hussein's Iraq as a place of primeval Evil. This had to be set right by the forces of Good. There is ample Old Testament backing for the vision of Babylon in particular, as a center of sin, corruption, and primal darkness. According to one typical commentary on Bible history circulated as the war of 2003 developed, "All false systems of religion began in the land of Babylon and will have their consummation from the spirit of Babylon in the last days." It also records how "God came down [to disrupt the erection of the Tower of Babel] and punished the people's arrogance by creating a confusion of different languages and possibly their racial distinctions."

A German scholar evokes Babylon's terrible reputation among Jews as an "anti-God state," seen by many Christians as "the mother of all harlots" and all the horror on earth. The Tower of Babel episode (Genesis 11: 1–9) is seen as the original source of the confusion of tongues and the dispersion of people around the world.[4]

Historians and travelers paint varied and sometimes conflicting images of what happened to Babylon. Its downfall appears to have been through gradual attrition, rather than sudden destruction from some kind of lightning bolt hurled by a vengeful God. In any case, the city's dissolution seems, to Biblical scholars and fundamentalists, to have fulfilled the prophecies of its downfall in the prophetic books of the Old Testament, Isaiah and Jeremiah. They see it as God's punishment of the Babylonians because of their destruction of Jerusalem and their deportation of the citizens of Judah. Greek travelers, beginning with Herodotus, the "father of history" (484–425 BC) describe it as a metropolis of vast proportions, with walls of a circumference of as much as 60 miles. By the time of the Romans, however, Babylon was gradually disappearing from maps and fading from memories.

With the fall of the Roman Empire and retreat of the Roman legions from the Middle East, Babylon's walls also crumbled and fell. Occasional historical mention of its ancient splendor served to emphasize that Christianity, the new and legal religion of Rome and of Byzantium, had won out. Babylon was a symbol of man's sins and turpitude and of God's wrath, like Sodom and Gomorrah. "Of Babylon," wrote the widow of archaeologist Claudius Rich, the first man of the modern age to systematically study Babylon's site, "[God] speaks only with indignation." The early Christian fathers saw it as a symbol of corruption. They used Babylon as a code word for pagan Rome, the enemy of the Church until the rule of Constantine (AD 306–337). By the eleventh and twelfth centuries, when the European Crusaders began their depredations against the domains of the newer faith of Islam in the early Middle Ages, Babylon was to Christendom only a shadowy legend, obscured by the all-too-real and menacing armies of the Muslims.[5]

THE JEWISH EXILES

Not so for the hundreds of thousands of Jews still living in the remains of the Persian Empire. These included descendants of those who chose to remain in Babylon after their captivity had ended, and were left behind by those who chose to return to Palestine. After the Arab conquest had ended Persian rule, the Jews of what had been ancient Babylonia, whose society had been weakened by social upheavals afflicting Persia, found new stability under the first Arab Caliphs, Omar and Ali. Jewish chroniclers record that the new Arab rulers, observing the Prophet Muhammad's injunctions against interfering with the lives of Jews and Christians, the "Peoples of the Book," encouraged a time of renewal and cultural revival among the Jews and Christians, who were to be respected. Under the peaceful coexistence between the Muslim bureaucracy and the autonomous institutions of the non-Muslims, the Jews were able to re-establish their ancient system of self-government.

The head of the secular part of the autonomous Jewish administration was called the exilarch. This office originated under the earlier domination of the Parthians and the Sasanids. The exilarch was supposed to be a descendant of Israel's King David (1000–961 BC), and his office was hereditary. One outstanding exilarch whose name has survived in Jewish history was named Bustanai. He passed the office to his sons by his Jewish wife and by a Persian princess: Jews of the period were as keen to mingle and intermarry with Persians as were the Macedonian Greeks in the time of Alexander the Great. Hereditary and elected representatives of Iraqi Jewry administered all taxes levied from Jews, with representation of Jews before the Muslim rulers. They were charged with certain communal and judicial functions in administering the *Yeshivot*, the Jewish community.

During the twelfth-century era of prosperity and a flowering of culture in Baghdad, the new Mesopotamian capital that had eclipsed Babylon in size and modernity, a Jewish traveler from Spain, Benjamin of Tudela, visited the city in about 1168. In his journals he graphically describes the "honor and splendor" surrounding the current Jewish exilarch, Daniel ben Hasdai (AD 1150–74) at the court of the caliph. Every Thursday, the caliph held audiences. Leaders of both the Muslim and Jewish societies were expected to appear. The exilarch sat beside the caliph, while the Muslim dignitaries had to stand. Another Jewish traveler, Petahya of Regensburg, reports that the administrative chiefs of the Jewish community in Mosul, northern Iraq (a mixed city of Arabs, Kurds, and Turcomans of various Muslim and Christian sects to this day, as the American occupiers of Iraq discovered in 2003, but virtually without any remaining Jews) punished offenders, even if one party to a civil or criminal case was a Muslim. Mosul had its own Jewish prison.

From the mid-thirteenth century AD Iraq was, for about a century, often a battle ground between Ottoman sultans and Persian kings. This continued intermittently until in 1638 the Ottomans finally annexed Baghdad and the rest of Iraq to their empire. However, the pashas in Baghdad and Mosul enjoyed more independence than in other regions of Iraq.

The Jewish and Christian communities and other minorities had to adjust to living in a remote province. It had been a flourishing center of culture, commerce and civilization, but now was a backwater wasted by wars and isolated from the main routes of international trade. A Jewish visitor from Yemen who visited Baghdad sometime after 1550 mentions the famous graves in Iraq of the Biblical prophets Ezekiel and Ezra the Scribe.[6]

A SHRINE RESTORED

In early August of 2003, while many of Iraq's ancient historical sites were still being looted or pillaged, Kate Seelye, daughter of former U.S. diplomat Talcott Seelye, and an enterprising correspondent for America's National Public Radio, came upon an ancient Jewish shrine south of Baghdad. It was reputed to be the prophet Ezekiel's burial place. She found the shrine and its synagogue near the village of Al-Kifi "lovingly cared for" by members of the local Muslim Bani Hassan tribe. Tribesmen had been safeguarding the site since departure of a small local Jewish community in 1948, following Israel's creation.

Seelye admired the landscape, where palm trees lined the banks of the nearby Euphrates River, looking as it must have thousands of years ago. Al-Kifi was apparently a suburb of ancient Babylon, 20 miles to the north. In King Nebuchadnezzar's time, it hosted many of the Jews he had exiled to Babylon from Jerusalem in the sixth century BC. Ezekiel is said to have settled and died in Al-Kifi, after reviving Jewish practice after the Babylonian exile. Today's synagogue was built some time after his death. Seelye, guided by the tribal sheikh and mayor of Al-Kifi, Sheikh Ahmed Habib al-Habut, saw elaborate Hebrew calligraphy on the walls. In a loft chamber, the mayor told her, Jews are believed to have written the Babylonian Talmud. He added that the room originally contained a library of ancient Hebrew texts, until Saddam Hussein ordered their removal to Baghdad in the late 1970s. An adjoining chamber with a dome and more Hebrew inscriptions contains a carved wooden shrine and a low stone tomb, said to be Ezekiel's. Next to it on the floor lay crumpled banknotes from Iraq, Iran, and Pakistan, apparently left by many Muslim visitors through the years. Seelye's guide told her how Muslims honored Ezekiel as a prophet of God. When about three dozen Jews who lived in Al-Kifi in the 1930s and 1940s left, he said, his father obeyed the Koran's instructions to guard holy sites of the Peoples of the Book. His father, he added, was persecuted by Saddam's regime for guarding the Jewish shrine, and was executed in the 1980s.

Michael Gfoeller, a civilian official of the U.S. occupation authority called the Bani Hassan's attitude "astonishing in its nobility." The shrine, he said, was a testament to Muslim–Jewish coexistence, and "one of the most important Jewish historical sites in the Middle East. There's always been a synagogue there, apparently for the last 2,600 years. Back in 1948, it probably would have been one of the oldest continuously functioning synagogues in the world."

Gfoeller said he was encouraging international experts to study and preserve the site. The mayor, Sheikh Shabut, voiced approval. He could imagine a time when Al-Kifi would flourish from tourism to the site "and a time when the Jews of Al-Kifi will be welcomed back."[7]

There were apparently few competent Iraqi Jewish scholars in the sixteenth century and afterward. This caused the Iraqi Jewish community to address questions on religious subjects to rabbis in Aleppo, Syria. Some Aleppine scholars moved to Baghdad and settled there. However, while the Iraqi Jews were importing scholars, by the late eighteenth century they were exporting the Jewish traders and merchants of Baghdad and Basra. Many emigrated to India. With the consolidation of British control there, a large British-protected Jewish colony gathered in Surat, India. By the early nineteenth century, the Iraqi merchants were moving to Calcutta, Bombay, and Poona. Especially prominent among the founders of these communities was the Sassoon clan, originally of Baghdad. Well-educated Sassoons contributed greatly to the religious and intellectual development of the Jewish communities in India. The merchants cultivated and kept close contacts with Far Eastern markets and with London, the rising British Empire's political and commercial metropolis. Links were formed in India between former Baghdadi Jews and trading giants like the British East India Company, which often exercised quasi-governmental functions. These links would influence relations and contacts within Iraq itself under the twentieth-century British mandate, which followed World War I.[8]

"SEEK THE PEACE OF THE CITY"

Jewish life in Iraq until the nineteenth and twentieth centuries flourished as much or more than anywhere else in the Jewish diaspora. In Bible history, the prophet Jeremiah, following the first Mesopotamian capture of Jerusalem in 597 BC and subsequent exile of the city's upper classes to Babylon, sent a letter to the exiles. He admonished them to quietism in their enforced new home, telling them to "Build ye houses, and dwell in them, and plant gardens and eat the fruit of them." They were instructed to:

take ye wives, and beget sons and daughters; and take wives for
your sons, and give your daughters to husbands, that they may bear
sons and daughters; that ye may be increased there, and not diminished. And seek the peace of the city.

These injunctions of Jeremiah shaped a political theory for Jewish life in
Iraq, including working for betterment of the society around them. The
Jews in Iraq held to these principles throughout the centuries of Persian,
Arab, and Ottoman Turkish rule following the fall of Babylon. During
these 2,000 years, no independent state of Iraq existed. The Ottoman
Turkish rulers, from the seventeenth century AD on, ruled each separate
component of Mesopotamian society in different ways. They favored
their Arab Sunni Muslim co-religionnaires, the Christians, and the Jews
over the Shiite Persians, mainly because the rival Persian Empire was a
religious and political threat to the Ottoman rulers in Constantinople.

But from the twelfth century AD, when Benjamin of Tudela reported
40,000 Jews in Baghdad, worshipping in 28 synagogues and enjoying
the favor of the Arab caliph, things began to change. The condition of
Iraqi Jewry slowly declined. So did the political and social power of a
Muslim (first Arab, then Turkish) establishment relatively well-disposed
toward the Christian, Jewish, and other minorities in its midst. After
AD 1500 the Iraqi Jews looked to their Sunni Muslim Ottoman neighbors for protection from the rising pressure of Shiite Islam in neighboring Persia. They celebrated the Ottoman victory of AD 1678 over the
Persians as a *Yom Nes*, or Day of a Miracle. But Jewish emigration to
India and elsewhere gradually increased, and the numbers of the Iraqi
Jewish community declined. By 1850, according to figures compiled by
the American Jewish Committee, Baghdad was host to only about 3,000
Jews. In 1853 they joined with the majority Sunni Arabs to fight against
one of the Kurdish rebellions in northern Iraq.[9]

OTTOMAN POWER DECLINES

One misfortune after another struck the Ottoman domains in
Mesopotamia in the nineteenth century. In 1831 an epidemic of bubonic
plague killed 3,000 people daily for weeks in Baghdad. The Tigris River,
in its spring flooding time, surged through Baghdad streets. It literally
dissolved hundreds of homes, mosques, and public buildings made of
mud bricks. The coming of the telegraph, commercial river steamers on
the Tigris, and the momentous opening of the Suez Canal in 1869, linking Europe with the eastern Ottoman domains and the Far East, were

too late to help the Ottoman rulers to keep their weakening grip on their Mesopotamian provinces.[10]

As Ottoman political power declined, however, the wealth and influence of the traders and merchants – Muslim, Christian, and Jewish – increased. It was probably during this period of growth that the seeds of animosity were sown between the Zionists, who came from the Western world and plotted and planned for a Jewish national state, and the self-appointed and comfortably established heirs of Babylonian Jewry, who had for the most part little interest in emigrating to Palestine or anywhere else. The Jewish traders of later nineteenth-century Iraq began to get seats in the Ottoman municipal and provincial administrative bodies that arose in the 1870s. However, they were unable to make policy in crucial local matters such as taxation, public works, or charitable activities. Most of the merchants and traders of whatever religion commonly bribed the Ottoman and Turkified-Arab bureaucrats to advance their interests. But the method, as Hanna Batatu, modern Iraq's most distinguished social historian remarks, "was expensive and could not always be counted on." Many of the big traders, impatient with the sclerotic old Ottoman bureaucracy, supported with sympathy and money the reformist revolution of the Young Turks in 1908, and its political expression in the reformist Committees of Union and Progress.

The development of the Young Turk movement was inspired by a highly enlightened Ottoman constitution of 1876. This was proclaimed by the reformist-minded Midhat Pasha, who had administered a growingly prosperous Baghdad from 1869–73. With associates, Midhat overthrew the tyrannical Sultan Abdul Aziz and installed his nephew, Murad V, as sultan. (Murad, judged insane by his peers, lasted only four months in power before the peers deposed him.)

Far more important, Midhat Pasha was the main author of an enlightened constitution in 1876. If it had been applied, some historians think it might have prolonged the life of Ottoman Turkey, dubbed by Western statesmen "the sick man of Europe" because of its unwieldy and growingly corrupt administration. The American–British occupying coalition, Iraq's de facto government in 2003 and 2004, might have been proud to adopt its principles in the new post-Saddam Hussein constitution they hoped to elaborate. They included: territorial integrity of the realm; liberty of the individual; freedom of conscience, the press, and education; equality of taxation; security of tenure for judges; and parliamentary government based on general representation.

The Young Turks, who had wanted from 1908 to put these lofty principles into practice, were mostly political exiles in France, Switzerland, and

Britain. They hoped to capitalize on the discredit of the sultan. They aimed at preventing further disruption of the empire, which had already lost most of Greece and the Balkans, as well as Libya. They wanted to reconstitute what was left on a liberal and national basis. In 1903 they had attempted some degree of cooperation with the Armenians (the Armenian holocaust of 1915 was yet to come) and the Macedonian and other revolutionary organizations, though not with the Arabs. Failure with the Arabs would prove fatal during the Arab revolt, which was aided by the British in alliance with the desert Arabs during World War I.

Efforts to reform and revive the decrepit Turkish Empire had some strange side effects. In 1909, a Jewish deputy for Thessaloniki in Turkish-occupied Greece (the birthplace of modern Turkey's founder, Mustapha Kemal Ataturk) named Carossa in 1909 "displayed ... a fierce zeal." He wanted to march on Constantinople and overthrow the despotic Sultan, Abdul Hamid. Carossa was spokesman for the delegation sent to tell the Sultan that he was deposed. Abdul Hamid was confined in a villa belonging to the Jewish bankers of the Committee of Union and Progress. Soon afterward, another Jewish parliamentary deputy from Thessaloniki became Turkish finance minister. The British ambassador to Istanbul, Sir Gerard Lowther, reported bitterly in a confidential dispatch to Foreign Secretary Sir Edward Grey that Jewish elements in the Turkish Admiralty and War Office had become so "impenetrable" that German diplomats began to pay "special court" to them to secure concessions and business deals.[11]

At the same time, a proto-Zionist group called The General Jewish Colonization Association tried to persuade the new Young Turk rulers to bring masses of Jewish settlers into Iraq, Palestine, Egypt, Cyprus, Syria, and eastern Turkey (Anatolia). They offered to finance this colonial enterprise fully, using the personal funds of the settlers and subsidies from banks and "societies formed with the object of facilitating emigration." In return, the Association promised that "our coreligionists who occupy high positions ... will use all their influence for the political and economic advancement of the Constitutional Ottoman Government." In a letter covering transmission of the offer to London, Ambassador Lowther remarked that the same group wanted to found "an autonomous Jewish state in Mesopotamia" which would be:

purely humanitarian and non-political. A partial success in the latter scheme has just been obtained by a group of Jews closely connected with the inner workings of the Committee of Union and Progress. Among them is a certain Jacques Menasche, whose brother-in-law is private secretary to the Grand Vizier and whose wife's charms have a special attraction for his Highness.[12]

Nothing came of this initiative, but the opening of worldwide communications through the telegraph and the Suez Canal benefited Arab and Kurdish merchants, traders, and landowners. One such was Muhammad Chalabi Sabunji, the son of a humble street peddler of soap. He became virtual dictator of Mosul from the 1880s until 1911. He achieved political power through the traditional Ottoman devices of generous hospitality shown toward people prominent in Mosul society; bribes, good relations with the local Christian clergy, and a liberal exchange of political intelligence about mutual adversaries with local tribal leaders.[13]

When they came to power in Constantinople, the Young Turks called elections for a new parliament in which the subject peoples, as provided in the 1876 constitution, would participate. The three Mesopotamian provinces (*vilayets*)—Baghdad, Basra, and Mosul—elected 17 deputies. All, however, came not from Shiite, Kurdish, Jewish, or Christian families, but only from old and solid Sunni families, a historical precedent for Saddam Hussein's Ba'athist Iraq in our own time. In Constantinople they discovered that they had far less in common with Turks, young or old, who were supposed to be ruling them, than they had with Arabs from other current or former Ottoman provinces, like Syria, Egypt, Arabia, or Yemen. When they went home, they shared with their countrymen the ideas and ideals of secular Arab nationalism, born during the nineteenth century and incubated in Christian educational institutions like the American University of Beirut.

The ideals of the "Arab Awakening" (the title of a seminal book by George Antonious, the distinguished Palestinian Christian historian), with its aspects of cultural and linguistic revival, universal education, women's rights, and other matters, spread like brushfire in most of the Turkish domains. In our own day, they still inspire attempts to bring about an Arab renaissance. They also drive efforts of anti-democratic Arab rulers to suppress them in today's world. These principles appealed mainly to educated urban Arabs. They had much less appeal in the villages and tribal backwaters of Mesopotamia and of the other Arab regions still under at least nominal Turkish rule.[14]

It would take two World Wars, the brief rise and almost equally rapid fall of British and French colonialism in the Middle East, and the subsequent rise of both the new state of Israel and of the influence of Israel's chief sponsor and ally, the United States of America, to turn ancient Mesopotamia into modern Iraq. It is these processes, crowding through the chaotic twentieth century, that we must next consider, in order to understand the deep antagonism in Iraq and most of the Arab and Muslim worlds in our own time first toward the colonial powers, then Israel, and ultimately, the United States.

2
The Ottoman Empire Divided

I asked Tom [Sawyer] if countries ever apologized when they had done wrong and he says "Yes the little ones does."
(*Mark Twain,* Huckleberry Finn)

Flying from Beirut into Baghdad in the spring of 1966, on my first newspaper assignment in Iraq, was for me a venture into the unknown. Our early-morning flight cleared the snow-dusted peaks of the Mount Lebanon range and the red hills beyond. These gave way to the dark-green patchwork around Damascus, then to the parched expanse of the Syrian Desert.

Joe Alex Morris Jr. of the *Los Angeles Times* and I wondered what we were letting ourselves in for. Joe had already been to Iraq several times since the July 1958 revolution when mobs had murdered and dismembered 23-year-old King Faisal II and his top advisors, including the wily, 70-year-old pro-Western Prime Minister Nuri al-Said, impaling Nuri alive before throwing him into a hasty roadside grave. General Abdel Karim Kassem, a soldier who admired Egyptian President Gamal Abdel Nasser's calls for pan-Arab unity and defiance of Israel and the West, then took over and ruled unsteadily until he too was murdered.

What followed was a succession of military rulers, punctuated by a bloody coup and brief rule by the Syrian-based Ba'ath party, instigated by an up-and-coming gunman-politician named Saddam Hussein al-Tikriti, with some help from the American CIA. Next was a restoration of "civilian" rule, supervised by General Abdel Rahman Aref after his brother, General Abdel Salem Aref, had been killed in a suspicious helicopter accident. (Helicopter or plane accidents in the Middle East involving dictators or ranking officers or politicians are often suspicious.)

After circling in the gusts of sand and dust, we made a bumpy landing at what was then Baghdad International Airport, in its more modest, pre-Saddam Hussein format. Inside the shabby terminal we were met by a "goon," a minder from the ubiquitous Muhabess, the security service which kept tabs on visiting journalists, businessmen, or diplomats.

Luckily for us, the goon was accompanied by a young, neatly dressed and American-educated diplomat, whom I remember as Adnan—the very one who had promised and delivered our visas in Beirut. By the time he and the minder had whisked us to a respectable hotel just off central Baghdad's Saddoun Street, Adnan told us that he had already arranged meetings for us with the reputedly liberal prime minister, Abdel Rahman Bazzaz.

"You'll find out," Adnan told us as we took tiny, ritual cups of acid Bedouin coffee from a copper tray in the somewhat threadbare lobby, "The new Iraq is going to surprise you. You're going to find out that we're not all the murderers some of your media makes us out to be."

Bazzaz was a shy, personable man, reputedly one of the main ideologues of the Ba'ath Party. He was also a friend of its two Syrian founders, the Christian Michel Aflaq and the Sunni Muslim, Salah al-Bitar. As Syrian prime minister in the pre-Hafez al-Assad era, Bitar had entertained me at breakfast in Damascus at the start of my Middle Eastern apprenticeship the previous autumn. Bazzaz was no fiery rhetorician. He was reticent during our meeting with him, with Adnan as interpreter: no rhetorical references to the Ba'athist slogan of "unity, freedom, socialism," only routine talk about Israel as a menacing enemy of the Arabs and of a recent ceasefire in the never-ending series of Kurdish revolts in the north of Iraq.

Joe voiced our wish to travel to Kurdistan and see the Kurdish situation first-hand. Bazzaz agreed that was a good idea, but would "take some time to arrange." Adnan gave us eye signals to drop the subject. On the way out, he said, "The only person who can lay on a fast trip to Kurdistan for you is the President. How would you like to have dinner with him tomorrow night?"

We enjoyed a relaxed dinner with President Aref Adnan; army officers in uniform and some anonymous gentlemen whom we assumed to be spooks shared the president's fare with us in his rather modest residence. Over coffee President Aref announced that a helicopter would whisk us up to Kurdistan first thing next morning.

At an ungodly hour, not one but three big Russian-made passenger choppers awaited us and our escorts in the pre-dawn darkness at a military helicopter pad for the flight north, first to Suleimaniyeh, then to Kirkuk, Dohuk, and Erbil. We had a couple of hours' stay and some desultory conversations with obviously tame official Kurds in each. The Iraqi officials with us confined themselves to vague generalities about the ceasefire being a good thing, and about the favorable prospects that at last, after so many generations, Kurds would get their "rights" (nobody said anything about Kurdish independence). There was no sign, naturally, of the Israeli advisers and trainers who had already been sent by Tel Aviv, along with small amounts of cash and weapons, to show Israel's appreciation and support for their aspirations, as well as to keep Kurdish pressure on the Baghdad regime. We found out about the Israelis later.

ANTECEDENTS OF WAR

Returning to base in Beirut, I dug out my history books and chatted with experts on the Arab world at the American University of Beirut (AUB). There was a growing awareness that a new general Arab–Israel war lay ahead; the third since Israel's creation in 1948. It would be the first since President Dwight D. Eisenhower had pressed Israel, Britain, and France to break off their Suez military expedition in 1956 and evacuate their troops from Egypt; an event that greatly encouraged and strengthened Egypt's President Gamal Abdel Nasser and his followers.

At the end of 1966, precursors of war were multiplying. One was a punitive Israeli raid on the Jordanian town of Samua in reprisal for cross-border forays by Palestinian fedayeen (terrorists to the Israelis; freedom fighters to the Arabs). There were clashes between Israel and the Syrian army in and near the UN-supervised demilitarized zone (DMZ) along the Jordan River and the area adjoining the Sea of Galilee and the Golan Heights. There was plenty of saber-rattling by both sides between Nasser's Egypt and an Israel governed by Prime Minister Levi Eshkol and the Labor Party. Israel's arch-hawk of the time, General Moshe Dayan, controlled Israeli military policy in the Defense Ministry. Iraq stood at some geographic distance from the expected fray. To understand why and how Iraq was involved when Israel on June 5, 1967 launched a preemptive war, changing the map and the history of today's Middle East, requires a backward look at the region.

At the dawn of the twentieth century, Britain had two main imperial concerns. One was securing the oil supplies she already needed to keep her global navy afloat and would soon need to keep the wheels of her industry turning. The other was protecting her sea communication lines (later to become air links as well) to India, the jewel in the crown of her empire. Iraq was an important key to both. By 1910, oil had begun to flow from the huge Masjid-I-Suleiman (Temple of Solomon) field nearby in Persia. The Anglo-Persian Oil Company was as great an asset to Britain as its East India Company had been in past generations. It was vital to protect the western flank and what were thought to be extensions of the Persian oilfields in southern Mesopotamia. The nearby port of Basra was already a strategic point on the combined overland and sea routes between Europe, the Middle East, India, and beyond. In 1903, the Kaiser's imperial German government and German financiers had coaxed and bought from the Ottoman government in Istanbul a concession to build the Berlin-to-Baghdad railway. If completed, it would have given Germany access to Basra and hence an open door on the Indian Ocean.

In 1914, the guns of August boomed into action in Europe and the Middle East: The Triple Entente, Britain, France, and Russia, went to war against the German, Austrian, and Ottoman Turkish empires. In November 1914, British-commanded Indian troops landed exactly where the U.S.-led coalition forces of Prime Minister Tony Blair's Britain would land in March 2003: on the slender Fao Peninsula, at the end of the Shatt al-Arab waterway. After moving on Basra and seizing most of the Ottoman province of that name in southern Mesopotamia, an army commanded by British Major General Charles Townshend in the fall of 1915 began moving northward toward Baghdad. Gradually, Turkish and Arab resistance stiffened. The advancing troop found themselves embedded in a literal quagmire, the Hawr al-Hammahur, the vast Iraqi marshland close to the Shatt al-Arab. It swarmed with flies, mosquitoes, and Arab guerrilla fighters, who resisted the British and Indians much as their heirs would resist Saddam Hussein's soldiers, secret police, and bureaucrats almost a century later. Saddam would finally punish them by draining the marshes. This nearly destroyed the tranquil culture of the Marsh Arabs, with their boats and houses made of reeds and their heavy dependence on fishing.

In 1915 The Turkish forces were commanded by Germany's Field Marshal Colman van der Goltz, a canny strategist. Heartened by the debacle and massacre of the British and Australian army in their disastrous campaign on Turkey's Gallipoli Peninsula west of Constantinople, which had aimed at capturing the city and the strategic Dardanelles, the Turks brought up reinforcements. Their forces counterattacked the British south of Baghdad. Near Ctesiphon, with its memorable antique arch built by the post-Babylonian Sassanians from Persia, the Turks pushed the British-led force back over 100 miles to Kut al-Amarah, a village situated in a looping bend of the Tigris river. Here, the Allied force endured a siege and war of attrition lasting 140 days. Finally, on April 26, 1916, 13,000 survivors, exhausted, sick, and demoralized, surrendered to the Turks. This was the biggest Muslim victory over Western military forces in centuries.

BRITAIN CAPTURES BAGHDAD

Determined to prevail, Winston Churchill, David Lloyd George, and the imperial military staff sent Major General Sir Stanley Maude at the head of a fresh force in December 1916 to advance again on Baghdad. Hearing from their spies that a rebellion in the Shia holy city of Najaf had expelled Turkish troops from that center—again crucial in the Anglo-American occupation of Iraq in 2003—British agents lobbied Shia tribal leaders to win them over. However, the British showed the same lack of understanding of the Arab mentality that the Americans would display in 2003. Neither the tribal Arabs nor the Turks proved cooperative. The Marsh Arabs, realizing that their quiet existence in the swamps was threatened, attacked and looted the weapons and stores of both sides. Finally, on March 10, 1917, General Maude's British force entered Baghdad. The British commander-in-chief, already ill, like so many of his troops, with cholera—there were no state-of-the-art clinics, hospitals, or medical supplies like those of the Anglo-American forces in 2003—issued a victory proclamation. It could have provided a basis for similar remarks made by President George Bush's civilian proconsul in Iraq, L. Paul Bremer III, in 2003. Henceforth the people of Mesopotamia (soon to be renamed Iraq) would have control of their own lives. The despotic and alien rule they had endured for so many generations was at an end. After intimations of a promised era of democracy and enlightenment, General Maude died of cholera.[1]

Meanwhile, the British Middle East staff in Cairo had enlisted the great talents and the devotion to the idea of Arab emancipation of Colonel T. E. Lawrence to launch an ultimately successful guerrilla war against Turkey in the Arabian Peninsula. Senior Arab leaders met in Damascus in 1915 to back it. They decided on conditions under which the Arabs were prepared to fight for full independence from the Ottomans. Their so-called Damascus Protocol envisioned a sort of free and independent Arab super-state, encompassing Palestine, the Arabian Peninsula (including the ancient independent kingdom of Yemen), and what would shortly become today's Syria, Lebanon, and Iraq.

This did not fit in with British and Allied plans. The Allies wanted to defeat Turkey as swiftly as possible, but not in order to establish a free Arab super-state. They wanted rather to give British and French soldiers access and passage across Russia and Romania so as to outflank and encircle the Central Powers. Any independent Arab kingdom would have to center not on Turkey or its northern Arab domains, but on Mecca and Medina, the Muslim holy places in Arabia.

Sir Percy Cox was chief political officer of the Allied expeditionary force that had captured Basra. Cox and his shrewd lady adviser, the Arabic-speaking English adventuress Gertrude Bell, were aware of the need to win the paramount Wahabi Arabian chieftain, Ibn Saud, to the Allied cause. They sent an envoy, Captain W. H. I. Shakespear, an admired friend of Ibn Saud, to accomplish this. But Shakespear's death in a battle with tribal enemies of the Saudis ended this hope. The British Arab Bureau, an intelligence and staff officers' "think tank" in Cairo, decided instead to anoint the Hashemite family of eastern Arabia's Hijaz province (which was Islam's official keeper of the Muslim holy places) to counter the Turkish call for a jihad against the "infidel" Allies. Britain negotiated an agreement with the Hashemite Sharif Hussein of Mecca to launch a revolt against the Turks in letters exchanged from July 1915 to February 1916 between the Sharif and Sir Henry McMahon, British high commissioner in Egypt. Britain promised "to recognize and uphold the independence of the Arabs within the frontiers proposed by the Sharif of Mecca." Hussein's original definition of these territories included all Arab provinces of the Ottoman Empire between Mersin on the southern Turkish coast in the north, the frontier of Persia in the east, the Mediterranean in the west, and the Red Sea and the Indian Ocean in the south, with the exception of Aden in South Yemen, which was already under British control.

What the Sharif got, especially as regards Iraq, was much less. McMahon reported that "as regards to the two *Vilayets* of Baghdad and Basra the Arabs recognize the fact of Great Britain's established position and interests there" which required "special administrative arrangements." There was ambiguity about French aspirations to rule Syria and Lebanon, and even more with regard to the future of Palestine, two-thirds of which was then constituted by the Turkish sanjak or sub-district of Jerusalem.

Sharif Hussein raised his battle flags on June 16, 1916 and captured Mecca from its Turkish garrison. The ensuing Arab revolt was at first confined to the Hijaz, western Arabia, because Britain was reluctant to inconvenience her French ally. France wanted Syria and Lebanon, so no British troops landed there. There followed long months of wheeling, dealing, and dickering between Britain, France, and the Arab leaders. Those in the future state of Iraq jealously tried to guard their independence of action. Sir Mark Sykes of Britain and Georges Picot of France negotiated the famous (to the Arabs, infamous) Sykes–Picot agreements. They partitioned all of Syria and Iraq and much of southern Turkey into spheres of British and French influence. France got today's Syria and

Lebanon; Britain was allotted Transjordan and Iraq. Britain received the Turkish *vilayets* of Baghdad and Basra, as well as the Palestinian ports of Haifa and Acre. The rest of Palestine was to be under some kind of ill-defined international control. An equally vaguely defined hinterland would, under British and French influence, be an "independent" Arab state or confederation, "under suzerainty of an Arab chief." Only the territory which is today Saudi Arabia and Yemen would be fully independent, with Britain retaining Aden and its quasi-protectorates, and the sheikhdoms of the Arab Gulf.[2]

The Arab revolt, driven by the genius and the zeal of the Amir Faisal, with the aid of Arab leadership and of the British Arab Bureau officers like Lawrence, drove the harassed Turkish forces northward through Arabia in the spring of 1917. In Gaza, an unsuccessful British commander, whose men were bogged down by the German-advised Turkish forces, was replaced at the end of June 1917 by General "Bull" Allenby, a brilliant and imaginative soldier. Allenby moved headquarters from Cairo to Palestine and began driving toward Jerusalem. His forces entered Jerusalem on December 9, 1917.

BETRAYAL IN THE LEVANT

Meanwhile, the Bolshevik Revolution in Russia had set in motion a train of political events affecting the political future of the entire Middle East, including Iraq and Israel. Lenin, Trotsky, and their fellow revolutionaries discovered in the Russian imperial archives documentary proof of the secret Sykes–Picot agreements and the promises to the Arabs. The new Bolshevik masters lost little time in informing the Turks, who in turn tipped off the Arab leaders. Here, the Ottomans told the Arabs, is proof that the treacherous Christian West is engaging in a monstrous conspiracy against the Muslims of the Ottoman Empire. When Sharif Hussein demanded an explanation from the British, he was told that the Sykes–Picot arrangements were only diplomatic exchanges, not binding agreements.

The Arab leadership was not convinced. Its confidence in the fidelity of the Western powers to their wartime commitments to the Arabs was further shaken by the publication on November 2, 1917, just before Sharif Hussein learned of Sykes–Picot, of a letter from British Foreign Secretary Arthur Balfour to a leader of the Zionist movement, Lord Rothschild. This was the Balfour Declaration. It assured Rothschild that "His Majesty's Government view with favor the establishment in Palestine of a National Home for the Jewish people." However, it added "nothing shall be done which may prejudice the civil and religious rights of existing non-Jewish communities in Palestine or the rights and political status enjoyed by Jews in any other country."

ENTER THE U.S.

The repercussions of this well-meaning but ambiguous document— which have been amply discussed in thousands of articles and scores of books—have continued throughout all of the Arab–Israel wars, cease-fires, armistice agreements and failed "peace processes" until today. What is most important here is how the contradictory promises to Jews and Arabs were followed by entry of a major new actor onto the scene, the United States of America.

Woodrow Wilson, the idealistic U.S. president who had brought the United States into the "war to save democracy" on the Allied side in 1917, formulated the lofty principles of his "Fourteen Points," about democracy and the self-determination of peoples. He tabled them at the Paris Peace Conference that convened in January 1919. Wilson faced an uphill battle. In addition to hundreds of diplomats, politicians, oilmen, financiers, and Christian missionaries and Zionist lobbyists who fought tooth and nail for their own interests, Wilson and his staff confronted French Prime Minister Georges Clemenceau and his British counterpart David Lloyd George. Clemenceau seemed to realize that France would become the junior partner to Britain in the division of the Ottoman spoils but he insisted that France keep Syria, Lebanon, and southern Turkish Anatolia. Lloyd George, determined that the British Empire would be the dominant ruling force in the Middle East, claimed Egypt, Arabia, Palestine, and all of Mesopotamia. Faisal, dressed in Arab robes, was allowed to speak once for 20 minutes, with Lawrence standing silently by. Faisal pleaded that Wilson's principles of self-determination and independence be applied to the foundation and recognition of an independent Arab state with clearly defined frontiers.

This was to no avail. British and French cartographers and diplomats, in closed committee rooms, drew the boundaries of what are essentially today's Middle Eastern states. The exception was Israel, still only a state of mind of the Zionist leaders. The British, in defining what was to be their mandate over Iraq, excluded Mosul, leaving it temporarily within the Syrian (and therefore French) sphere. They concentrated on grabbing the Turkish *vilayets* of Baghdad and Basra. With a ruler they drew a straight line across the map of the northern

Arabian desert, thus arbitrarily setting an artificial southern boundary. The nomadic desert Arabs have never respected it.

The whole artificial Mesopotamian mandate, with its conglomerates and islets of majority Shia, minority Sunnis, Kurds, Jews, Assyrian (Chaldean) Christians, Turcomans, Yazidis, and other smaller sects, was formally presented to the new League of Nations, the post-World War I predecessor of today's United Nations. Woodrow Wilson had helped to conceive the League and acted as midwife to its birth, only to find that the isolationist U.S. Congress refused to join it. The League, without the United States, divided up the post-war mandates among the victors. Mesopotamia, of course, was left to Britain. The League formally confirmed this at the San Remo Conference in April 1920.

Working with models borrowed from British India, including every-thing from legal codes to postage stamps, the British mandate officials descended on "liberated" Baghdad and Basra with the troops. Like the American and British "liberators" of 2003, they faced a host of differ-ent opponents. There were thousands of unemployed former Ottoman soldiers and bureaucrats. Often they were as disaffected as members of Saddam Hussein's ex-power structure after the American-led conquest in 2003. In 1920 as in 2003, the Shia clergy in Kerbala, Najaf, and the other Shia power centers detested the new Christian rulers. Arab nation-alists, bitter over the Allies' broken promises, formed secret societies in Baghdad. Shia clerics in Najaf coalesced in the *Jamiyat an-Nahda al-Islamiya*, or League of Islamic Awakening. Muslim religious leaders in Baghdad, along with landlords, merchants, journalists, and civil servants, formed *Haras al-Istiqlal*, the Guardians of Independence. These groups had very diverse views but most agreed that they must get rid of the British.[3]

It was tribal revolt, rather than urban political upheaval, that most sorely tested British patience and British power in Iraq. The British ruthlessly suppressed the insurgents using the Royal Air Force and chemical warfare—mainly mustard gas bombs—against the fractious tribesmen, as they had done in India a year earlier against tribesmen in the Punjab territory. Winston Churchill, the Secretary of State for War and Air, made this official. He ruled that Iraq "could be cheaply policed by aircraft armed with gas bombs, supported by as few as 4,000 British and 10,000 Indian troops" on the ground. These tactics, already in use, were formally endorsed and adopted at an imperial conference in Cairo in 1921.

In somewhat the same manner as the world community and U.S. Secretary of State Colin Powell felt the need, in the face of White House unilateralist policies, to lend respectability to and win international approval for the U.S.–British coalition's war on Saddam Hussein's Iraq in 2003, the British foreign secretary Lord Curzon decided to make a display of political responsibility. Britain, wrote Curzon, wanted in Iraq:

> [An] Arab façade ruled and administered under British guidance and, as far as possible, by an Arab staff. ... There should be no actual incorporation of the conquered territory controlled by a native Mohammedan [sic] and, as far as possible by an Arab staff. ... There should be no actual incorporation of the conquered territory ... in the dominions of the conqueror, but the absorption may be veiled by such constitutional fictions as a protectorate, a sphere of influence, a buffer state, and so on.[4]

THE HASHEMITES ARRIVE

Sir Percy Cox, with Lord Curzon's approval, proclaimed the state of Iraq, to be a monarchy. The British enthroned the World-War hero Emir Faisal of the Hashemites, the Meccan family that the French had expelled from their Syrian mandate after he was proclaimed king of the Arabs in Damascus. Faisal quickly signed an alliance treaty with Britain. Its terms remarkably resembled those of the League of Nations mandate. Nationalist and religious groups protested so violently that the royal cabinet had to resign. The British high commissioner assumed dictatorial powers and the British carried out mass deportations of real or suspected nationalist leaders. A fresh British-drafted constitution gave King Faisal I almost total authority over the new Iraqi legislature. In 1925 huge demonstrations swept through Baghdad. They delayed the assembly's approval of the Anglo–Iraqi treaty. The British high commissioner forced ratification through by threatening to dissolve the assembly.

In 2003, another Hashemite prince, Hassan bin Talal, brother of the late King Hussein of Jordan, and his cousin, Sharif Ali, who got a seat on L. Paul Bremer's temporary governing council, would both bid for influence on the post-Saddam Hussein scene in Iraq. In a July 2003 op-ed article in *The New York Times*, Prince Hassan praised the accomplishments of what Arab nationalists considered to be the puppet regime, under the British, of King Faisal I. He called him "a man of wisdom and foresight," who "brought together all of his country's disparate communities in a spirit of genuine friendship and reconciliation despite the constraints of the largest hegemonic power of that time, Britain." Under Faisal I, wrote Hassan, Iraq "was a country whose citizens participated in building the nation, no matter one's denomination or affiliation, whether Shiite or Sunni, Chaldean or Sabaean [another Arab Christian sect], Arab or Kurd, Circassian or Turkman." Hassan even went so far as to assert that Iraq, as the first Arab member of the League of Nations, "became a model for other emerging nation-states in the Middle East and beyond."

Rather than openly calling for a Hashemite restoration in Baghdad (which found some favorable echoes in Israeli media), Hassan disguised his apparent hopes by wishing that:

> Iraq could again be the model for the developing nation-state if it is able to humanize economics and politics, putting its citizens' well-being at the center of policymaking. ... It is the historical legacy of King Faisal I, who enabled Iraqis to be stakeholders in their political future. The development—not imposition—of democracy in Iraq is vital.[5]

Other commentators and historians have a less rosy view of Faisal I's heritage. Most, however, agree that his rule, which lasted until his sudden death in 1933 and the succession of his son, Ghazi, was the period of most successful governance during the period of preponderant British influence.

Direct British colonial power in Iraq gradually diminished. T. E. Lawrence, in a prophetic article in the London *Sunday Times* of August 22, 1920, called Iraq:

> a trap from which it will be hard [for Britain] to escape with dignity and honor ... [and] worse than the old Turkish system. They kept fourteen thousand local conscripts and killed a yearly average of two hundred Arabs in maintaining peace. We keep ninety thousand men, with aeroplanes, armoured cars, gunboats and armoured trains. We have killed about ten thousand Arabs in this rising this summer. ... How long will we permit millions of pounds, thousands of imperial troops, and tens of thousands of Arabs to be sacrificed on behalf of colonial administration which can benefit nobody but the administrators?

A constituent assembly, convened in 1924, in 1925 approved an Anglo–Iraqi treaty and an Organic (quasi-constitutional) Law made Iraqi ministers responsible to a bicameral parliament. After long delay due to Arab opposition to British tutelage, and the insistence by France and others that Iraq was not ready for full independence, an Anglo–Iraqi treaty in 1930 set up a 25-year alliance. Both governments were supposed to consult one another on foreign policy. Britain got air bases and control of communications, and provided a military mission to train the Iraqi army.

DIVIDING THE OILY SPOILS

The colonial regime, using the British army and the RAF gradually subdued Kurdish and Bedouin tribal revolt and lawlessness. It also managed to control the Shia clergy in Baghdad, Najaf, and Kerbala, most of whom were of Persian origin. Saudi–Iraqi boundary disputes along the line drawn by the World War I victors were aggravated by bitter rivalry arising from the civil war between Hashemite losers and Saudi victors in the Arabian Peninsula.

The toughest foreign problem for Faisal I and the British was their relationship with the former Turkish overlords of Iraq. The 1923 Lausanne peace conference regulated (without definitively settling) disputes, especially Greco–Turkish ones, arising from World War I and its aftermath. President Kemal Ataturk's new Turkish Republic demanded the return of most of the former *vilayet* of Mosul, which insiders knew was rich in oil. In 1925, after two years of bitter diplomacy, involving much double-dealing and efforts by major international oil companies to get the drop on each other for oil concessions, Turkey yielded to British pressure and reluctantly accepted a treaty awarding Mosul to Iraq.[6]

From that 1925 treaty until autumn of 2003 when Turkish "peace-keeping" forces were frustrated by domestic Iraqi opposition from moving back into Iraq, as invited by the Bush administration, the industrial world's thirst for oil and the claims and hopes of rival companies and nations, including the oil-poor state of Israel, for access to Iraq's oil, have been behind much of the Middle East's turbulent history.

By the outbreak of war in 1914 the Anglo-Persian Oil Company's refinery at Abadan, near the Iraqi border, was exporting a quarter of a million tons of oil annually. After prodding by Winston Churchill, who in 1911 was First Lord of the Admiralty (hence his World War II code name, in messages to President Franklin D. Roosevelt, of "former naval person") and who promoted the transition of the British fleet to oil, Britain on the eve of World War I in 1914 acquired a 51 percent interest in Anglo-Persian. Germany had already made its bid for Mesopotamian oil. In its agreement with the Ottoman Empire in 1903 to build the never-completed Berlin-to-Baghdad railway, an ambitious undertaking of the Deutsche Bank, the Germans had been granted mineral rights over land for 20 kilometers either side of the track. In 1911 and 1912, the so-called Turkish Petroleum Company (TPC) was created. It was Turkish in name only: the owners included Royal Dutch/Shell, the British-owned "National Bank of Turkey," the Deutsche Bank, and an imaginative and aggressive Armenian entrepreneur named C. S. Gulbenkian. He became known as "Mr. Five Percent," since that was his share of this and several future major oil concessions. In 1913 the TPC merged with Anglo-Persian, with shares divided among the British, German, Dutch, and Gulbenkian interests in the TPC. This gave Britain a major oil stake in the Middle East just as she was entering World War I and landing troops in Mesopotamia.[7]

Before the war's outbreak, the Ottoman government had granted a concession to this enlarged TPC consortium. Its individual members pledged not to get involved in production or processing of oil in the Ottoman Empire in Europe and Asia, except through the TPC, with the exclusion of certain areas delimited by a red line drawn on a map. This became known as "the Red Line agreement." When the war ended in 1918, the British occupied Mosul, having already expropriated the German interests in the TPC. However, due to wartime inter-Allied agreements like Sykes–Picot, Mosul was supposed to be within the French (Syrian) sphere of influence, not the British. In 1919, Britain succeeded in persuading the French government to transfer Mosul to British political control, in return for a secure and guaranteed role for the Compagnie Française des Petroles in developing the Mosul oilfields. France also agreed to construction of two pipelines to transport crude oil from Mesopotamia and Persia to Syria's Mediterranean seaports.[8]

Although post-war America was retreating into political isolation, its economic, commercial, and hence long-term strategic role in the Middle East was just beginning. Oil was the key force in this role. Up to the end of the war, over 80 percent of Britain's oil came from the United States. Persia was the only important Middle East producer, with an insignificant share in total world production. In 1913 the United States (mainly Texas and Oklahoma) produced 140 times more oil than did Persia.[9]

WILSON OPENS DOORS

Woodrow Wilson, the son of a Presbyterian minister, was a professor of law and government and both president of Princeton University and governor of New Jersey before he was first elected U.S. President in 1912 (re-elected in 1916). He was a high-minded man of lofty, nearly theological, principles who was not enthusiastic about backing World War I European Allies. At Germany's request, he had in 1916 even tried to mediate and end the war. Only after German submarines began sinking American merchant ships in the Atlantic did he draw the United States into the war and send over a million Yankee soldiers to fight in Europe's trenches. At the peace conferences following the war, he opposed, in vain, the secret undertakings of Britain and France to carve up the Middle East between them. He advocated and promoted short-lived independent states for both the Kurds and the Armenians, millions of whom had died in conflicts with the Turks.

One thing that Wilson and his American envoys did insist upon and obtain, however, was an "open door" commercial policy in the mandated territories, including Iraq. Oil was very much on the mind of the State Department. It engaged in long paper arguments with the British Foreign Office, which felt that Texas and Oklahoma had more than enough oil to satisfy America's needs. The big American oil companies aggressively promoted their new interest in Middle Eastern oil. When the former Turkish Petroleum Company metamorphosed into the Iraq Petroleum Company (IPC) after the 1925 accord, the IPC's owners with 23.75 percent shares each were Anglo-Persian (which later became British Petroleum, BP), Royal Dutch/Shell, an American group which later narrowed to Standard Oil of New Jersey and Socony-Vaccum (later Mobil), and the Compagnie Française des Petroles (CFP), with Gulbenkian getting his customary five percent cut.

This was, in effect, a breakthrough by the State Department in favor of Big Oil in the United States. It tacitly accepted the Red Line provisions, which Britain considered still valid, and excluded all non-IPC participants.[10] Major oil discoveries in the Kurdish areas near Kirkuk in 1927 boosted IPC further. By the mid-1930s, IPC's oil production provided a major part of Iraq's national revenues. At the same time, the American oil companies were capturing the main concessions in Saudi Arabia, Kuwait, and the rest of the eastern Gulf region.

In the meantime, Britain's colonial mandate had ended in 1932 and Iraq had entered the League of Nations as a sovereign member. But powerful religious and nationalist groups still resented continuing British influence, as well as the growing power of the IPC. In August 1933 an Iraqi army unit massacred about 300 Assyrian Christian villagers in northern Iraq. The atrocity found broad approval in Muslim public opinion. When the soldiers were not punished, many Assyrians emigrated westward to Syria, which with Lebanon was to remain under French mandate until World War II.

PALESTINE TO CENTER STAGE

It was following King Faisal's sudden death in 1933 and the accession of his handsome and popular, but rather unstatesmanlike, son Ghazi, that Iraq began its fateful embroilment with the problems of what was then another British mandate, Palestine. These problems would grow to dire proportions. Eventually they led first Israel in 1948, 1967, 1973, and 1991, and then in 2003 the United States and Britain, now a junior ally of Washington, all to become involved in war with Iraq.

The Iraqi state and society struggled to form a viable and modern political system. The dominating political figure throughout the inter-war period, and indeed up until his murder by the enraged Baghdad mobs during the Iraqi revolution of 1958, was Nuri al-Said. He became a key figure in the interplay between the Zionist makers and founders of Israel and the Arabs of Iraq. Nuri, born in 1888 (officially in Baghdad but quite possibly in a village with the Turkic-sounding name of Tuzkhurmtu), was both a product of the dying Ottoman Empire—his father was a government auditor in the Ottoman bureaucracy—and a servant of the Arabs who broke away from it. Gifted with a keen sense of the history and politics of his time, he shrewdly anticipated the coming Arab Revolt. As a young officer, Nuri became a military adviser to Sharif Faisal in 1918. He fought with Lawrence and the Arabs north-ward from Arabia as far as Damascus. When the French colonial army kicked the self-proclaimed "King" Faisal out of Syria, he traveled with Faisal to Baghdad to join the new British-controlled regime.

Like a successful player in a game of musical chairs, until his long reign ended with his murder in the1958 revolution Nuri moved between top jobs in the Iraqi kingdom: prime minister, defense minister, sensitive diplomatic posts abroad. One of the main foreign-policy problems preoccupying him—as it was to be with all of his successors, including Saddam Hussein—was Palestine, and the rival Arab and Zionist move-ments there, under a growingly shaky British administration.

The prelude to Baghdad's long-lasting (and long-range) duel with the Zionists and later with the Israeli state was orchestrated by British statesmen, especially Winston Churchill. As a member of Prime Minister David Lloyd George's cabinet, Churchill played a role in the Middle East roughly comparable to a hybrid of Colin Powell and Donald Rumsfeld in the George W. Bush administration from 2001 onward. Wilsonian and post-Wilsonian America stood on the sidelines. It was far more concerned with the growing race for Middle Eastern oil than with the clash of Arab and Jewish nationalism. Churchill's first concern after the end of World War I had been keeping France, already installed in Syria and Lebanon, out of Palestine, as well as out of Iraq. His solution was to offer the throne of the artificial new mandate-state of Transjordan to King Abdallah I, the Hashemite grandfather of King Hussein of Jordan and the great-grandfather of today's King Abdallah II. Churchill sought to persuade Abdallah, in return for giving him the Jordanian throne, to avoid attacking the French in Syria, and thus refrain from provoking them to move into Palestine or to insist on keeping Mosul. As historian David Fromkin writes, "Churchill's advisers concluded that Britain could fully reconcile and fulfill her wartime pledges [the basically contradictory Balfour Declaration and Sykes–Picot agreements] by establishing a Jewish National Home in Palestine west of the Jordan and a separate Arab entity [Transjordan] in Palestine east of the Jordan," with Abdallah in charge of the latter.[11]

Churchill and his advisers believed, and told Prime Minister David Lloyd George, that Abdallah could curb both the anti-French and anti-Zionist Arab movements that could possibly develop bases in Transjordan, east of the Jordan river. In March 1921, after setting down this policy in a series of meetings in Cairo, Churchill took a train to Jerusalem. He met with Abdallah, whom he found "moderate, friendly," and amenable to agreement with the British. Abdallah allowed them to govern Jordan, without British ground troops but permitting the RAF to maintain air bases, a decisive instrument of control.

Soon, H. St. John Philby, the British Arabist explorer and adventurer, became an official adviser to Abdallah. British officers began forming and training a Bedouin army, later called The Arab Legion, commanded by General Sir John Glubb, whom the Brits and others in the Middle East journalistic fraternity soon dubbed "Glubb Pasha."

The idea of a Jewish state in Palestine had of course arisen long before World War I, during the declining years of the Ottoman Empire. Theodor Herzl, generally credited as the founder of Zionism (defined as the return of the Jews to Zion, a Jewish refuge and state, preferably in their Biblical and historic ancient homeland in Palestine), tried to persuade the Ottoman Sultan and the pre-war German emperor to grant Jews a colonization charter. He did not succeed. An alternative British plan for such a charter was withdrawn, after disagreement among the would-be Jewish founders. When Britain in 1917 issued the Balfour Declaration to win and keep Jewish support against its World War I enemies, David Ben-Gurion and the other Zionist leaders saw their opportunity.

The Balfour document, most Jewish and some Arab historians believe, was validated legally when the League of Nations made Britain the mandatory power in Palestine, Iraq, and Jordan. The Palestine Mandate's language assured British support for creation of the Jewish "National Home." The Zionists were certain that this was the foundation of a future Jewish state, even though in 1917 the Arab population of Palestine (as Nuri al-Said in Iraq and many other Arab leaders were fond of pointing out) outnumbered the Jews there by almost ten to one.[12]

Churchill and Lloyd George, as they installed the Hashemite Arab rulers in power in Iraq and Jordan, faced a basic contradiction. Although Iraq had its large, secure, and thriving Jewish population, which considered itself an extension of the ancient Jewish community of Babylonian times, there were very few indigenous Jews in Transjordan. If Transjordan was to remain exclusively Arab, with Jews barred, then the Balfour policy of fostering a Jewish National Home was not being strictly observed—especially since Britain was deemed to be preparing its Palestine mandate to be a state eventually ruled by Jews, and Jordan's territory represented 75 percent of what the Jews considered to be historic Palestine. So, since Churchill had made an ad hoc decision to keep the Jewish National Home west, not east, of the Jordan river, Churchill had the terms of the Mandate redrafted to specify that Britain did not have to apply the Balfour policy east of the river.[13]

The World War I victors were now in more or less firm possession of the spoils—the remnants of the old Ottoman Empire. Their contradictory promises and goals had set the stage for a colossal Arab–Jewish struggle for the same land. This struggle would eventually overshadow the Middle East. Late in the twentieth century, it would drag the United States of America, as it emerged from the Cold War with the Soviet Union, into assuming one of the biggest overseas burdens in its history: a war to fight its terrorist enemies, and to build a worldwide military network to defend its own interests and those of a chosen few allies. Among these, Israel was privileged. We must next consider how early stages of this struggle changed both Iraq and Israel.

3

"Operation Ezra and Nehemiah": Bittersweet Flight to Zion

While gathering our strength, reinforcing and getting ready to return
to Palestine—let us show to the whole world that we are as fit as any
people to live in an independent political community.
(Chaim Weizmann, 1914)

On a gray morning late in January 1969, about 15 non-Arab journalists met our bus and our appointed minder in front of the old Baghdad Hotel. Our editors had sent us to Iraq to report the aftermath of the grisly public executions of January 27, 1969, shown on TV, of 14 Iraqis, nine of them Jews, including boys of 15 and 16. They were hanged before big crowds, encouraged to watch, in downtown Baghdad's Liberation Square.

All 14 had been convicted of spying for "the Zionist entity," the standard Arab propaganda name for Israel. In some broadcasts, the phrase "and for the United States" had been added, almost as an afterthought. That made the sharp Ba'athist line on Israel conform to the legend, often heard since the Arab defeat in the war of June 1967, that Washington connived in every anti-Arab conspiracy that Tel Aviv inspired.

Although the hanged victims, who had remained on public display after thousands of spectators watched their final convulsions, had been finally cut down and could no longer be photographed, we were bent on observing whatever reactions we were allowed to see or hear. Our young minder assured us from his microphone at the front of the bus that we could go "anywhere" and talk to "anyone" we wished.

Our response was swift: a Jewish district, please. (At the time, according to later Israeli estimates, only 3,300 remained[1] of the 5,000 left after the "rescue" by Israel of the large majority of a Jewish community that, at the time of Israel's birth and Nuri al-Said's ascendancy in the former Iraqi monarchy, had numbered close to 300,000 souls).

A GUIDED TOUR

Our supervised expedition began in a quarter of narrow streets and alleyways near the city's center. Some of our fellow newshawks were

40

already calling it "the ghetto." The bus parked across a dark intersection and our minder ushered us into a synagogue. In the gloom inside, relieved only by a couple of naked 10 or 25-watt bulbs, a bent-over rabbi, perhaps in his eighties or nineties, extracted from a cupboard a huge scroll of the Law. Speaking haltingly in Arabic, translated by our minder and by a younger Jew wearing a *kippah* who stood by the rabbi, he told us, "See, we keep our Torah safe. There is freedom for all religions in Iraq." When asked how many worshippers still attended services, his muttered answer was not translated. It seemed to satisfy our minder.

A posse of secret policemen, dressed in shiny, tight-fitting black suits waited outside. One sported a revolver in a highly visible shoulder holster. Perhaps, we thought, all of us—including our minder from the Information Ministry—faced imminent arrest; possibly worse.

Our escort seemed to sum up his courage. After assuring the Gestapo-like group that we were all on an officially approved mission, he talked on a walkie-talkie radio, a badge of officialdom in the Iraq of 1969. After a terse two-way conversation, he handed the radio to the chief cop. "Naam, Sidi, naam Sidi," equivalent to "yes, boss," the cop repeated laconically. Then he waved us off with a word or two and a dismissive, if liberating, gesture. The ITV crew got one quick shot and we climbed back into the bus. The driver accelerated with squealing tires, as though he were glad to be leaving a scene of iniquity.

As we approached the Tigris river bridge, bound for a mainly Shia neighborhood. I remembered that I was the proud owner of a brand-new Canon still camera. Although there was film inside, I had not yet tried it out. As we crossed the Tigris bridge, I raised it to the bus window to click a view of the river.

That was a serious mistake. Two black cars, Peugeots as I remember, obviously shadowing us, overtook the bus. One pulled ahead and then stopped sideways in the middle of the bridge, cutting us off.

The cop with the visible revolver, now joined by others whom we had not seen at the synagogue, had drawn his piece from his shoulder holster. He extended the other hand toward me. "Camera, camera," he demanded. My colleague Eric Pace of *The New York Times* remarked ruefully, "He thinks we're spies and that you were shooting a view of the bridge." As I reluctantly handed over my camera, the ITV crew was discreetly veiling their own big film camera and sound gear under a cover on a rear seat in the bus.

The cops (or spooks) used their own walkie-talkie to talk to headquarters. Our release came somewhat faster than it had at the synagogue—but not before the boss cop had extracted my new film, with the one exposed picture, and rather grudgingly handed my empty camera back to me. Next, we spent a few short minutes admiring the busy market area and the golden-domed Shia mosque in the quarter of Al-Qadimain, the site of the tombs of the seventh and ninth of the twelve Shia imams, and for centuries a pride of the Shia majority in Iraq. Our minder, probably a Sunni himself, seemed a bit ill at ease. Later, the ITV crew succeeded in persuading him and the driver to park the bus at the end of a grove of stately palm trees, where their correspondent wanted to do a stand-up piece to camera. Another raid interrupted this. A squad of uniformed, beret-wearing military police descended on us in two station wagons, accompanied by a couple of the men in shiny black suits.

This time things looked somewhat grimmer. "They're taking us to the TV station," said our minder, who looked distinctly worried. "We go on the air with our confessions in 20 minutes," quipped Eric Pace, trying to cheer us up with his inimitable black humor. But when our bus reached the TV station, our minder said with a wan smile, "We probably won't have to stay long, you'll see."

For over two hours we were served stale Arab tea and glasses of water by our hosts. They did not question us (although they were interrogating the minder in another room). The ITV cameraman lamented the loss of usable daylight.

When liberation came at last, the sun was sinking rapidly in the west. As the dark winter night spread over Baghdad, we shuttled back to the city center and parked near the scene of the January 29 hangings, by a huge piece of avant-garde sculpture on Liberation Square. Some of us risked still snapshots and the ITV crew unlimbered their big camera, tripod, and sound gear to do a stand-upper on the square.

Reader, you have probably guessed it by now! Our final detention of this busy day happened as our ITV correspondent declaimed on camera. The resourceful correspondent signaled his cameraman to keep shooting. He managed to film his own arrest. This time, our weary custodian performed valiantly: in a tone of righteous indignation, he actually rebuked the arresting policemen, this time uniformed traffic cops. They soon relented without outside intervention. Relieved that the adventure was over, we hoped to be able to file uncensored stories or, in the case of the AP photographer with us, send a "Belino" or photo transmission by wire. (In both the print and photo cases, we had to transmit from the pressroom at the Ministry of Information, as occurred later during most of the rule of Saddam Hussein.)

JEWISH SURVIVORS

Thirty-four years later, after President George W. Bush's forces and the "coalition of the willing" had invaded Iraq and toppled Saddam Hussein, European reporters sought out the tiny group of Jews who still survived in Baghdad. Philippe Broussard described in *Le Monde* of May 8, 2003, the lonely life of those 26 lone survivors, out of 32 before the 2003 war. Of the hundreds of synagogues once distributed around the city only one now remained open. It was in the Bedawin portion of the poverty-stricken suburb of al-Habibia. A handful of old folks, all over 70, prayed there. When Deborah Parmentier, an AFP (French News Agency) correspondent found it later, in October 2003, the synagogue was closed. Rabbi Emad Levy, aged 38 and the son of the last rabbi, who like five or six others had been whisked away to Israel on special flights during the summer, was now tending a flock of two families, including eight men; less than the ten required to read the Kaddish, or prayers for the dead. Except for one teenager and a "young" doctor of 50, the other family members were septuagenarians. The last Jewish religious marriage was in 1978; the most recent bar-mitzvah ceremony in 1979.

On Yom Kippur, the Day of Atonement, in October 2003, Rabbi Levy stayed home to pray with a friend. The locked synagogue was guarded by an armed Muslim employed by the tiny Jewish community. "We could reopen the synagogue when a real government is in place. [Otherwise] it could be attacked," Rabbi Levy said. "The neighbors used to work for Saddam Hussein's secret services, and today they call the guard a Zionist." He added that the little community was frightened, noting that local newspapers, proliferating under the nearly total media freedom allowed by the American occupation authority, had been reporting that Jews from abroad had been secretly buying Iraqi properties.

Real or imagined pressure caused the group to keep an even lower profile than before the war. In June 2003, a U.S. Defense Department official paid a discreet visit to the rabbi to offer special protection. Fearing that might be seen as provocative, the rabbi turned down the offer.

The fateful interaction of Israel/Palestine and Iraq had begun, although slowly, back in the 1920s and 1930s. Palestine was then still a British-ruled dependency, and Iraq was a monarchy under British protection. To fully understand what happened then and later, we must return to the life of Iraq's Jews in the times when they were numerous. Some historians insist that in the nineteenth century, the Jewish population of Baghdad (though not of Basra or the other centers of Jewish life) occasionally outnumbered the Muslims, and certainly the Christians. Like the other minority communities, such as the Assyrian or Chaldean

Christians, the Turcomans, and Yazidis, the Jews lived within either Arab or Kurdish districts of Mesopotamia in neighborhoods or *mahallahs*. Certain families or clans were predominant and enjoyed religious and social autonomy. So did larger minority communities of Jews and Christians, called *millahs*.[2]

Believing themselves to be the natural heirs of the ancient Babylonian Jews and successors to their high culture, the Iraqi Jews were often leaders in their trades, professions, and communities. As well as merchants, traders, and money-changers, they were also successful bankers, lawyers, doctors, and businessmen, sometimes very prosperous ones. In 1927, when the monarchy's Baghdad Chamber of Commerce was organized, scholar Hanna Batatu records that British firms, or companies with mixed British, French, and American capital, formed a majority of the Chamber's so-called "first-class" members. Each had to have capital of over 22,500 Iraqi dinars (a respectable sum at that time, when the Iraqi currency had gold backing and was fairly sound). They had a large business turnover. Only one was a Muslim Arab concern, and its director was the son of the owner of a British firm called Allen Bros. of Aberdeen, Scotland. Later, in 1938–39, just before World War II engulfed the Middle East, 215 out of its 498 total members were Jewish.

Batatu cites a British consular report of 1879, during the Ottoman era. At that time, the Jews were "the most important mercantile group," dwarfing the Shia and Sunni Arab or Christian communities. Again, in 1910, the Jews had "literally monopolized" trade and neither Muslims nor Christians could compete, especially in Basra. By 1920 the Jews were extending their influence to the transit trade with Persia.

The Jewish traders competed with the British colonial merchants who had established themselves in Iraq. The Jews imported mostly British goods directly from India and Britain, depriving resident British merchants of their Iraqi commissions.[3] By the start of the twentieth century, most of Baghdad's leading Jewish merchants owned their own commercial firms in India or England. One such tycoon was Ezra Sassoon Suhaiyik, worth nearly $2,000,000 in 1919. He owned a big trading house, J. S. Sykes and Co., in Manchester, England. Zion Bikhor and Ezra Ishaq Salih, both Baghdad merchants, possessed companies in Bombay and London.

By far the biggest, wealthiest, and most powerful of the Iraqi Jewish commercial dynasties were the Sassoons, sometimes called "the Rothschilds of the East," with roots back in Ottoman times. Like successful businessmen of all eras and faiths, they understood how to ride out the ebb and flow of wars, economic booms, and depressions. The founder of the commercial house, David Sassoon, who by 1850 was active in China and Japan as well as India and Europe, took advantage of the 1861 cotton famine in the mills of Lancashire, England, caused by the American Civil War when the Confederacy's cotton exports were throttled; Sassoon replaced American cotton with Indian cotton yarn at up-market prices. He died in 1864. His heirs acquired banks, trading companies, and other firms from London to Singapore and Tokyo. The Sassoon empire is remembered today, if in name only, in products like Vidal Sassoon beauty products. Over 250,000 Iraqi-born Jews who have emigrated since 1948, mostly to Israel but also to the Americas and Europe, count many Sassoons among their social elite, including the Israeli diplomat who at this writing is ambassador to Greece: David Sassoon.

In Iraq, the upper layers of the Jewish trading class during the period of British influence and rule (1917–32) generally prospered in good harmony with their Muslim and other fellow citizens. They avoided politics. Like Nuri al-Said's bankers, the Zilkhas family, they did favors for the rulers (once placing a country house and horses at Nuri's disposal when he visited King Farouk's Egypt). The Jewish family of Lawi, important automobile dealers and agents, made it a point to offer discounted cars to high Iraqi officials. However, when Arab–Jewish riots erupted, as they periodically did in British-mandated Palestine, the financially strong but politically inactive Jews, largely unaffected by the Zionist movement, did not get involved. The bulk of the top jobs in government went to Muslims. In the period 1921–58, encompassing both the British mandate and the independent monarchy, out of a total of 575 ministerial appointments, 95 or 16.5 percent went to members of merchant families. Of these, 84 were held by Muslims, and 59 of those appointments went to members of only six big Muslim families.[4]

The Iraqi Jews throughout history never renounced their religion, but they did adopt Arabic language, culture, food, proverbs, and superstitions. In 1915, when the Ottoman reformers issued a revolutionary manifesto, they called on "Arabs of the Christian and Jewish faiths to join ranks with your Muslim brethren" to fight Turkish rule.

It was this partial cultural amalgam with Arab society which probably kept most Iraqi Jews before World War II, and those still living in Iraq after it, from embracing Zionism. However, the Iraqi Jews did begin to feel pressures when, in 1929 and 1936, Arab rioting and revolt broke out against both the Jewish residents and settlers and the British rulers in Palestine. Some of Nuri al-Said's close associates began smuggling arms to the Arabs during the 1936–37 Palestinian Arab revolt, led by Ezzedine al-Qassem's armed Palestinian guerrillas.

INDEPENDENCE ... SORT OF

Iraq in 1932 became the first Arab remnant of territory of the old Ottoman Empire to achieve independence of a sort. As conflict in Palestine developed in the 1930s, Iraqi army officers with nationalist sentiments made strong bids for power in Baghdad. Batatu points out that the Iraqi royal army officers' corps was split. Its three main factions were Kurdish, pro-Arab or pan-Arab (thus, by definition, anti-Zionist), and Iraqi nationalists (or "Iraqists"), focused on their own homeland rather than on dreams of pan-Arab unity. General Baqr Sidki, who led a coup in 1936 just as the Arab revolt against Britain was erupting in Palestine, is said to have left behind documents projecting a military dictatorship and ouster of the king. Sidki's coup was led by Kurds and Iraqists, whereas the main roles in counter-coups by other officers in 1937 and 1938, and in the pro-German coup of Rashid Ali during World War II, were played by pan-Arabs. During this last upheaval, Nazi Germany, after encouraging it, was too late in sending airborne support. Well over 100 Iraqi Jews were killed in a short but deadly pogrom that erupted on June 1, 1941. This gave David Ben-Gurion and other Jewish leaders in the West a strong impetus toward the eventual "rescue" of the Iraqi Jews and their extraction to Palestine.

Pan-Arab and anti-Zionist nationalism among the Muslims (and some Christians) of Iraq was generated by the arrival in Baghdad a few months before World War II of the charismatic, pro-Nazi Haj Amin al-Husseini, the Mufti of Jerusalem. When the 1936 revolt began, the British authorities in Palestine correctly identified Haj Amin as its spiritual or ideological leader. They fired him from his official job as mufti and deported him to Syria, to the annoyance of the French authorities in Damascus. The French were relieved after King Ghazi had died in April 1939 and been replaced by his son, Faisal II, when Haj Amin showed up in Baghdad in October of 1939, invited by the extreme pan-Arab and pro-Palestinian faction, to the embarrassment of the government of Prime Minister Nuri al-Said and the British diplomats who stood behind him. The ex-mufti gathered several thousand disciples. He cemented links with like-minded Iraqi army officers and watched approvingly when Rashid Ali and his rebellious generals and colonels of the "Golden Square" drove al-Said and the pro-British regent, Abdulillah, temporarily out of Iraq. British forces landed in Basra and others attacked from the west. The pro-Axis and pan-Arab, pro-Palestinian factions were defeated, and the old regime was restored.[5] Yet the Iraqi Jewish community, as one of the undercover Zionist agents later assigned to bring them out to Israel, Shlomo Hillel, records in his memoirs, had been rendered more conscious of the problems in Palestine and more nervous about their own possible fate. The restoration of British-backed rule did not remove this nervousness. It also stimulated renewed interest among the *Yishuv*, the Jewish population of Palestine, in the fate of their Iraqi co-religionnaires.

VIOLENCE AND RESCUE

Inter-communal violence was not unusual in the Iraqi monarchy of the 1930s. On September 17, 1936, to mark the outbreak of the Arab revolt in Palestine, the government in Baghdad declared "Palestine Day," on which several Jewish passers-by were killed in the street by a bomb. Shlomo Hillel recalls that during that decade, Hebrew-language teachers who the *Yishuv* sent to Iraq were expelled. The Iraqi community was pressured to end Jewish cultural activities and movements. Despite this, Hillel notes, younger-generation Jews in Iraq studied Arabic literature and culture. Until this period of heightened inter-communal tension, most Iraqi Jews had spoken their own Arabic dialect, writing it in Hebrew letters learned in their homes or their own schools. Now, however, Iraqi Jewish writers and poets sought to join the mainstream Arabic culture of the Iraqi Muslims and Christians by writing in proper modern Arabic. In return they were identified more as Iraqis of the Jewish faith than simply as Jews.[6]

Benny Morris, one of the most thorough Israeli historians of Israel's covert intelligence activities, relates in a book co-authored by Ian Black, a *Guardian* newspaper journalist who long served in Jerusalem, the checkered history of the Zionist "rescue" of the Iraqi Jews. Reacting to the upheavals of the Rashid Ali period in 1941, the Haganah Jewish militia in Palestine in 1942 organized and trained a small clandestine force called *Shura* (Line) or Babylonian Pioneer Movement. It smuggled agents and material into Iraq to form small "self-defense" cells for Iraqi Jews. Haganah emissaries, notably three men named Shaul Avigur, Enzo Sreni (an Italian Zionist), and Smarya Guttman, moved in from British-controlled Palestine. In Iraq they selected a core of young Zionist-inclined men considered potential leaders. They set up pipelines for clandestine arms supplies, smuggled through Transjordan, Turkey, or Iran and, from 1947 on, by air from Palestine. They also began training programs. From 1943 on they used constant short-wave radio communication, most of it coded or encrypted, with the headquarters in Tel Aviv of Mossad LeAliya Bet, or "Mossad B." A predecessor of the present-day Mossad, Israel's main non-military external intelligence service, Mossad B was charged with facilitating illegal Jewish immigration, to circumvent British restrictions and to build up Jewish manpower for the *Yishuv* as a military and civilian demographic base for a future Jewish state. The clandestine armed *Shura* cells in Iraq bridged the period between the first clandestine flights of Jews from Iraq to Palestine before Israel's independence, and the time from 1948 onward, when David Ben-Gurion and the other founders of the state pursued a systematic policy of "in-gathering" Jews from abroad, especially from Arab and Muslim countries, as well as ones with only small Jewish minorities, like Turkey, Iran, and India. During the wars with Arab neighbors in 1948, the *Shura* cells in Iraq continued to move the Jewish community out of Iraq. By 1951, the *Shura* organization had 16 branches and 2,000 members inside Iraq, 300 of whom had taken military training.

Shlomo Hillel has described in detail his own major role in "Operation Ezra and Nehemiah," the Biblical reference used as a code name. Hillel, whose Mossad code names were "Emil" and "Shamai," was a Jew born in 1923 in Palestine (as a *sabra*, as native Palestinian Jews are today referred to in Israel) and educated there. Before Israeli independence in 1948, Hillel shuttled between Palestine and Iraq, hitching rides on British and private planes at times; at others, dressed in Arab robes, moving by local taxis and other conveyances into and out of Iraq, Iran, Turkey, and Palestine. The clandestine Mossad B station in Baghdad, consecutively codenamed "Berman," "Dekel," and "Oren," organized the outward-bound "shipments," as they were often referred to, in coded messages exchanged with Tel Aviv. The second-biggest Mossad B station was in Tehran, codenamed "Goldman," "Nuri," and "Alon" in the radio traffic and in occasional written messages carried by couriers.

At first, many Iraqi Jews crossed the Shatt al-Arab waterway from Iraq to Iran, or traveled through Kurdish country to the north. (The complicity of some of the Iraqi Kurds in this early traffic helped to establish the later covert, but firm, ties between the state of Israel and the Iraqi Kurds.) Inside Iran, the emigrants, facilitated by bribery, tribal connections, payoffs to smugglers, and other devices, moved through Abadan, Khorramshar, and Ahvaz, or further north through Dezful and Kermanshah, to Tehran From there, they were sent either by air or overland to Turkey and on to Tel Aviv.

Shlomo Hillel was based in Baghdad in 1947–48 and 1950, and in Tehran in 1949. In 1947 he managed to scrape together the funds, the planes and the personnel, including European and American mercenary pilots, to start the first direct flights from Iraq to places in Palestine like Beit Sean, where British surveillance was lax or non-existent. In 1949–50, he adopted a new Mossad identity: that of "Charles Armstrong," of "Near East Air Transport Incorporated," a cover name for his clandestine charter operation.

WHEELING, DEALING, AND MISHAPS

In his book *Operation Babylon*, Hillel describes how in 1949 "Charles Armstrong" successfully made deals with Nuri al-Said's Iraqi regime for what became a legal, two-year-long airlift of Iraqi Jews to the new state of Israel. Unlike the other Arab regimes in the Middle East, Nuri, with King Faisal's approval, was willing to push through the Iraqi parliament a law allowing Iraqi Jews to leave legally if they chose to do so—but automatically depriving them of their Iraqi nationality if they did, while also despoiling them of most of their property, businesses, cash, and other valuables. The offer was to expire in March 1951.

Israel's founders conceived of "in-gathering" a demographic pool of over 100,000 Jews, many of them well educated and provided with skills the new state needed. However, the exodus frustrated the Israeli founders' hopes of acquiring extra wealth as capital for the new state.[7]

In 1950 the entire operation began to crumble. In May 1948, the conflict between Iraq and the new state of Israel had begun. The first action had been the dispatch by Nuri al-Said's government of Iraqi troops to join the other Arab forces fighting the Israelis west of the Jordan river; like subsequent Iraqi military campaigns against Israel, this will be examined in detail later in this book. Active fighting with Israel worsened the situation of the remaining Jewish community in Iraq. Clandestine emigration to Palestine had already reduced it by roughly one-fourth to one-third in size.

Naim Giladi is an Iraqi-born Jew who eventually made it to the United States and who was interviewed in New York by a newsletter on Middle East affairs, *The Link*, in 1998. His forebears were the Haroon family, one of the largest and most venerable of the descendants of those who had built the Prophet Ezekiel's tomb near the ruins of ancient Babylon. Giladi worked for Mossad B in the Iraqi Jewish underground. In 1947 at the age of 18 he was unfortunate enough to be caught by the Iraqi secret police while running other young Iraqi Jews ("like myself," he said) in the underground railroad of clandestine emigration. Trying to learn the identities of other members of Giladi's colleagues, his Iraqi torturers pulled out his toenails with pliers, exposed him naked on a cold rooftop in January, and threw buckets of cold water over him. He was transferred to prison near Baghdad at Abu Ghraib—which Saddam Hussein's men later used to incarcerate, torture, and execute prisoners and which the conquering U.S. Army captured in the spring of 2003 and turned into a jail. Ex-Ba'athists, Saddam supporters, and miscellaneous other captives were also abused and tortured, as the world learned in spring of 2004.

Giladi was tried by an Iraqi military court, as were many of his fellow citizens. The Nuri al-Said regime and much of the Arab population bitterly resented Israeli victories and futile United Nations mediation efforts in Palestine. When he was sentenced to be hanged, Giladi speeded up escape plans he had made before his trial. He stuffed himself with bread, the main prison fare, "to put on fat in anticipation of the day I became 18, when they could formally charge me with a crime and attach the 50-pound ball and chain that was standard prisoner issue."

Once his leg was shackled, Giladi went on a starvation diet, thinning down his leg under the shackle, making it easier to slip off when greased by a pat of butter he had managed to purloin. A visiting friend had brought him some army clothing—a long green coat and stocking cap, obscuring part of his face. He escaped by mixing with a group of soldiers leaving the prison. A friend was waiting with a car and the Jewish underground sped him eventually to Israel, where he arrived in May 1950.

Like many immigrants evacuated from Iraq, Yemen, and other Arab countries, Giladi got off to a bad start. An immigration official could not pronounce the Arabic-like "gh" in his name, and changed it to "Hlaski." This made it sound like the name of an Ashkenaze, European-born Jew. The mistake introduced him to how the caste system in Israeli society worked. Since he knew farming, he was sent to Dafnah, a farming kibbutz in Upper Galilee. There, he recalls, the accommodations for immigrants were "the worst of everything. ... I left." He next found himself in Ashkelon (then still with an Arab name, al-Majdal). The local Arabs were under the authority of an Israeli military governor. Giladi's new employers, discovering that he spoke Arabic and Hebrew, wanted him to get local Arabs to sign "petitions" to the United Nations that they be transferred out of Israel and into the Gaza Strip. He claims that the Israeli authorities were preventing the local farmers from watering or tending their orange trees and otherwise pressuring them to depart. So he refused the job. Eventually, he adds:

those Palestinians who didn't sign up for transfers were taken by force—just put in trucks and dumped in Gaza. About 4,000 people were driven from al-Majdal in one way or another. The few who remained were collaborators with the Israeli authorities.

When Giladi applied for a new government job, his government interviewers discovered that his face did not match his seemingly Ashkenaze name. When asked whether he spoke Polish or Yiddish, he had to admit he did not. Eventually he legally changed his name to Giladi. When he applied for a job with the Socialist/Zionist party to work on their Arabic newspaper, he was sent to a "department of Jews from Arab countries." Disgusted, he reflected, "It's segregation ... just like a Negroes' department. I turned around and walked out. ... That same year I organized a demonstration in Ashkelon against Ben-Gurion's racist policies and 10,000 people turned out." Dutifully he served in the IDF after the 1967 war in Sinai, during the fighting of the post-1967 "war of attrition" along the Suez Canal. After the 1970 ceasefire, Giladi organized demonstrations for equal rights for Iraqi and other "Oriental" or "Arab" (Sephardic) immigrants. He compares the struggle he led in a movement, which the Israeli authorities dubbed the "Black Panthers," with what "blacks" in the United States were fighting against: segregation, discrimination, unequal treatment. Rather than reject the "Black Panther" label, he adopted it proudly. "I had posters of Martin Luther King, Malcolm X, Nelson Mandela, and other civil rights activists plastered all over my office."

Giladi says he was disgusted by the events of 1982, when the then Defense Minister Ariel Sharon led the Israeli invasion of Lebanon in an effort to smash the PLO. Sharon was found by an Israeli commission of inquiry to be "indirectly" responsible for the massacre by Lebanese Christian militia of hundreds of Palestinians at the Sabra and Chatila camps outside Beirut in the fall of 1982. Giladi then emigrated to the United States. He renounced his Israeli citizenship, acquired American nationality and used the proceeds of the sale of his house in Israel to pay for publication of his book, *Ben-Gurion's Scandals: How the Haganah and the Mossad Eliminated the Jews*, dealing with what he claims was violence by the Zionist underground in Iraq to pressure the Iraqi Jews into emigrating. Since 1998 Giladi has lived in New York City with his family. John F. Mahoney, one of the editors of *The Link* newsletter, says Giladi told him, "I am Iraqi, born in Iraq, my culture still Iraqi Arabic, my religion Jewish, my citizenship, American."[8]

"ARAB" JEWS WHO MADE IT

There are other, similar accounts by Iraqi and other Arab Jews who found that in Israel, they did experience various forms of social and job discrimination. However, as the case of General Shaul Mofaz illustrates, many of the "Arab Jews" opted to embrace the system and succeeded in rising to the very top of the Israeli body politic. Mofaz is an Iraqi-born Jewish immigrant whose spectacular rise in the IDF eventually raised him to the cabinet post of Defense Minister under Ariel Sharon's leadership in 2002.

When I lived in Casablanca, Morocco, during the late 1950s and early 1960s, I met the young David Levy, born in the Moroccan Jewish community, who eventually became Israeli Foreign Minister. When I first met him (in 1960, as far as I can remember), he was not yet 20. He was a wannabe entrepreneur and the inseparable friend of a Muslim youth from a merchant family named Larbi something-or-other: "David and Larbi." When Levy emigrated to Israel for the first time, he seems to have been so dissatisfied with the conditions which other Arab Jews like Giladi experienced that he returned to Morocco. But he returned to Israel and worked his way upward in the construction business from menial jobs. Levy embarked on a political career that took him to the Knesset and eventually into the government as foreign minister, the pinnacle of government. In 2003 and early 2004, he served on a Knesset committee investigating why Israeli intelligence had overestimated weapons of mass destruction in Iraq and had ignored those in Libya, which Muammar Qaddafi had just declared to the Americans.

Dr. Yehouda Shenhav, with degrees and teaching experience from both Israeli and American higher institutes of learning (a PhD at Stanford University, California; teaching at both Stanford and Princeton University), has written on the problem of the Sephardic Jews in Israel, especially the Iraqi ones. In his book, *The Arab Jews: Nationalism, Religion and Ethnicity* (in Hebrew, publisher Am Oved, Tel Aviv) he links the *Mizrahim*, the Israeli term for the Jews born in Iraq and the other Arab states, with the treatment of the Palestinian Arabs.

Dr. Shenhav was born in Petah Tikvah, near Tel Aviv, in 1952 as Yehouda Shaabani. His mother, Esparant Mualem, of a wealthy Iraqi Jewish family, arrived in Israel at the age of 18 from Baghdad. She and her parents were part of the arranged exodus of Operation Ezra and Nehemiah, which in all brought over 120,000 Iraqi Jews to Israel between March 1950 and July 1951. At the immigrant absorption camp of Sha'ar Aliyah and the transit camp for new immigrants, Esparant met Eliyahu Shaharbarani. The couple married in 1951. Like many other

Iraqi Jews, they remained at first on the margins of mainstream Ashkenazi society in Israel, living on an army intelligence base in Beersheba.

Salah Shenhav, Yehouda's father, was one of the more mobile Iraqi Jewish merchants who were able to commute more or less regularly between Iraq and Palestine in the 1930s. During one visit, he bought a plot of land in Petah Tikvah. Shlomo, their eldest son, settled in Palestine, eventually becoming a well-to-do industrialist. In 1946, when Ben-Gurion and the other elders of the Palestinian *Yishuv* were beginning to plan the "in-gathering" of the Arab Jews, he joined Kibbutz Alonim, entering a branch for Jews of Iraqi origin with about 40 members, called the "Babylonian" group. Dr. Shenhav's father then went to become a settler in Kibbutz Beeri in the western Negev desert. This was built on the ruins of a former Arab village.

Yahouda's father left the kibbutz to join the Haganah, Israel's pre-state army. By 1950, without telling his son, he had been recruited into Aman, the Hebrew name for Israeli military intelligence. One day an elderly man with a heavy Iraqi accent encountered Shenhav's son Eliyahu in a Tel Aviv café and introduced himself as the man who had recruited his grandfather into the Israeli intelligence community. When he gave Eliyahu two pictures of his father with other young twenty-something men, Shenhav recognized that they were all *Mizrahim*, Arab Jews. Shenhav said he recognized his father in the photographs "by his flowing mane of hair." (Shenhav added that it reminded him of the character Kramer on the popular American TV show, *Seinfeld*).

After serving Israeli military intelligence on many missions abroad, Eliyahu worked as a security guard in a supermarket. Ironically, death came for him at the age of 62—from one of the 29 Scud missiles which Iraqi dictator Saddam Hussein fired at Israel—during the 1991 Gulf war.

After his first years of university studies in business management, Dr. Shenhav began to agitate for more recognition in Israeli society of the values and the grievances of the *Mizrahim*. He fueled acrimonious debates in Israel with an article he published in *Haaretz* magazine in December 1996 called "A Conspiracy of Silence," claiming that the political Left in Israel, in its obsession with the tragic problems of the Palestinian Arabs, was ignoring or obscuring what he considered the equally serious "*Mizrahi* problem," the Arab Jews, because the Left could neither deal with it properly, nor make it go away.

Another Shenhav article, even more central to today's Israeli–Iraqi enmities, appeared in the same magazine in April 1998, entitled "The Perfect Robbery." Shenhav railed bitterly against the Israeli establishment for "deceiving" the Iraqi-born Jews and for allegedly using the pretext of their assets, seized or frozen in Baghdad (and in 2003, after the American occupation, already the subject of hundreds of Jewish claims against the Iraqi state), as a means of evading responsibility for compensating Palestinians who were dispossessed refugees from the 1948 Arab–Israel conflict. (In 1949, Israel, victorious in the conflict, was asked to sign the Lausanne Protocols, obligating it to pay compensation to the Palestinian refugees before it was admitted to the United Nations.)

In 2003, Shenhav found Israel's society to be in sad straits—sad, because, he said, "it could have been paradise here." All the possible phobias have piled up about anti-Semitism, about homosexuals, about Palestinians, and about *Mizrahim*. The *Mizrahi* politicians in all the parties, instead of being sensitive to these questions and to questions of suffering and social justice, have themselves become oppressors. For Prime Minister Ariel Sharon's ruling Likkud party, he had a parting shot: Now, of all times, the poor treatment of the weaker classes, who [including the *Mizrahim*] are considered Likkud voters, is coming from Likkud itself.[9]

WHOSE TERRORISM?

The most persistent and controversial of the many accounts of the Jewish exodus from Iraq in 1949–52 is the story—if you believe the accounts published in Israel; or the legend, if you believe the results of the official Israeli government inquiry ordered by Prime Minister David Ben-Gurion—of terrorist bombings, mostly of the Jewish community in Baghdad, during the emigration period. Early eyewitness accounts of Jews claim that these were perpetrated by Israeli secret agents in order to speed up the arranged and legal departures of Jews. If, however, you believe the official Israeli inquiry results and mainstream official Israeli doctrine, these terrorist acts were the work of Iraqi officials or provocateurs.

One account is by Naim Giladi in the United States. Reports by him and others in the Hebrew-language *Black Panther* magazine, and in books by such other critics of Israel as the late American, Rabbi Elmer Berger, agree in the main with the names and dates, if not the deeds, narrated by Mordecai Ben-Porat. Mossad B sent Ben-Porat, an Iraqi-born Jew, back to Iraq to supervise the operation. Later, commissioned to investigate by an embarrassed Ben-Gurion government, he gave the Israeli agents a clean bill of health. The fundamental difference between the two versions lies not, in most cases, in the facts about the bombings themselves, but rather in the question of who were the guilty parties.

On March 19, 1950, a bomb caused damage and injured several people at the American Cultural Center and Library in Baghdad. This was a favorite meeting place for young people, especially students, and for many Jews. Next, on April 8, 1950, the last day of the Jewish Passover, there occurred the first terrorist attack directed specifically at Jews. A car with three young passengers tossed a grenade at the Dar el-Beida (Casablanca) café in Baghdad's Abu Nawas Street. Many Jews had been strolling along the banks of the Tigris in celebration of the ancient Jewish ritual, the so-called Sea Song, and had gathered afterwards in the café. According to the *Black Panther* account, no one was injured. Ben-Porat, however, counted six Jews injured, one in a critical state. He cabled this to Tel Aviv, mentioning that "there were other provocations and throwing of stones at Jewish citizens in various parts of the capital."[10] That night and the next day, leaflets scattered in Jewish neighborhoods called on Jews to leave Iraq immediately. Many responded to this and to their own fears by jamming emigration offices, set up in schools and synagogues, to fill out declarations that they were willingly renouncing their Iraqi citizenship and applying to leave Iraq. The crowds, especially of poor Jews with little to lose who hoped for a better life in Israel, grew so large that the Iraqi authorities had to open new registration centers.[11]

On May 10, 1950, at 3 a.m. a grenade was hurled at the display window of a Jewish-owned car dealership, the Beit-Lawi Automobile Company. There was structural damage but no one was hurt at this early hour. On June 3, 1950, someone in a speeding car threw another grenade in the El-Batawin area, an up-market Jewish neighborhood where wealthier Jews and middle-class Muslims lived. Again, no one was hurt. The Zionist emigration activists asked Tel Aviv to raise the quota for immigration from Iraq. On June 5, a bomb exploded next to the Jewish-owned Stanley Shasghura building on central Baghdad's Al-Rashid street (where many of the Iraqi terrorist insurgents struck at American troops in 2003). There was property damage but no casualties.[12]

Most members of the Baghdad Jewish community believed that extremist Iraqis, probably all Muslims, wanted to kill them or drive them out, so as to seize their property and money. Their right to emigrate had been recognized by the Nuri al-Said government. Iraqi police officers appeared at synagogues, seeking to persuade Jews to fill out the necessary forms and leave legally. Some Jews were hesitant, believing that the whole operation was simply a trap to unmask Zionists among them. Zionism, under Iraqi law, was a serious criminal offense.[13]

The most complete published accounts of the bombing offensive, including the official one of Mordecai Ben-Porat, concern the Ma'suda

Shemtov synagogue in Baghdad, a main gathering point for immigrants. Here, Ben-Porat points out, the emigrants experienced final processing. They completed their formalities for departure and lined up for transport to the airport and for the flights that were leaving for Nicosia and, sometimes, directly for Tel Aviv. The temple's first floor contained prayer halls and offices, and the organizing officials had offices on the second floor. An active, noisy courtyard surrounded the synagogue, filled with Jews and other Iraqis connected with the operation or who had nearby shops.

On the evening of January 14, 1951, the synagogue was full of Kurdish Jews from Suleimaniyeh. Leah Cohen, near the bus that was to take emigrants to Baghdad airport, was hanging onto the hand of her five-year-old son, Eli when a grenade was thrown. She fled with him to a local Muslim doctor, who removed a splinter from the boy's bleeding hand. In all, three people were killed by the grenade: two boys, Sassoon Yitzhak and Saleh Shaba, and an adult, Moshe Baghnou, who died from his wounds on the next day. Six were seriously and 19 lightly injured. Ben-Porat records that when the grenade exploded he was at the home of Flora and Haim Shamash. They were the parents of Eitan Shamash, one of the leading organizers of the emigration campaign. Ben-Porat rushed to the synagogue, then informed Sassoon Abed, chief of the public committee for emigration affairs. Moshe Baghnou, before he died, testified that he had seen "a Muslim dressed in khaki" throw the grenade from the balcony of an Arab house facing the synagogue.

After this, fear seized the Baghdad Jews that an anti-Jewish organization was definitely plotting to harm or kill them, and that anyone in a position to leave should do so at once. Queues thickened at the Ezra Daoud synagogue, another registration point. On the night before the Iraqi government's period for legal departure expired (March 19, 1951), some prospective travelers were paying as much as £200 sterling, a very large sum for most of them, to guarantee that their names were on the "legal" list. Before the end of March, the Iraqi parliament passed a law confiscating the property of all Jews who had renounced their citizenship. The maximum cash sum anyone was allowed to take out of the country was £70 sterling. The tempo of flights increased to three or four a day. At first, an Iraqi police officer would accompany each flight to Nicosia airport in Cyprus. Ben-Porat describes how, to spare the officer the embarrassment of seeing the same plane take off for Tel Aviv's Lydda (now Ben-Gurion) airport with the emigrants, he would be given a "grand tour" of Cyprus or entertained in a café or restaurant until the travelers had flown eastward to Israel, sometimes in different aircraft from those they arrived in. He would then return to Baghdad, on the same or another plane. As David Hirst reports, "Before long all that was left of the 130,000 abandoning home, property and an ancient heritage was a mere 5,000" Iraqi Jews.[14]

It was not long before recriminations began over who was responsible for the terrorist campaign. Giladi and others allege that the attacks were the work of the clandestine Mossad B agents and the so-called "Movement" to encourage emigration and discourage those Jews who wanted to stay on in Iraq. A Palestinian Arab working as a salesman in Baghdad's big Uruzdi Beg department store told police that he recognized a well-dressed customer in the shop from the time he had been a coffee-boy in Acre, Israel, as Yehudah Tajjar. The police arrested Tajjar, who confessed his identity and claimed he had come to Baghdad to marry his Jewish sweetheart. He gave the police names of other Israelis who were arrested, 15 in all. One of them, Shalom Salih, who allegedly managed clandestine Haganah arms caches in Iraq, is said to have led police to these caches, some dating back to World War II. During the Iraqi court trial of those arrested, the prosecution claimed they were Zionist underground agents charged with scaring the Jews into leaving as soon as possible.

It was Tajjar who apparently turned state's evidence against his fellow Jews. Sentenced to life imprisonment, he was released after serving ten years. On May 29, 1966, the Leftist Israeli newspaper *Ha'olam Hazeh* published what it said was a full account of the exodus, based on Tajjer's account. On November 9, 1972, *Black Panther* magazine published further extensive accounts of the events, including the trial, mainly from two Israeli citizens present in Baghdad at the time. One of them, Kadduri Salim, had been injured by the Shemtov synagogue grenade. When he reached Israel he applied, in vain, for compensation from the Israeli state, citing the Iraqi court decision that the "Movement" had thrown the grenade. Another account, by an Iraqi-born lawyer, described the contradictory opinions of two Iraqi judges, from South and North Baghdad respectively, who at first set free several Jewish suspects after the first bombings, then sided with the police and the prosecution and eventually condemned the other suspects to death.[15]

According to Mordecai Ben-Porat, bombings after the synagogue attack continued at other sites: at the U.S. Information Center (which he, unlike the *Black Panther* accounts, places in March 1951, not March 1950), near the big Rafidain Bank on June 6, a letter bomb at the home of a Jewish attorney, Jamal Baban, and on August 19 at the office of the *Al-Yaktha* newspaper in Basra.

Ben-Porat acknowledges how widespread the opinion was that those Jews charged and convicted were indeed guilty of the attacks, and that even Prime Minister David Ben-Gurion believed this for a time, which is why he ordered an official investigation. However, Ben-Porat argues that the Iraqi Jews were leaving anyhow in large numbers, before the exodus was legalized by the Iraqi authorities, escaping often at great risk. Many of the Jews contacting the clandestine Halutz Movement for assistance in leaving, Ben-Porat says, had to wait two years for departure. He estimates that about 12,000 Jews escaped via Iran alone, about 10 percent of the entire Iraqi Jewish community. In the appendix of his book, *To Baghdad and Back*, Ben-Porat reproduces the documents concerning the official investigation, which cleared (or whitewashed, in the opinion of his skeptical adversaries) the Jews involved. A series of letters and affidavits, attached to the official Israeli findings, seem to show that the three Jews executed were innocent and framed, and that the attacks were the work of Iraqi officialdom.

Although most who chronicle these events are too young to have witnessed the Iraqi Jewish exodus, the subject revived in Israeli consciousness as a result of the fall of Saddam Hussein. Massive property claims are surfacing against the post-Saddam Iraqi state by émigré Jews. Some aimed to recover or acquire real estate or businesses in a future, "democratic" Iraqi state, and in spring of 2004 the Israeli Justice Ministry was giving them official attention. These claims are closely linked in some Israeli minds with the explosive issue of a future Iraqi "normalization" of relations with Israel. How these relations became a permanent state of war from 1948 on is our next subject.

4

Iraq Enters the Palestine Arena

Anyone who works for peace in the Middle East gets clobbered by both sides.
(Former U.S. Secretary of State Dean Rusk)

Roughly contemporaneous with the exodus of the Jews came Iraq's first involvement in the long series of armed Arab–Israeli conflicts, fundamentally about the fate of Palestine. It has continued until today.

World War II and what followed until the 1948–49 Arab–Israel war saw the infancy of Israel's formidable intelligence and security services, destined to bear the brunt of future confrontations with Iraq and the other Arab states. Their antecedents were rooted in the Jewish underground resistance to British rule, as well as activities to do with Jewish immigration from the Arab countries. The Zionist founders realized that before they could build a state, they must first join with the World War II Allies against their common enemies, the Nazis. Adolf Hitler was bent upon exterminating the Jews in Europe. The Allies wanted help from the Arabs in the Middle East to defeat him.

The Jewish Agency for Palestine, founded in 1929, coordinated immigration and settlement for the *Yishuv* in the territory of the Mandate. Its political department kept careful tabs on the Arab communities and states, inside and outside of Palestine. The Haganah militia, an embryo of the post-1948 Israel Defense Force (IDF), was closely connected to the Histradut labor federation. It operated throughout Palestine with its own covert agents and informants. However, The Jewish Agency's Arab "experts" completely failed to predict that anti-Jewish and anti-British Arab riots in Jaffa, arising from Arab labor strikes in 1935, were going to explode into the major Arab revolt of 1936–39. Individual Jews who were in contact with the Arab community were chosen by the *Yishuv* leaders to report on Arab activities and intentions. One offered the advantage of belonging to the British police in Tel Aviv. Another, in Haifa, was Emmanuel Wilensky, an archaeologist. He tried to organize Jewish intelligence activities on a "scientific" basis. Arab informants were recruited—for the most part not regularly paid agents, but rather individuals who had quarrels over real estate or other matters with their fellow Arabs.

In their history of Israeli intelligence, *Israel's Secret Wars*, Ian Black and Benny Morris identify key figures active during the 1936–39 warfare with the Arabs. One of them, Reuven Zaslani, the Jerusalem-born son of a Russian rabbi and a scholar and teacher of both Hebrew and Arabic, was energetic, tough, and dedicated to the full-time intelligence job he undertook in 1937 for the Haganah. He was so secretive that the late Teddy Kollek, one of Israel's pioneer founders who later became a long-remembered Mayor of Jerusalem, once joked about Zaslani that when a taxi driver asked him where he wanted to go, he replied, "There's no need for you to know."[1]

With others like him, Zaslani formed a strong team, which tried to work with the British services against the Arab movements. In early 1939 the British army managed to kill the Arab commander-in-chief of the revolt, Abdel-Rahim Haj Muhammad. Many Arab insurgents fled into Syria and the revolt petered out, with the Palestinian Arab community badly divided. A British government White Paper of 1939 had ended hopes of a partition proposed in the summer of 1938 by the Peel Commission, an Anglo-Jewish-Arab group. The White Paper discouraged the Zionist leaders by restricting the sale of land to Jews and by envisioning the creation of an independent Palestinian state within ten years. The British soon cracked down hard on Haganah activities and rounded up its agents.

THE ROOTS OF ISRAELI INTELLIGENCE

A right-wing armed faction opposed to the Haganah was the Irgun Zwei Leumi (IZL or Irgun). This had been founded in 1931 by Avraham Tehomi, but split in 1937 because one of its leaders, Zionist theoretician Ze'ev Jabotinsky, would not support indiscriminate retaliation against the Arabs. The split resulted in the establishment of a new underground terrorist group, Lohamet Herut Israel or Lehi, the Israel Freedom Fighters, which came to be known as the "Stern Gang" after Avraham Stern, its chief. Stern created an anti-British underground, which instigated violent terrorism, including the bombing, shooting, capture, and hanging of British soldiers. Menachem Begin, the Zionist leader who as Israeli prime minister in 1979 would conclude peace with President Anwar al-Sadat of Egypt, re-established Irgun in 1944. It soon rivaled the Stern Gang in violence. Ben-Gurion's group declared against the Irgun what almost became a civil war. It was aggravated when Lehi gunmen assassinated Lord Moyne, the senior British Minister-Resident in the Middle East, in Cairo.[2]

During the wartime British crackdown in 1940, the Haganah set up a counter-intelligence department (*rigul negdi* in Hebrew). Its main jobs were to watch Jews who collaborated with the British occupiers and the Irgun activists. During the turbulent months from June 1940 to March 1942, which included the Rashid Ali drama in which British reinforcements were rushed to Iraq to thwart Axis plans there, Moshe Shertok (who later became Moshe Sharett) and others set up the first country-wide Jewish intelligence service, under the very noses of the British authorities. It was called in Hebrew *Sherutt Yediot*, Shai for short. Its headquarters was a Tel Aviv office supposed to be the premises of the welfare committee serving Jewish soldiers in the British army. It included an "internal" or counter-espionage department dealing with Jewish affairs, a British or "political" department charged with infiltrating the British military and government establishments, and an Arab department, headed by Arab linguists. Shai also became involved in buying captured German and Italian weapons smuggled into Palestine by Australian troops who had been fighting General Rommel's Axis armies in North Africa. It stockpiled the arms for what the Zionist leaders knew would be a serious conflict with the Arabs. Eventually Shai moved into more permanent Tel Aviv headquarters. Under the leadership of a diminutive but tough young man named Isser Halperin (later Harel, who would head independent Israel's Mossad in the 1950s), Shai created comprehensive intelligence files listing thousands of Arab names.

After France fell to the Nazi armies in June 1940, the Zionist leadership and Shai began to work more closely with the Allied military, gaining experience with them in intelligence operations outside Palestine. In addition to Operation "Ezra and Nehemiah" to bring out the Iraqi Jews, the Haganah cooperated with British and Free French preparations for the invasion of Vichy-French-ruled Syria and Lebanon in June 1941. Their activities included the sabotage of oil refineries in northern Lebanon's port of Tripoli in order to deny fuel to Hitler's Luftwaffe planes, operating from French-controlled Syria since France's fall. It was these bases that the Germans hoped to use to support Rashid Ali's May 1941 coup in Baghdad. In one joint operation with Allied officers reconnoitering Vichy French positions in south Lebanon, a young Haganah officer, Captain Moshe Dayan, lost his left eye when his binoculars were hit by a bullet fired by Senegalese colonial troops. Dayan's lifelong eye patch became the best-known badge of recognition of this soldier-archaeologist and leader of Israel's military forces in future wars.

During the Allied military campaign to free Syria and Lebanon from Vichy control and German influence, the Haganah deployed a new combat and intelligence unit known as the *Plugot Mahatz*, (strike companies or Palmach; also Palma). This included an elite unit called the Syrian Platoon. Its members were mostly *Mizrahim* or Arab Jews who knew or learned local Syrian and Lebanese Arabic dialects, just as the Iraqi Jews knew and used idiomatic Iraqi Arabic.

After the defeat of Rommel's Afrika Korps at El Alamein in the summer of 1942, the SOE trained about 100 Palmach operatives. Moshe Dayan commanded the Jewish trainees. They benefited from the skills of operatives working with the pro-Zionist British officer Orde Wingate, known and trusted by the *Yishuv* for the exploits of his "Special Night Squads" against the Arabs in Palestine in the 1930s.

By 1943, the British had begun to fall out with their temporary Zionist allies. The Palmach had begun to steal British weapons. Syria and Lebanon were now firmly in Allied hands. In May 1943, the Palmach set up its own Arab Platoon to serve its own interests. It also created a Palmach German Platoon of German speakers.[3]

RESISTING THE BRITISH

Soon, all of the Zionist underground and paramilitary groups were targeting the British occupation, while gearing up for war with the Arabs. The end of World War II speeded this up. One event in the new Jewish anti-British terrorist offensive did much to draw world attention to the Zionist cause and hasten the departure of the British: the blowing up of British headquarters in Jerusalem's famous and (still today) luxurious King David Hotel on July 22, 1946. The hotel, near the edge of West Jerusalem and a famous landmark, built of the solid, golden-colored carved blocks of Palestine stone, was the nerve center of British military power in Palestine. This author remembers standing on its steps in November 1977 amid cheering crowds of onlookers, journalists, and Israeli officials, as President Anwar al-Sadat of Egypt arrived in Jerusalem to make his historic declaration of "no more war." He made it to Prime Minister Menachem Begin, the 1946 planner of the King David's destruction—and ultimately the signatory of a peace treaty with Sadat under President Jimmy Carter's watchful eye in Washington in 1979.

In 1946 the King David Hotel had defenses, in terms of the technology of that time, comparable to those of the Hotel Al-Rashid and other American power centers in occupied Baghdad of 2003. The Zionist leadership and the Haganah approved the Irgun plan, drafted and proposed by Menachem Begin, in order to shake British rule to its foundations. The Irgun's assault unit packed a set of milk churns, of the sort regularly delivered to the well-fortified hotel, with about 500 pounds of a mixture of gelignite and TNT, attached to a timer, and delivered to the Regence Café, next to the kitchen. Disguised as Arabs, Begin's attackers temporarily held the café staff hostage, placed the milk cans, then released the hostages, telling them to run for their lives. The huge explosion demolished the entire wing of the hotel used by the British military, with a roar that shook all of Jerusalem. Around 90 people died in the rubble, including British personnel, Arabs, and 15 Jews. As he wrote in his book of memoirs, *The Revolt*, Begin and his men had put the world on notice that "a new generation" of fighting Jews had replaced the timid generations who had suffered oppression: "[W]e gave up our arms when we were exiled from our country. With our return to the land of our fathers our strength was restored."[4]

In April of 1947, Britain turned the Palestine problem over to the United Nations which had established UNSCOP, the UN Special Commission on Palestine, to seek an Arab–Jewish settlement before the British left. Ben-Gurion announced on April 1 that the Jewish Agency now officially aimed at establishment of a Jewish state, followed by a "Jewish–Arab alliance." This gave rise to the plan to partition Palestine into two independent states, one Jewish and one Arab. Ben-Gurion and his advisers began to study Arab military strength. They determined that the two main Arab forces were those of Egypt (35,000 regular troops) and Iraq (about 30,000). Most Arab forces, with the exception of Transjordan's British-trained and led army, were ill-trained and ill-prepared. Altogether, Egypt, Iraq, Syria, Transjordan, and Lebanon could field 150,000 men, though it was doubtful that they could get all of them into Palestine at once. The Jews, who had been killing British soldiers, did not count on British help.

THE ARABS PREPARE FOR WAR

By the time that Ben-Gurion, on June 18, 1947, had ordered the Haganah to prepare for war with all of the Arab states, Azzam Pasha, the Egyptian secretary-general of the newly British-created Arab League, put the Jewish leadership on notice that the Arabs "would fight as fiercely against them they had fought against the Crusaders." Fawzi al-Kawakji, a veteran of the former Ottoman Turkish army, was named commander of a volunteer "Liberation Army." The Mufti of

Jerusalem, Haj Amin al-Husseini, who had backed the Axis during World War II, was promised funds and freedom of movement for his militia forces. At a meeting in Aley, Lebanon, the Arab League decided that as soon as Britain withdrew, Arab regular armies would occupy all of Palestine. In all, 41,000 Arab troops were supposed to participate, including 7,000 soldiers of King Farouk's Egyptian army. The Aley decision called for the Egyptians to serve solely in a rear support role and not enter Palestine, because of a cholera epidemic in Egypt. Abdallah of Transjordan, who held secret contacts with the Jewish leaders, including with Mrs. Golda Meyerson (later to be Prime Minister Golda Meier), abandoned the enterprise. Ben-Gurion praised Abdallah as the "only voice of peace" among the Arab leaders. Privately, Ben-Gurion had severe misgivings because of the strength and probable intentions of the Arab Legion.[5]

On November 29, 1947, came the crucial vote in the United Nations General Assembly on the resolution to partition Palestine, a resolution supported by the United States and the Soviet Union. Resolution 181 provided for the creation of two states, one Arab and one Jewish, in Palestine. Jerusalem was to be put under an international regime. The Zionist leaders approved it. The Arabs, who had already rejected an earlier (more favorable for them) two-state offer from Britain and demanded full sovereignty over all of Palestine, refused to accept partition. The first general Arab–Jewish fighting, mostly between the Haganah and Palestinian irregulars, began immediately after adoption of the resolution.

The reasons why Israeli strategists, until Iraq's conquest by the United States in 2003, viewed Iraq as one of Israel's greatest—even its greatest—long-term strategic enemies, lie back in this crucial period of Israel's birth as a state. Iraqi Jews were under pressure at home, and beginning to leave for Palestine. The Iraqi royal governments considered Arab Palestine to be a "sacred" cause. Iraq's perception of Israel as a principal adversary, exacerbated by the animus aroused by the mid-twentieth century Jewish exodus, like the Iraqis' still-enduring pan-Arab sympathies for the Palestinians (heightened, if anything, by the U.S.-led war and occupation of 2003), can also be traced directly back to the same era.

In Iraq, the Allied armies and the goods and services they purchased during World War II had contributed both to population growth, and to the prosperity of a population that, in Baghdad, had doubled in number between 1922 and 1947. Partial industrialization spawned a large labor force. Marxist sentiment spread with Western education and the rise of communist and nationalist parties. The British authorities licensed many of these, such as the National Democratic Party and the Istiqlal (Independence) Party. Opposition to the monarchy and the British, as in Palestine and other parts of the Arab world, began to rise. Under the governments of prime ministers Hamdi al-Pachachi and Tawfiq al-Suwaidi in 1944–46 (Nuri al-Said was temporarily sidelined after the regent, Abdulillah, got tired of taking orders and advice from him), 16 labor unions, twelve of them Communist-controlled, were licensed. Soon they controlled Basra port and the British-managed railways. Strikes broke out. When they spread to the British-directed Iraq Petroleum Company (IPC) in 1946, ten people were killed in clashes between unionists and police.

Such events were a prelude to a massive national uprising, called *al-Watba* (The Leap). Its immediate cause was the Anglo–Iraqi agreement initialed at Portsmouth, England, on January 15, 1948 after long negotiations. If implemented, it would have extended the British quasi-protectorate over Iraq for another 20 years. Istiqlal and the Communists began to stir up their followers against the treaty and against British policy favoring the Zionists in Palestine, even before the Iraqi delegates reached Portsmouth. On January 20 the police shot and killed a number of demonstrating railway workers and impoverished people. The next day, the Regent announced he would not ratify the Portsmouth Treaty. He recalled Prime Minister Salih Jabr, the first Shia Muslim to hold the post, from Britain. Major clashes with the police and army killed hundreds. The violence foreshadowed the revolution of 1958. It demonstrated the fury of an aroused Baghdad mob, which the Americans and coalition allies were to learn about, to their grief, during their occupation in 2003 and 2004. The opposition demanded abolition of the Anglo–Iraqi Treaty, dissolution of parliament, free elections, and "a prompt supply of bread" for everyone. Jabr's government resigned and was replaced, from January to June 1948 by a caretaker cabinet headed by another Shia with an anti-British record, Muhammad al-Sadr. It had to organize new elections in the summer of 1948. These were again rigged in favor of the "old gang," the pro-British political establishment. New resistance erupted in strikes and marches. A major revolt followed when an IPC oil pumping station near Haditha (sabotaged by the anti-American underground in 2003) was crippled by a strike organized by Communist strikers demanding huge wage rises. After weeks of bloody clashes, the government and IPC management cut off food and water to the strikers, who then organized a march on Baghdad. At Fallujah, security forces stopped and arrested them.[6] The unrest overheated the atmosphere for the 1948 elections, and for the imminent start of Iraq's decades of war, lasting into the twenty-first century, against Israel in Palestine.

IRAQ FIGHTS THE NEW ISRAELI STATE

Iraq's direct involvement in the 1948–49 war began in May 1948, when the last British soldier left for home and the Star of David flag replaced the Union Jack in Palestine's Jewish regions. Some fighting had begun in December 1947, with the gradual division of the country into Arab and Jewish enclaves. As British forces began a slow withdrawal, sniping and terrorism escalated into urban and rural guerrilla warfare between Arabs and Jews. By May 1948 the combined Jewish forces, which included Palmach, Irgun, and another guerrilla group called Hish, controlled the coastal strip and much of eastern Galilee. The Arabs, for their part, held most of the West Bank and western Galilee. Jerusalem was divided. Since it contained a sixth of all of the Jewish population of Palestine, the Haganah fought desperately to break through the encirclement of the city by British troops and Fawzi al-Kawakji's 4,000-man Arab Liberation Army, which had infiltrated into Palestine from Syria.

Through the winter and until spring of 1948, armed Jewish convoys trying to open the road to Jerusalem suffered heavy losses from Kawakji's Arab guerrillas. In April 1948, the Jewish high command, certain that Britain would not help them, launched its first big offensive, Operation Nachshon, part of Plan *Dalet* (Plan D). This aimed to gain control of areas of Jewish population and settlement and of strong points along the roads to Jerusalem. The Jewish forces finally secured most of West Jerusalem and its approaches, but the Palmach and Irgun troops were repeatedly driven back from the Old City of East Jerusalem by the well-trained and disciplined Arab Legion of Transjordan, commanded by Sir John Glubb with other seconded British officers. However, by the time the state of Israel was proclaimed on May 15, with Ben-Gurion as prime minister and defense minister, much of Plan D had been fulfilled, except for Jewish capture of East Jerusalem, western Galilee, the West Bank highlands, and the heights dominating Jerusalem.

Arab historians have consistently remarked that the Arab campaign against the new Jewish state, including the Iraqi contribution, was doomed from the outset, because there was no real joint Arab operational plan. Instead of the 41,000 Arab troops originally envisioned, the total strength of Arab forces committed during the first phase of the war (May 15 to June 11, 1948) was only 21,000. Israel, in contrast, was able to muster 65,000 men of the Haganah and the various militias. The

Arab forces were, at the outset, better equipped. Later Czechoslovakia, with the USSR's support, and with volunteers from the American and Western European Jewish communities, rushed weaponry to the Israeli forces. While the Arabs began the war with about 150 armored cars, 20 tanks and some artillery, the Israelis at first had practically no such equipment. But not only were the Arabs handicapped by lack of planning and coordination, they had the huge strategic disadvantage of exterior lines. Arab logistic bases were distant: for the Egyptians, 250 miles across the Sinai Desert to the Nile Delta; 80 to 90 miles back for the Arab Legion.

The Iraqis, for their part, had to cross 700 miles from their main base, Baghdad. The Arab operational plan, hastily cobbled together on May 13, 1948, called for a multi-pronged advance from Lebanon, Syria, Transjordan, and the Sinai. Its aim was to destroy the Haganah and occupy all of the territory of the former Palestine mandate. The army of Lebanon—traditionally identified by the Israelis as the least threatening of their adversaries—assisted by Fawzi al-Kawakji's Arab Liberation Army, was to occupy northern Israel from the port of Haifa in the west to Nazareth in the east.

The Syrian army was supposed to capture the district of Galilee, and the Iraqis the coastal plain around Tel Aviv. From the south, the Egyptians forces, no longer inhibited by cholera in Egypt, were to advance in two prongs: through Gaza toward Tel Aviv and through the central Negev desert toward Beersheba. Once Beersheba and Tel Aviv had fallen to the Arabs, the Egyptians were to advance along the Tel Aviv–Jerusalem axes, afterward linking up with the Arab Legion operating in and around Jerusalem. The Legion had secured the eastern part of the city before May 15. Then, with five-pronged concentric thrusts, the Arab forces would move along a 180° arc, reaching from Acre on the sea through Galilee and the central highlands to Gaza and Beersheba. These final moves were supposed to end Israeli resistance. The Arab forces initially sent in were 1,000 Lebanese (a battalion); 3,000 to 4,000 of Kawakji's guerrillas; a Syrian brigade of 3,000 men; two brigades of the well-trained and disciplined Arab Legion totaling 10,000 men including an armored unit, and a small Saudi Arabian contingent. The Iraqi contribution, hastily dispatched from Baghdad by Salih Jabr's government on the eve of May 15, consisted of about two battalions, with one armored car. Its mission was to move across Transjordan and into the West Bank at Beisan; then to seize and hold the city of Nablus, in liaison with the Arab Legion forces in the Jerusalem and Bethlehem sectors.[7]

The under-strength Iraqi brigade crossed Jordan successfully; at that time, unlike future Iraqi crossings in 1967 and 1973, there was no Israeli air power to harass it. One of its two battalions crossed the Jordan near Beisan and joined up with the Arab Legion temporarily to occupy the Old City of Jerusalem, Nablus, and the strategic British-built police fort, nicknamed the "Tiger's Eye," at Latroun. The Iraqis captured a couple of kibbutzim and a Jewish-run power station on the way. The Latroun fort was an important tactical position: it guarded the western end of the Bab al-Wad defile. The road from Tel Aviv winds uphill here to the 2,700-foot highlands of Jerusalem. At the time of the first truce concluded on June 11, arranged by UN negotiators under the direction of Swedish Count Folke Bernadotte (assassinated by Israeli gunmen on September 17, 1948), combined forces of the Arab Legion and the Iraqis had occupied a zone reaching from Jerusalem's Old City, westward along the main Jerusalem–Tel Aviv road to Latrun, and northwest to Ramleh and Lydda (Lod). From there the zone reached northward along the railroad line to Qalqiliya and Tulkarm, swinging east to Nazareth and the Sea of Galilee (Lake Tiberias) at Samakh.

The other Iraqi battalion met heavy Israeli resistance on the Jordan River. Its assault crossing was repulsed with heavy losses by Israelis entrenched in the West Bank hills dominating the Jordan valley. Later, the Iraqis successfully beat back an Israeli counterattack by the Carmeli or Golani brigades directed at Iraqi forces around Jenin. This time the Israelis suffered heavy losses. They retreated to the ancient site of Megiddo, the Armageddon of Biblical prophecy. However, the Israelis increased pressure on Jerusalem. The Arab Legion left Nablus and moved to reinforce the garrison of Jerusalem's Old City on May 22, 1948, leaving the Iraqi force in sole possession of Nablus. The Israelis were unsuccessful in attacking Latroun, losing hundreds of casualties there and in their unsuccessful siege of Jerusalem's Old City. Latroun remain in Arab hands until the June 1967 war. In the sector of Qalqiliya-Tulkarm, Arab forces were now only twelve miles from the Mediterranean and six miles from the strategic coastal road between Tel Aviv and Haifa.[8]

STALEMATE AND ISRAELI VICTORY

By June 1, only two weeks after it began, the Arab offensive had lost its steam. The Iraqi force was strung out along a line running from Jenin to Tulkarm and Qalqiliya. The newly-commissioned Israeli Air Force planes from Czechoslovakia, piloted by Israelis, brought the

Arab forces under heavy fire. On the ground, the newly-formed IDF under General Yigal Allon consisted of five brigades. Three of these were at the time the elite brigades of the Israeli army, named Harel, Yiftah, and Hanegev. Commanding the Harel brigade was the future Israeli commander-in-chief, defense minister, prime minister, and peace negotiator, Yitzhak Rabin. There was a 15-mile gap between the Arab Legion, whose brigade and regimental commanders were mostly British officers, and the Iraqi force, based at Majdal Yaba. This gap included the two Arab towns of Lydda and Ramleh, still in Arab hands, and precariously garrisoned by Arab Legion Bedouins from Transjordan. The nominal supreme commander of the Arab Legion, King Abdallah of Jordan, and the real commander, General Sir John Glubb, were under strict British government orders not to cross lines drawn on the maps by the UN General Assembly partition resolution of November 1947. The resolution had assigned both Lydda and Ramleh to the Arab state, not the Jewish one. However, by July 10 advancing Israeli pincer forces had captured both these Arab towns and had nearly surrounded the Jordanians in Latroun and the Iraqis at Majdal Yaba.

From this time on, the Iraqis hunkered down. They were reinforced by a more or less steady supply line across Transjordan. By October 1, 1948, when the Israelis launched a victorious offensive against Egyptian forces in the Negev, two Iraqi brigades, at nearly full strength and totaling nearly 15,000 men, held Nablus and its suburbs. When it became evident that Egyptian and Sudanese troops in the Negev (two Egyptian majors, Gamal Abdel Nasser and Muhammad Naguib, who were destined to become future presidents, served with them), were under relentless pressure in Falujja, in the northern Negev, the Arab high command thought of calling on the Iraqis for help.

At an Arab summit conference on October 23, the high command proposed that the Iraqi forces should extend their front to include the Arab fortress at Latroun. This would have relieved the equivalent of six Arab Legion companies in the Hebron area. It might have lifted the Israeli siege of the Sudanese and Egyptian troops, including Nasser and his men. The conference rejected this. The outcome was that the Lebanese, Syrian, and Iraqi armies all refused to budge from the positions they held. This put the whole burden on the Arab Legion to defend their original positions, as well as to spread themselves thinly to secure all of the Hebron district and also try to aid the Egyptians and Sudanese in the Falujja pocket. As a Pakistani military historian who chronicled the war puts it, "It was only his kingly forbearance and his responsibility as official host to the conference, that prevented King Abdallah from losing his temper with the distinguished conferees."[9]

According to Sir John Glubb's memoirs, the reinforced Iraqis at this time numbered 19,000 men. They were the only effective force left in the field. However, they lacked air cover or ground defenses against the growing Israeli air power. So they accomplished little and suffered heavy losses. Discontent with the war grew among informed people at home in Iraq, who had learned not to believe the empty claims of Arab victories propagated by the government's radio in Baghdad.

Facing efforts by the Egyptian army to break out of various traps in Gaza and the Negev, General Yigal Allon, commanding the southern front, launched Operation Horev, the major Israeli offensive of the 1948 war, on December 22, 1948. Its purpose was the total annihilation of the Arab forces in the Negev and northern Sinai. The Iraqis, Syrians, and Lebanese never got involved. Allon launched two Palmach brigades (Harel and Hanegev), one Haganah brigade (Golani), and the 8th armored brigade. Another brigade was assigned to keep pressure on the Sudanese in the Falujja pocket. The IDF attacked on an east–west axis toward the coast and advanced into Egypt's Sinai Peninsula, wiping out Egyptian strongholds along the way. Deep penetration raids further into Sinai were designed to confuse the Egyptian command and to sow panic, if possible, behind the Egyptian lines.

After a week of Israeli advances, the British government intervened. By threatening British military intervention, the government in London forced Ben-Gurion to order an immediate ceasefire and withdrawal on January 8, 1949. The British ultimatum, delivered within the legal framework of Britain's 1936 treaty with Egypt, caused shock and surprise to both Egyptians and Israelis. Ben-Gurion's government had wrongly believed that U.S. President Harry Truman and international support for the new state would prevent any British interference. King Farouk's Egyptian government had repudiated the 1936 treaty, and Egypt neither asked for nor wanted British intervention. On January 7, 1949, the day the Israelis halted their advance, the Egyptians had been chased out of all of former Palestine except for the Gaza Strip. The silver lining for the Egyptians, however, was that the British ultimatum saved the Egyptian army from a huge impending disaster. It lived to fight another day.

Israel's War of Independence, as Israeli historians call it, had ended, with the capture of 30 percent more territory than the UN General Assembly had allotted it in the partition resolution. Because upwards of

300,000 Palestinians had fled or been forced to flee by Israeli excesses such as the notorious massacre at the Arab village of Deir Yassine on April 9, 1948, when the Irgun and Lehi killed 254 Palestinians, there was now a Jewish majority on the territory held by the IDF. As Israeli historian Michael B. Oren, in his recent history of the 1967 conflict and its antecedents, *Six Days of War*, recalls, only the threat of conquering more Arabs and so ending the Jewish majority, and the specter of possible war with Britain, the protector of King Farouk's Egypt and King Abdallah's Jordan, held the IDF back from conquering the West Bank and Gaza.[10]

A torrent of Palestinian Arab refugees crowded into Egyptian-held Gaza. They were soon compressed into its tiny area, "like peas into a pressure cooker," as one Gaza resident (Sobhi al Terrazi, principal of the Gaza College) reminisced to the author in the summer of 1967. In one final operation, carried out after the UN-sponsored armistice with Jordan and after the removal of a British threat posed by the landing of a small British force at Aqaba in October 1948 under terms of a British–Transjordan defense treaty, Israeli troops captured the Arab village of Umm al-Rashrash on the Red Sea. On the partition map it was included in the Jewish state. Renamed Eilat, it became Israel's only Red Sea port, the Jewish state's lifeline down through the Gulf of Aqaba and the Straits to Tiran toward the ports and markets of Africa and Asia.[11]

ARMISTICE AGREEMENTS—MINUS IRAQ

In mid-February 1949, Dr. Ralph Bunche, the brilliant Afro-American statesman who emerged as the main United Nations peacemaker after the Israeli assassination of Count Bernadotte, issued an invitation to King Abdallah's Jordanian government to send a delegation to the Greek island of Rhodes. Its task was to negotiate an armistice agreement with Israel under UN auspices. The Jordanian delegation reached Rhodes on February 28. An Egyptian delegation had already arrived, and had rather quickly signed an armistice with Israel on February 24. Lebanon followed on March 23. A Syrian delegation finally put its signature to armistice documents on July 20, only after the new American CIA had helped to engineer a military coup in Syria by the amenable Colonel Husni al-Zaim. He was murdered for his trouble in another coup six months later. This inaugurated a long period of turbulence in Syria, ending only when air force commander and Defense Minister General Hafez al-Assad took power as president in 1970.[12]

The first armistice accords brought no let-up in Israeli political pressure on Jordan. With a total force of just over 11,000 men and the

19,000 Iraqis, Jordan faced an IDF that now numbered about 120,000. Although what the media at the time termed a "real" ceasefire, preceding the armistice, had been signed in Jerusalem by Jordan's Colonel Abdallah al-Tel and Colonel Moshe Dayan on November 28, 1949, IDF pressure in the south continued, as we saw. After the Jordan–Israel and Egypt–Israel armistice accords were signed, Transjordan and its British-officered Arab Legion still held one card: part of a wedge of territory in the Negev Desert, with its point at Aqaba and its base 55 miles inland at Bir Ibn Auda.

Rather than clash again with the Jordanians and so irritate the British, the Israelis held off. Later they forced out the Arab Legion and occupied the Negev enclave. In a decision fateful for the future of the Middle East, King Abdallah's Jordanian government on December 1, 1948, acceded to requests from Palestinian leaders: he incorporated the Jordanian West Bank into the Hashemite Kingdom of Jordan. Henceforth, the West Bank was to be known in Amman, even after it was conquered and lost to the Israelis in June 1967, as "West Jordan," while the kingdom of Transjordan was called "East Jordan." Journalists and statesmen from that time on referred to the "West Bank" and the "East Bank." The Arab League in Cairo issued loud protests. At the insistence of Egypt, then as now its strongest member, it proclaimed a rival shadow "Government of Palestine" in Egyptian-occupied Gaza, scarcely recognized elsewhere in the world. In terms of realpolitik, Arab historians attribute Jordan's 1948 formal annexation of the West Bank to the fact that the only effective Arab military force remaining in the area to face the IDF was Jordan's Arab Legion.[13]

The Iraqi expeditionary force was already discounted as a serious military factor. It was further devalued, both in the eyes of its Israeli adversaries and in those of its Arab allies, by the actions in 1949 of the Ben-Gurion government. The Israeli delegation at Rhodes on March 11, a day after the Israeli capture of Eilat, began turning up their psychological pressure against the losing Arab states, especially Jordan and Iraq. They threatened to occupy Nablus once the Iraqi army had withdrawn, and they continued to grab parcels of territory in the Hebron area, the scene of serious Jewish–Arab violence under British rule. In his memoirs, Sir John Glubb recalls:

> It is impossible to reproduce the tension and anxiety of those days, the constant reports of fresh Israeli advances ... the Iraqis gradually slipping out [of their West Bank positions], and the 11,000 Arab Legion (still without ammunition) facing ten times their numbers.[14]

Israel then made a direct military threat to resume fighting the Arab Legion unless the Jordanians agreed to pull out of a slender strip of territory, one to two miles wide and 110 miles long, the length of the ceasefire line in the north. The total area Israel wanted was about 400 square miles. This would give the IDF a foothold on the low line of hills overlooking the coastal plain near Jenin, Tulkarm, Qalqiliya, Kafr Qasim, and Majdal Yaba. In return, the Israelis offered to allow the Arab Legion to replace the Iraqi expeditionary force in the Nablus area. Jordan reluctantly gave in, since the UN seemed unable and the United States unwilling to prevent the Israelis from advancing again and occupying the entire West Bank. So on April 3, 1949, the Jordanians and Israelis finally signed their armistice. Nine days later a 2,000-man Arab Legion force relieved the Iraqis in Nablus. The Iraqis retreated back across Jordan and went home. They found their country in a ferment over dissatisfaction with the war and their performance in it. Unrest, mainly in Baghdad and Basra, affected the local Jews and their relations with the Muslim population and the government.

The Rhodes armistice agreements left Jordan's Arab Legion holding Nablus, East Jerusalem, and Hebron. The Egyptian army kept the Gaza Strip and the city of Gaza, as well as the rapidly growing camps of Palestinian refugees from Israel. A UN-supervised Mixed Armistice Commission (MAC) was formed in Jerusalem, with two Jordanian and two Israeli members. A UN representative acted as chairman. During the troubled years from 1949 until the June 1967 war, the MACs had limited success in the mission they were supposed to carry out: regulating border disputes and trying to settle cross-border conflicts.

One essential point must be kept constantly in mind. It concerns the 1948–49 armistice accords, and all of the many Arab–Israel ceasefires that followed. It also relates to the formal peace treaties that the Carter and Clinton administrations in the United States managed to mediate between Egypt and Israel in 1979, and between Jordan and Israel in 1994. Iraq, humiliated by its performance in 1948–49, remained scornfully aloof from all of these agreements. It never participated in a single real peace meeting of any kind, and never signed any armistice or peace document.

Long before Saddam Hussein's reign, every Baghdad government kept its distance from real compromise with what it called the "Zionist entity." As the United States and Britain hunted for an exit strategy from their ill-planned and misconceived outright military rule of Iraq after the war of 2003, it was sheer wishful thinking on the part of the neoconservative policy-makers in Washington to believe that a "new, democratic Iraq" which they were trying to will into being would ever change its stance against Israel. As long as the fundamental questions of Palestinian freedom and emancipation of an independent Palestinian state remained unsolved, no Iraqi politician or intellectual, other than some returned, pro-American exiles like Ahmed Chalabi or Kanan Makiya, would dare publicly to support Israel or "normalization" of any sort with the Jewish state.

BEN-GURION SPEAKS

In early 1968, after my first two years of covering the Middle East from my Beirut base for the *Christian Science Monitor*, I succeeded in persuading the Jerusalem government press office to arrange an interview for me with David Ben-Gurion. He had long since retired to his native kibbutz of Sde Boker in the Negev. During one of his stays in Tel Aviv in March 1968, a government minder took me to meet him at an open-air café on a tree-lined street in Tel Aviv, near Ben-Gurion's apartment. With his familiar shock of white hair, rising from a tanned and partially bald scalp, the patriarch was easily spotted, sitting alone with only a handful of indifferent patrons sitting at tables distant from his.

The central theme of our conversation, which lasted the better part of an hour—my minder had stipulated beforehand that in view of the statesman's advanced age and probable fatigue, it should not last more than 20 minutes or so—centered around Israel's relations with Jordan and the two sovereigns he had dealt with: King Abdallah and Abdallah's grandson King Hussein, who as a teenager had witnessed his grandfather's assassination by an angry Palestinian at the Al-Aqsa Mosque in Jerusalem. Iraq, until 1958 the other Hashemite kingdom, was a secondary subject.

After sipping some thick, dark, Arab-style coffee, Ben-Gurion reminisced that in 1948 and 1949, and even more so after Israel's triumph in the six-day June war of 1967, the IDF could have gone on to conquer the East Bank, Transjordan, after securing all of the West Bank. That the IDF did neither, Ben-Gurion assured me, was due to the earlier contacts, friendly and otherwise, with the Hashemites in Jordan and the subsequent "understanding" (the word I remember him as using) with King Hussein. Perhaps Ben-Gurion, without saying so out loud, was remembering that British pressure on both sides in 1948–49 had prevented the war from widening into a conflict and eventual Israeli conquest in Transjordan. Ben-Gurion certainly must have known that King Abdallah had been fighting mainly for his own political survival, rather than for the pan-Arab cause, let alone that of the Palestinians.[15]

As for Iraq, Ben-Gurion repeated to me the often-heard axiom of mainstream Israeli leaders and commentators that he probably did much to father himself: any new movement of Iraqi troops into Jordan or Syria would be seen instantly as a threat to Israel. Such movement would be perceived as a *casus belli* by any Israeli government, which would act accordingly. This is a pillar of Israeli policy, accepted in Washington and embedded over the years in American cooperation with Israel.

Israel has been ever watchful for signs that Arab neighbors to the east, Jordan, Syria, and Iraq, might some day patch up their disagreements and ideological quarrels and join in a unified "Eastern Front" against their Jewish adversary. This is why Israel has always regarded Iraq as a principal strategic enemy. And this, of course, is why when Saddam Hussein al-Tikriti, the Iraqi dictator who threatened Israel, especially during the final years of his reign in the 1990s, was ousted by the United States and Britain in 2003, the Israelis heaved a huge sigh of relief. For a short time, at least, they were pleased with the military victory which saw a U.S.-ordered dissolution of the entire Iraqi army and early, unsuccessful U.S. efforts to build a new, tame one. David Ben-Gurion's perception of Arab threats led the state to look for new, non-Arab allies. A generation before the Iraqi Kurds fought as war partners in 2003 with the United States, Israel's main Iraqi ally had become the Kurds, our next focus.

5
Ménage à Quatre: The U.S., Israel, Iran, and the Iraqi Kurds

The Kurds' only friends are the mountains.
(Kurdish proverb)

Shortly after Baghdad fell to American forces in spring of 2003, a senior official of the Kurdistan Democratic Party (KDP) let a cat out of the bag in a conversation with a European journalist. His disclosure pleased President Bush's neoconservative advisors in the Pentagon. It nourished the view that the U.S. plans to add Iraq to over 100 other countries where it maintains military bases termed "the new American empire."

The head of the KDP in 2003 when the disclosure was made was Massoud Barzani, the son of the late Mullah Mustafa Barzani. The elder Barzani had told me during my visit to him in the Kurdistan mountains in 1972 how welcome U.S. "influence and presence" would be if the United States extended its powerful reach into Kurdistan.

Massoud's deputy, Brusik Nuri Chawais, an engineer educated in Germany, was more specific. His words were music to the ears of the Bush administration in Washington. Chawais announced that:

> the Americans ought to stay to restore security, get the adminis-tration and public enterprises running again, and to reconstruct. After an interim period of about a year, the coalition forces should leave Iraq, but we can consider the United States having military bases there afterward. We need a strong alliance with the Americans.[1]

Rumors and echoes about permanent U.S. bases caused satisfaction in Israel, the firmest ally in the Middle East of the United States and a past helper of the Iraqi Kurds as well. In 1973 General Ezer Weizman, Israeli pioneer, combat pilot, and former Israeli Air Force commander who was later to become president of Israel, told officers in a briefing of his wish that "Israel had bases on the Euphrates."[2]

Turkey's parliament in March 2003 narrowly rejected the U.S. mili-tary's request for rights of passage on land through Turkey to invade

Iraq. This had been requested by Defense Secretary Donald Rumsfeld's deputy, Paul Wolfowitz, in return for an offer of new multi-billion-dollar U.S. loans. U.S. troops still urgently needed access to northern Iraq, by air if not overland. The KDP and the other principal Kurdish group running the northern Kurdish enclave, the Patriotic Union of Kurdistan (PUK) of Jalal Talabani, had welcomed the idea. Working with U.S. engineers, technicians, and equipment, they prepared several "temporary" airstrips capable of taking both large troop-carrying helicopters flying in from Turkey, and even larger C-130-type transports from further afield, if necessary. (Turkey was slow, in that spring of 2003, about even granting overflight rights, but it finally did so before the invasion began on March 19, 2003. The entire American 4th Infantry Division, waiting on troopships off Turkey, had to be shipped down to the Gulf and enter Iraq from Kuwait.)

The most likely permanent site for the U.S. military in Iraqi Kurdistan was a big former base of Saddam Hussein's air force at Bashur, on a level plain north of Erbil. Others were also considered: Baghdad International Airport; Talil, near the southern Shi'ite city of Nassiriya; and a field near the site called H-1 in the western desert were a few. This program would replace bases in Saudi Arabia. The U.S. Central Command had already moved its main headquarters and aircraft to the Gulf emirate of Qatar and to Kuwait; since the 1991 Desert Storm campaign to expel Saddam's forces from Kuwait, these units had been located at Prince Sultan air base in the Saudi desert.

Bases in Iraq were projected as only one more step—a giant one in strategic terms—in the vast and continuing expansion of American military facilities that had begun in the Middle East, including Israel and Central Asia in the previous two years.[3]

Israel and later the United States had laid the groundwork for what were to become long relationships with the Kurds. The Shah of Iran temporarily joined, to make a foursome out of a threesome, after the overthrow of Iraq's monarchy in 1958. The Shah's involvement lasted until his betrayal of the Kurds in 1975.

THE KURDS' FADED DREAMS

The Kurds have a convoluted story, built around a never-fulfilled yearning for an independent state of their own, and their more modest hope, equally unrealized except in northern Iraq since 1991, for some real freedom and autonomy within the borders of host countries Turkey, Iraq, Iran, Syria, and the former Soviet Union.

In the early twentieth century, during the dying decades of several empires—the British, the French, the Ottomans, and the Russia of the imperial Czars—the geographical area known as Kurdistan lay at the seams where these empires touched and clashed with one another in various places. The region is mainly mountain valleys, overlapping the borders of Turkey, Syria, Iraq, and Iran. During the territorial bartering of the immediate post-World War I period, British statesmen including Winston Churchill eyed Kurdistan as another possible British protectorate, like Egypt, Iraq, or Palestine. However, much of Kurdistan had been promised to France in the Sykes–Picot Agreement, so British planners rethought the problem. Why not, some suggested, set up several autonomous Kurdish states? British political advisers could "guide" the tribal rulers. Clemenceau's French government was asked to concede this in a spirit of Allied brotherhood. British troops began several futile attempts to organize and dominate the Iraqi Kurds in 1919. The Kurds, in three separate uprisings, turned against them, and the British had to pull out[4]—only to return later, once the control apparatus of the British mandate over Iraq enabled the RAF to subjugate them with bombs, including chemical ones, the "weapon of mass destruction" most favored at the time.

When the Allies and the defeated Ottoman Empire signed the Treaty of Sevres in 1920, the idealist U.S. President, Woodrow Wilson, at first had his way. The treaty provided for independent states for the Armenians in Turkey and in the then Russian empire, and for Kurdistan, in adjoining areas of Syria, Turkey, Iran—and in Iraq, where 18 million Kurds then lived. The proposal was met with fierce opposition by the Turkish nationalists and with indifference by the Allies. Wilson, crippled by serious physical illness which wore down his will, would soon turn his back on his grandiose visions of self-rule for the former colonized peoples. Free Kurdistan never saw the light of day.

After quashing talk of a U.S. mandate for Palestine, Britain suggested that the United States should instead have League of Nations mandates to occupy and rule parts of Eastern Turkey, Constantinople (Istanbul), the Dardanelles Straits, the Caucasus, and Armenia. Most of these ideas withered away, except for Armenia. When Wilson suggested a U.S. mandate there, the U.S. Senate rejected the idea within days.[5] The short-lived "independent" state of Armenia, shadowed by the devastation and refugee exodus caused by the Ottoman massacres of 1915 and later fighting, soon collapsed, after some of Turkey's Kurds had joined both the Russian and Turkish forces.

Kurdish tribal uprisings, especially those of the important Barzan clan—at first led by Sheikh Ahmed of Barzan, a formidable foe of both the Turkish and British forces, and later by his brother, Mullah Mustafa Barzani—were crushed in the 1920s and 1930s. Iran's Shah Reza, the post-Ataturk rulers of the Turkish republic, and Nuri al-Said's Iraq, with Nuri's British backers, often cooperated. Once the July 1958 revolution had literally killed off Nuri and Iraq's monarchy and instituted a succession of military rulers (and later Saddam Hussein), the Kurdish situation changed drastically.

Barzani had withdrawn to the Soviet Union before World War I. He reappeared with the Red Army to lead the short-lived Soviet-sponsored Kurdish Republic of Mahabad in 1946 (ending the Soviet military presence in Iran's provinces of Kurdistan and Azerbaijan was one of President Harry S. Truman's first Cold War triumphs). After 1958, Barzani uneasily coexisted for a time with the military rulers in Baghdad. Kurdish fighters even helped Iraqi generals to massacre their Ba'athist opponents in the period before the Ba'ath seized power.

THE KURDS' NEW FRIENDS: THE STATE OF ISRAEL

Under successive Baghdad regimes, relations between the Kurdish clans and the Iraqi leaders oscillated between fighting each other and kissing and making up. One major complicating factor was the growing hostility of imperial Iran. From 1947 onwards, Iran was under the iron rule of Shah Reza's son, Muhammad Reza Pahlevi. A brief interlude of quasi-democratic rule under Prime Minister Muhammad Mossadeq ended in 1953 when the Shah's rule was restored by the CIA at the behest of the U.S. and British governments and oil companies. The new Shah abandoned his father's policy of working with the rulers in Baghdad against the Kurds. Instead, he began using the Kurds as an instrument to weaken central authority in Iraq, which the Shah, like his secret but increasingly close ally Israel, regarded as a threat.

An Israeli–Kurdish connection soon began. The predecessors of Israel's Mossad had suffered reverses following the exodus of Iraqi Jews in 1948–51. In May 1951, only nine weeks after Ben-Gurion signed the order creating Mossad as a fully fledged foreign intelligence agency, Iraqi security cracked down on the ring, arresting two Israeli agents and dozens of Iraqi Jews and Muslims who had been bribed to run the escape networks. In all, 28 people were charged with spying. Both agents were condemned to death, 17 Iraqis were given life sentences, and the others were set free. Both Mossad agents were eventually released, but only after they had been badly tortured. A substantial amount of money was paid into the Swiss bank account of the Iraqi Interior Minister in exchange for setting them free.[6]

It was highly desirable, Ben-Gurion and his advisers believed, not only to recoup this setback in Iraq and some other intelligence failures in Egypt and elsewhere, but also to establish a foothold in Kurdistan, which could be immensely valuable to Israel in the future. The Israeli founders looked to non-Arab peoples like the Kurds, the Turks, the Ethiopians, and other African peoples as counter-weights inside and outside the Middle East to the Muslim Arab peoples surrounding Israel.

This tendency was strengthened following the Suez War of 1956. U.S. pressure exercised by President Eisenhower and Secretary of State John Foster Dulles on Britain, France, and Israel had forced all three to withdraw their troops from President Gamal Abdel Nasser's Egypt. Nasser himself had come to power in 1952 with the knowledge and approval of the American CIA station in Cairo. He was emerging as a regional leader of the vast Muslim Arab majority. To oppose Nasser, his Western and Israeli adversaries established links with non-Arab states (including nominally Muslim ones, like those in Turkey and Iran) who had their own reasons for resisting Nasserism and the Soviet Union, which was arming and helping to train Nasser's military. Israel's Mossad, under one of its most effective chiefs, Isser Harel, was an architect of this strategy. Harel explained later that "my aim was to build a dam against the Nasserist–Soviet flood." Nuri al-Said's Iraqi government, a member with Turkey, Iran, and Pakistan of the 1955 Western-sponsored Baghdad Pact, was part of this alliance until the 1958 revolution.

Mossad established its own foreign relations department just before that revolution. Its head was Ya'akov Caroz, an operative who had transferred from the Shin Beth, the State's internal security service in 1954, and had then served Mossad in Paris. The Shah's Iran soon became the kingpin of what Israelis called their "peripheral" strategy. Iran had quietly given de facto recognition to Israel in 1950, soon after Turkey had done so. An operative of Aman, Israel's military intelligence, Max Binnet, was sent to Tehran in the early 1950s. From there he directed intelligence operations against Iraq and supported the continuing exodus of Iraqi Jews headed for Israel. Another key operative was the Iraqi-born Yaacov Nimrodi, who spent over two decades in three different periods between 1955 and 1978 in the Shah's Tehran as representative of the Jewish Agency and of Mossad, as an Israeli military attaché, and finally as a highly successful businessman who made a fortune as an arms trader.

After the Suez War, covert relations between Israel and the Shah improved rapidly. In September 1957, General Taymour Bakhtiar, the first head of Iran's new SAVAK intelligence and internal security service, met in Paris with Ya'akov Caroz. Isser Harel recommended to Prime Minister Golda Meier that Israel pursue the relationship. Bakhtiar and Harel developed a close personal friendship. Bakhtiar kept this up, as well as close relations with the American CIA, until the Shah fired him in 1961 (SAVAK later had him assassinated while on a hunting trip in Iraq). The Shah appointed in Bakhtiar's place the tough and sinister Lieutenant General Nimatullah Nassiri, who worked with the Israelis until he was sacked in 1978 as the Shah's regime began to totter. In the spring of 1959 Chaim Herzog, head of Aman, was the guest in Tehran of the Iranian military intelligence chief, General Alavi Kia. With the personal approval of the Shah and Ben-Gurion, they agreed to continue military and intelligence cooperation. A CIA report stolen from the American Embassy in Tehran, along with many other documents, by the revolutionary "students" who stormed the Embassy and took its personnel hostage in November 1979, confirmed that Israel "aided SAVAK activities and supported the Kurds in Iraq."[7]

KASSEM CONTRA KURDS

Soon after seizing power in the July 1958 revolution, Iraqi General Abdel Karim Kassem invited Mullah Mustafa Barzani to leave his exile in the USSR and return to Iraq. There was a very brief honeymoon between the regime and the Kurds, then more bitter fighting, some of it between Barzani's forces and pro-government Kurdish tribes. They provided Kassem and subsequent rulers with Kurdish mercenary fighters (collectively and contemptuously called *josh*, or donkeys, a play on words on the Arabic *jeish*, which means "army.") During the first year of fighting, Kassem's forces destroyed about 500 Kurdish villages in air attacks. During the winter of 1958–59, 80,000 people had become homeless refugees. At the same time, Baghdad resumed the process of "Arabizing" the oil-rich Kirkuk region. This dated back to the discovery of major oil reserves there during the British mandate in the 1920s. The government-controlled oil industry had then begun trying to "Arabize" the industry by bringing in large numbers of Arab workers instead of hiring the local Kurds. The British and subsequent Iraqi regimes gradually turned Kirkuk into a rich farming region Beginning in the 1930s, massive irrigation projects were launched on the Hawjia, Qaraj, and

Qari-Teppa plains around Kirkuk. Several large nomadic Arab tribes from southern Iraq were settled on the newly fertile lands.[8]

General Abdel Salem Aref overthrew and killed Kassem in Baghdad on February 8, 1963. The CIA assisted in this process for reasons connected with the Soviet–U.S. Cold War, which we will examine later.

Aref tried to promote relations with Egypt's Nasser, whom the Shah detested almost as much as Israel did. The Shah showed renewed interest in weakening Iraq. The Iraqi Kurds under Barzani had begun new rebel operations in 1961, and both Israel and the Shah believed it was a good idea to help them. Aref clamped a ruthlessly reactionary rule on the country. Sporadic but savage fighting with the Kurds continued.[9]

Serious Israeli support for the fight of the Iraqi Kurds began in 1964. Harel's replacement at Mossad, Meier Amit, was targeting hostile Arab regimes more aggressively. Defense Minister Shimon Peres met secretly with an ageing Kurdish leader, Khumran Ali Bedir-Khan, who had spied for Mossad during the early years of Israel's independence. In August 1965, Mossad organized an initial three-month training course—the first of others to follow—for officers of Barzani's "Pesh Merga" (Kurdish for "those facing death" or sacrificers) fighters. The operation was codenamed "Marvad" (carpet).

In the late summer of 1966, according to Black and Morris, Israeli Prime Minister Levi Eshkol deputized Ariyeh ("Lyova") Eliav, the Labor Party secretary-general who was then a member of the Knesset and deputy minister for industrialization and development, to conduct a survey in Iraqi Kurdistan and contact Barzani. An Israeli assistance program was set up under Haim Levakov, a Palmach veteran and specialist of Arab affairs. An Israeli delegation with a complete Israeli field hospital and a small Israeli staff of doctors and nurses was sent to Barzani's forces in jeeps and trucks, probably from Iran. (Eshkol and Foreign Minister Abba Ebban had both secretly visited Tehran in June 1966.) Eliav disclosed the covert mission in a newspaper article in 1978 entitled "A Secret Mission to Mustafa Barzani—in an eyrie in Kurdistan." He said that when the Israeli convoy arrived at the rendezvous with Barzani's forces (probably somewhere near Haji Omran, where I entered on my own visit to Kurdistan, arranged by Ahmed Chalabi in 1972), Barzani's men and a small force of armed Pesh Merga fighters awaited them. After nightfall, the Israeli visitors rode on horseback to Barzani's secret headquarters. There they had an "emotional" meeting with the Kurdish patriarch. They spoke Russian, a language familiar to Eliav and the Israelis with him, and which Barzani spoke fluently after his long exile in the USSR.

THE ISRAELI–KURDISH HONEYMOON

Eliav greeted Barzani solemnly in the name of the Israeli government. He presented greetings from the Knesset to Barzani in the form of a special gold medallion, struck to commemorate the opening of the newly-elected Knesset. What forms Israeli assistance could take, besides arms and military training, was discussed. The field hospital, described by Eliav as a "big present" to Barzani, was set up. One of the medical members of the party was a dentist, who fixed Barzani's teeth, which had been causing him "hellish pain." Before the Israelis departed, Barzani asked Eliav to "tell the prime minister and the ministers that we are brothers and we will never forget that you, the Jews, were the only people and country to aid us in our hour of need." He then took his curved Kurdish dagger from his belt and presented it to Eliav and gave him another for the chairman of the Knesset.

When Eliav's account appeared in Israel in May 1978, Barzani, a sick, broken, and discouraged man, was living out his last months as a pensioner of the CIA in Washington hotels and hospital rooms. Eliav commented:

> Barzani is now drawing close to the end of his life. ... A few months ago, I received warm regards from him by way of Congressman Stephen Solarz, a Jew and one of the best friends Israel has in Congress. ... I hope and believe that it is not all over for the Kurds and that the final chapter has not been written about the deeds and the brave aspirations to break the stranglehold of strangers and to live their lives in liberty and freedom.[10]

During the period of the secret Kurdish–Israeli honeymoon, Barzani made several covert trips to Israel. He was taken on guided tours of kibbutzim and met editors and politicians, including Menachem Begin, all sworn to silence. Apparently Mossad and SAVAK both helped the Barzani Kurds set up a Kurdish intelligence service, called the Parastin. The IDF general staff officer in charge of coordinating activities with Barzani was reportedly Colonel Mordecai Hod, who later became IDF chief of staff. The Israeli officer sent to Barzani's headquarters for liaison work was Major Eliahu Kohen.

One of the keenest contemporary American observers of the developing Israeli–Kurdish relationship, before it was so rudely interrupted by the Shah's 1975 deal with Saddam Hussein, was the American syndicated columnist Jack Anderson. On September 17, 1972, Anderson reported that a courier from Israel would appear in Barzani's mountains every month with $50,000 in cash for Barzani. This was later vehe-mently denied. Quoting a CIA report, Anderson noted that in return Barzani was at the time "continuing to gather men and equipment together" to prepare for future hostilities with the Iraqi army. Anderson added that Mossad chief General Zvi Zamir had visited Barzani at least once to discuss renewed or continuing Kurdish assistance to the trickle of Iraqi Jews still leaving for Israel.[11]

Lee Dinsmore, a U.S. Foreign Service Officer who served as American consul in Kirkuk during the early Israeli–Kurdish flirtation, was a passive observer. The United States, before 1972, was hardly more than a silent, though not disapproving partner in the Jerusalem–Kurdistan relationship. Dinsmore wrote in 1977 that "Israel has trained Kurdish insurgents in Iranian territory," an operation arranged by the Shah's SAVAK.[12]

In view of the close U.S.–Israeli–Kurdish ties, strengthened after Saddam Hussein's downfall in 2003, some academics sympathetic to Kurdish and Jewish causes claim that the majority of the world's Jews are genetically more closely related to the Kurds (who are not, anthro-pologically speaking, Semites) than they are to the Arabs, who are Semi-tes. A team of Israeli, German, and Indian scientists reported in 2001 that they had examined a total of 526 Y-chromosomes from six popula-tions—Kurdish Jews, Kurdish Muslims, Palestinian Arabs, Sephardic Jews, Ashkenazic Jews, and Bedouin from southern Israel's Negev region. Kurdish Jews and Sephardic Jews, the research study concluded, "were very close to each other." The same researchers found that:

> the Jewish Judean people ultimately began their existence in an area within or near Kurdistan, prior to migrating southwest to Israel. This exciting research showing that Kurds and Jews may have shared common fathers several millennia ago should, hopefully, encourage both Kurds and Jews to explore each others' cultures and to main-tain the friendship that Kurds and Jews enjoyed in northern Iraq in recent times.[13]

In a candid discussion of the value of the Kurdish connection to Israel, Israeli writer Eliezer Tzafrir, author of a book called *Ana Kurdi* ("I am a Kurd"), says the project was "an opportunity to keep Iraqi forces busy, away from Israel. It enabled us to smuggle out some 2,000 Jews who still lived in Iraq, and it gave us an opportunity to strengthen ties with the Iran of Shah Muhammad Reza Pahlevi." Israel regarded the Shah as its close ally, and Tehran as the "rear command post of the Israeli operation in Kurdistan."

Israeli commentators credit their state with one of the biggest early Iraqi-Kurdish victories over Iraqi government forces under the presidency of General Abdel Rahman Aref. The Israeli claim, not publicly reported at the time but known to U.S. and other diplomats near the scene, is that on May 12, 1966, a young Israeli paratroop officer named Tzuri Sagui directed Barzani's fighters in an ambush which wiped out an entire Iraqi army brigade.[14]

UNCLE SAM'S ROLE

The American role in this U.S.–Israeli–Kurdish *ménage à trois* gradually grew from more or less sympathetic observation to at first token, then more active participation. In August 1969, Barzani is reported to have welcomed at his headquarters two U.S. officers working with CENTO, the U.S. Central Command, which had grown out of the 1955 Baghdad Pact. They were U.S. General Anthony Devery Hunter and another officer, identified only as Perkins. Their plane landed at an airstrip somewhere near Barzani's headquarters (possibly one of the strips later expanded into an American base by 2003). After long discussions they left. Perkins returned with four other U.S. personnel two days later to sign a secret accord, giving Mullah Mustafa Barzani $14 million.

The agreement, which was a kind of founding charter of the abiding U.S.–Kurdish alliance, called originally for total secrecy. The purpose of Kurdish insurgency was said to be the overthrow of the Ba'athist regime (which the CIA had actively helped into power). Once this had been accomplished, the United States was to be sole arbiter of whether the Kurdish rebel movement should continue. However, this movement could be supported by the United States only if the Kurds did not go beyond the bounds of autonomy and seek an independent Kurdish state (which would have riled everyone in the region except possibly Israel). The Kurds had to obey U.S. orders or risk losing U.S. aid. Nothing the Iraqi Kurds might do, especially in support of Iranian Kurds, could be allowed to harm the government or stability of Iran. In return, the Shah would undertake not to harm the Iraqi Kurds. Communists (who were, until their CIA-assisted massacres by the Ba'athists, important supporters of the Kurds) had to be excluded from the movement, not protected by it. This also meant no more support by Barzani's former host and ally, the Soviet Union. If Moscow made any offers of aid, the Kurds should immediately inform the United States. Amounts and levels of both military and financial aid would be decided by Washington.[15]

Henry A. Kissinger, who served as U.S. Secretary of State from September 1973 to January 1977, and as National Security Adviser from January 1969 until November 1975, decided most U.S. foreign policy during those years, and subsequently exercised great influence as a consultant to governments and corporations who regulate the world's affairs. In the third and final volume of his memoirs, *Years of Renewal* (Simon and Schuster, 1999), Kissinger devotes an entire chapter to the convoluted U.S.–Israeli–Iranian–Kurdish tragedy played out in the 1970s. It should be re-read by anyone seeking to understand origins of the Bush administration's Iraq policies from 2003 onwards.

Kissinger explains that "saving" the Iraqi Kurds from being crushed by the Baghdad regimes would have required a huge U.S. commitment near the Soviet borders, of a size close to that being sent to fight the losing war in Indochina. This would have been difficult, he implies, because East–West relations were "weakening" and Arab–Israel peace negotiations were not going well. The Nixon administration was under congressional fire because of Vietnam and "rogue" CIA operations. Desire to support the Kurds had to be weighed against the logistical difficulties of supplying them in their remote mountains, and the danger of alienating oil-rich Arab friends and allies.

Kissinger observes that under his stewardship the Nixon and Ford administrations, both close allies of Israel and the Iranian Shah, were the first to commit direct U.S. aid to them. The 1972 alliance resulted from Nixon's visit to the Shah in Tehran in May of that year, following his summit meeting with Soviet President Leonid Brezhnev in Moscow. As Nixon and Kissinger saw it, the increasingly powerful vice-president Saddam Hussein was moving Iraq closer to Moscow. This was happening at the precise time when President Anwar al-Sadat of Egypt, following Nasser's death in 1970, faced the problem of dislodging thousands of Soviet military advisers, trainers, and military personnel (including combat pilots), who constituted a growing Soviet strategic presence in the Middle East.

THE NIXON–KISSINGER–SHAH AXIS

By the fall of 1971, the autonomy agreement between Saddam Hussein's regime and the Iraqi Kurds, signed on March 11, 1970, had virtually collapsed. After an assassin sent by Saddam failed to kill Mustapha Barzani, the Barzani Kurds returned to the warpath, with, as we saw, Israeli and Iranian help. The Shah appealed at least twice, in November 1971 and March 1972, to Nixon to join him in assisting Barzani. On

March 28, 1972, King Hussein of Jordan, another silent partner of the Iraqi Kurds, passed on an appeal for help from Barzani to Nixon. Kissinger held back from sending direct U.S. aid until Soviet Premier Alexei Kosygin's friendship treaty with Iraq of April 9, 1972. This secured new large-scale Soviet arms supplies for Saddam Hussein. While Nixon and Kissinger were being entertained in appropriate royal fashion by the Shah in Tehran, May 30–31, 1972, the Shah reminded them that a budding Soviet–Ba'athist alliance was in the offing. He asked for more new U.S. arms, especially planes, to keep pace with the Soviet deliveries to Iraq. He was authorized to order his choice of U.S. Air Force F-15s or Navy F-14s. This kept the quality of the arms sold to the Shah on a par with those given to Washington's other main Middle East ally, Israel.

After much internal deliberation and some wrangling between and among administration and congressional forces, Nixon approved the covert program of aid to the Kurds, described above, on August 1, 1972. Together with Israeli, Iranian, and some British help for the Kurds, the total allied aid effort amounted to the rather paltry sum of about $1 million per month.

President Sadat upped the Cold War ante in the Middle East in July 1972 when, to the immense satisfaction of Washington, he expelled the Soviet troops and advisers from Egypt. Immediately, the Kremlin, in the person of Politburo member Mikhail Suslov, exerted pressure on Barzani to make things up with the Baghdad regime, and pressed that regime to draw closer to Moscow.

Kurdish fighting with the Iraqi army continued, broken by brief ceasefires. With help from Ahmed Chalabi, then teaching mathematics in Beirut, I traveled to Tehran, and Kurdistan for my meetings with Richard Helms (ex-CIA director and now U.S. Ambassador to the Shah), Barzani, and finally, on my return from Barzani's headquarters, with the Shah, to whom I passed on Barzani's requests for more help. I had no inkling of an almost simultaneous joint effort by Kissinger and new CIA director James Schlesinger, which Nixon approved, for additional U.S. aid for the Kurds. Kissinger argued that Ba'athist Iraq was now the main Soviet client in the region. Saddam Hussein, moreover, was now supporting Palestinian terrorism and parallel "rejectionist" efforts by anti-Sadat Arab states to sabotage Arab–Israel peace initiatives led by Sadat. The Shah more than matched the U.S. and continuing Israeli efforts with more cash and logistical and artillery support from his side of the Iranian border.

Israel entered more actively into the Kurdish game when the October 1973 Middle East war erupted with the surprise Arab attack, intended to recover the Israeli-occupied Sinai and Golan from Israel, and also, in Sadat's perspective, to draw the United States actively into Middle East peacekeeping. Israeli liaison officers with the Kurds suggested that the U.S.-led coalition should encourage a major Kurdish offensive in Iraq in order to destabilize and if possible to overthrow Saddam Hussein's regime. Nixon and Kissinger rejected this. Some critics see this as the first wasted major opportunity to get rid of the Ba'athists.

In *Years of Renewal*, Kissinger shows uncharacteristic blindness about Iraqi military participation in the 1973 war, which we will look at in greater detail in the next chapter. He correctly states that the Kurdish forces managed to tie down two-thirds of the Iraqi armed forces, thus keeping them away from Syria's front with the Israelis. Incorrectly, however, he minimizes the impact on the fighting of the Iraqi tank brigades, which belatedly arrived at the front to defend the crucial approaches to Damascus from the Israeli armored counter-offensive. William Colby, who had just replaced Schlesinger as CIA director, and the Shah both said no to Barzani when he asked whether he ought to undertake an offensive outside the Kurdish highlands. Barzani's guerrillas were too ill-equipped to fight Iraqi armor and air power in the lower hills and flatlands. Kissinger records that deciding otherwise "would have risked the destruction of the Kurds without helping Israel." At the moment that Barzani received Kissinger's edict, Israeli forces under General Ariel Sharon's leadership were crossing back across the Suez Canal in their successful counter-offensive against Sadat.[16]

THE OIL EQUATION

As the October 1973 war ended, an oil crisis enveloped the West. It was spurred by the oil production cuts and export embargoes imposed by Iraq, Saudi Arabia, and other leading Arab oil producers. It helped to generate the curious ambiguity that was to characterize America's relations with Iraq from then until the final showdown with Saddam Hussein in the 2003 war. Whereas America's close ally Israel had ample reasons to regard Iraq as a major strategic enemy, U.S. policymakers began to recognize it as possibly a useful partner.

On January 1, 2004, under a rule allowing declassification of secret and confidential materials after a 30-year delay, Prime Minister Tony Blair's government, President George W. Bush's closest ally in the Iraq adventure, released some extraordinary and hitherto secret documents on the Middle East of the 1970s.

Files released from No. 10 Downing Street showed that British Prime Minister Ted Heath's government feared that President Nixon and

Henry Kissinger planned to invade Saudi Arabia and the Arab Gulf states to seize their oil installations and so secure fuel supplies for the United States, where Arab and OPEC price hikes of up to 100 percent had panicked industry and consumers.

Prime Minister Heath commissioned a report from Percy Craddock, chairman of Britain's joint intelligence committee. The 22-page survey delivered to Heath in December warned that the most likely American action was indeed seizure of the oil-producing regions. This, it added, could trigger a new Arab–Israel war, led by such states as Iraq, and protracted oil sanctions against the West. Craddock's report warned that:

> The United States might consider it could not tolerate a situation in which the U.S. and its allies [including Israel] were at the mercy of unreasonable countries. We believe the American preference would be for a rapid operation conducted by themselves to seize oilfields.

One of the most senior CIA field officers then serving in the Middle East, himself a player during these events, disputes the thesis held by some Israelis as well as the senior British analysts, that the Kissinger–Nixon duo actually planned to carry out such an operation. He believes that James Schlesinger made such "grandiose pronouncements," as the ex-CIA officer calls them, with the intention of provoking his listeners and exaggerating his own importance. This could have been partly due to jealousy of his rival in Washington's power games, Henry Kissinger, also given to such tactics upon occasion. My informant acknowledges that American contingency plans—such as are formulated by all major governments to meet hypothetical strategic situations—to seize Arab oilfields certainly existed. It is also true that some well-known American commentators did publicly advocate military conquest of the oilfields to ensure the availability of reliable, fairly priced oil for American consumers, oil then coming predominantly from Saudi Arabia, Iran, the Arabian Gulf, and Iraq. However, my ex-CIA informant believes that Prime Minister Edward Heath's fears of such rash action by his American ally were unjustified, as were the anxieties of Lord Cromer, provoked by James Schlesinger, which caused Heath's fears.[17]

IRAQ AND THE KURDS IN THE COLD WAR

In the months and years following the 1973 Middle East war, both Israeli and American interest in Iraq greatly increased. For Jerusalem's planners, Iraq was looming larger as a strategic enemy and had to be carefully watched. The Soviets, seeing that massive American military aid was now flowing into Egypt, increased theirs to the Iraq of President Hassan al-Baqr and his more powerful partner, Vice-President Saddam Hussein. They began to send heavy Russian artillery. This enabled the Iraqi forces to stop withdrawing from their strong points in the Kurdistan mountains after each summer's campaign against the Kurdish rebels, and to fortify those positions. This gave them more advanced positions to attack from during the eventful summer of 1974, which would see the Nixon–Kissinger leadership severely hampered and temporarily paralyzed by the Watergate scandal and Nixon's resulting resignation.

Prior to this, on March 11, 1974, precisely four years after the Ba'ath's original "autonomy" offer, Baghdad offered the Kurds a new plan, mentioning autonomy but in fact proposing tighter central control of Kurdistan by Baghdad. Since Mullah Mustafa Barzani's rejection was a foregone conclusion, the new March 11 proposals amounted to an ultimatum.

Alarm bells sounded in Tehran and Tel Aviv. The Shah warned Washington that Kurdish defeat would increase Baghdad's power, as well as that of its Soviet supporters, threatening Iranian and Western oil and other interests in the Gulf region. In several talks with Kissinger during his "shuttle" peace missions between Jerusalem, Cairo, and Damascus, Israeli Prime Minister Golda Meier suggested that Israel should beef up its own aid to the Kurds. Accordingly, Barzani dramatically boosted his financial and political demands. On March 16, 1974, he asked the United States for $180 million to support "full autonomy," or alternatively $360 million to create what he called an adequate infrastructure for creation of a fully independent Kurdish state. Kissinger confided to correspondents traveling with him on his shuttle missions that he thought Barzani's demands were excessive. The U.S. Congress, in the shadow of Watergate, was drastically slicing away appropriations for the wars in Indochina. CIA director William Colby opposed increased aid to the Kurds. However, Kissinger, as National Security Adviser, finally agreed with the Shah and with Israel. He asked Ambassador Richard Helms and senior White House advisor Brent Scowcroft to submit a proposal for such an increase. In early April 1974 they recommended almost doubling aid by increasing the covert U.S. contribution from $5 million to $8 million. Overt relief aid provided another $1 million for Kurdish refugees. The Shah boosted his share of the Kurdish aid program from $30 to $75 million annually. Israel and Britain kept their shares at prevailing levels.

The resources were unevenly used, because the various active players—

Israel, the Shah, Barzani, and the CIA—had differing agendas. William Colby's CIA was concerned chiefly with keeping at bay a U.S. Congress that was deeply unhappy about Vietnam and past CIA messes. The Shah wanted both to defend Iran's frontier from Iraqi aggression and to insulate Iran's Kurds from a possible contagious rebellion. Israel wanted simply to keep the pot boiling in Kurdistan, and so keep Baghdad's generals off balance and too preoccupied to support any new campaigns against the Jewish state.

Barzani, however, was still ambitious. In early September of 1974, with Washington hit by Watergate's near-paralysis and by negative U.S. Congressional reaction to Turkey's summer invasion of Cyprus, resulting in the closure of most U.S. bases in Turkey, Barzani suddenly demanded that the United States support a Kurdish drive to seize the Kirkuk oilfields. Kissinger rejected this, he said, in order to avoid aggravating what was already a serious energy crisis in the United States by touching off violence against Middle East oilfields, inside and outside Iraq. He also convinced Gerald Ford, now President following Nixon's Watergate-induced resignation, that a scheme of the Shah to send regular Iranian troops into Kurdistan to reinforce auxiliaries already deployed there, disguised as Kurds, was "too dangerous." Together with Israel's influential Ambassador to the United States, Simcha Dinitz, Kissinger got Ford on August 26 to approve transfer to the Kurds of Soviet equipment worth $28 million, which Israel had captured from the Arabs during the 1973 war. Israel was recompensed with "equivalent" American weapons.

Barzani and his men continued to appeal to all of their foreign allies for more aid against Saddam's forces, which in late 1974 were gaining ground. By the winter of 1974–75, the Shah was considering placating Saddam Hussein with a settlement of all their fractious problems. During a meeting with Kissinger in Zurich on February 18, 1975, between the Shah's skiing runs at Gstaad, Switzerland, and at the end of one of Kissinger's "exploratory" Middle East peace shuttles, the Iranian ruler suddenly told Kissinger that he planned to negotiate with Saddam Hussein. Kissinger immediately informed President Ford that the Shah wanted "to move in the direction of some understanding with Iraq, regarding the Kurds," but would continue to aid them for the time being.

Kissinger writes of his personal distaste for the Shah's apparent intention to sacrifice the Kurds in return for a better relationship with Saddam Hussein. On February 22 he told Israeli ambassador Dinitz of the Shah's signals. His fears were immediately fulfilled. On March 6, the Shah and Saddam met privately on the sidelines of the Algiers OPEC oil conference. In the words of one senior Kurdish leader to this author, they "dumped the Kurds into the shit." Saddam formally acceded to Iranian territorial demands, including an adjustment of their Shatt al-Arab river boundary in favor of Iran. In return, the Shah did indeed dump the Kurds. He immediately closed Iran's borders with Iraq. Within hours, Iranian personnel were withdrawing from Barzani's fiefdom. All Iranian supply lines to the Kurds were cut. Kurdish resistance began to crumble and within days came near to total collapse. Saddam's government resumed mass Kurdish deportations. He resettled thousands of Kurds in southern Iraq and sent Arabs to Kurdistan to take their fields, flocks, and other assets as well as their real estate.[18]

Kissinger strongly implies that the Shah fooled him about his imminent intentions in a message to Israeli Defense Minister Yitzhak Rabin on March 9, insisting that the Shah had mentioned the coming deal with Saddam only as "hypothetical." Kissinger records that he sent a "frosty" telegram to the Shah on March 10, neither endorsing nor openly opposing the Algiers deal, but stating that "[T]his is obviously a matter for Your Majesty to decide in the best interests of your nation," and that U.S. support for Iran as a "close and staunch friend of the United States" would continue. He reflects that despite a storm of criticism of himself and his Kurdish policy in Washington and abroad, and CIA director Colby's proposals to continue aid, the decision had been the Shah's. The United States, mired deeply in Watergate's consequences and in the Indochina wars, could not alone continue the policy of helping the Kurds. "Covert operations," Kissinger replied in his oft-quoted response to criticism from Colby and others, "are not missionary work." Rabin and the rest of the Israeli leadership decided to follow the Shah's lead. They withdrew Israel's modest support, as did Britain.

In ruminations that seem to have foreshadowed recriminations following Saddam's further aggressions against the Kurds, including his murderous gas attack on Halabja and many other targets during the Iran–Iraq war in the 1980s, Kissinger shows some regret. However, he closes his recollections of the Kurdish adventures of the 1970s with the reflection that if the Shah–Israel–U.S. triumvirate had acted differently, things might have turned out even worse.

This was the tragic ending for the Kurds of this sorry episode in the story of the tripartite alliance against Iraq. It took place as both the United States and Britain were beginning to consider the possible advantages of a partnership, at least a covert one, with Saddam Hussein. The help given Saddam and the subsequent partnership form the next focus of our attention.

6
How the CIA Gave Saddam a Leg Up

Permit me to tell you that I know for a certainty that what happened in February [1963] had the support of American Intelligence.

(*King Hussein of Jordan*)

When my late friend King Hussein made this statement to Egypt's leading publicist Muhammad Hasseinine Haykal in September 1963, Hussein, as usual, knew what he was talking about.[1] His reference was to the 1963 Ba'athist coup against President Abdel Karim Kassem, in which the young Saddam Hussein, although an exile in Cairo, was involved as more than a distant observer.

The background to the CIA's first step in boosting Saddam Hussein toward absolute power began in 1959, only months after the 1958 revolution led by General Abdel Karim Kassem had liquidated the monarchy and its loyal, pro-Western servant, Nuri al-Said. In his 2003 book, *Bush and Babylon*, the Pakistani author Tariq Ali depicts the Arab world's (especially Egypt's) retrospective hero-worship of Napoleon Bonaparte as one of the foundations of Gamal Abdel Nasser's charisma and personality cult on "the Arab street. This made "Nasserism," as it has come to be called, "the religion of military-populists throughout the Arab world [including Iraq] and elsewhere." The Baghdad mobs who in July 1958 had murdered King Faisal II, his uncle, and Nuri, did not cheer the revolution's leader, Kassem, but shouted instead, "We are your soldiers, Gamal Abdel Nasser. Your soldiers!"

Once in power, Kassem used the powerful Iraqi Communist Party as a buffer against Nasser's Iraqi followers, and against the clandestine Ba'ath party, which had seized power in neighboring Syria in 1965 under the leadership of the Christian Michel Aflaq and the Sunni Muslim Salah al-Bitar. The Syrian Ba'athist founders hoped to extend their program to Iraq. It at first paralleled and later rivaled that of the Nasserists: to unite all Arab nations under a single system of "Arab socialism." In Syria, the successful 1965 Ba'athist coup had severely curtailed the traditional power of city elites. It was supposed to promote citizens with rural and small-town backgrounds—like the soldier from a minority mountain religious sect, the Alawites, President Hafez al-Assad, who dominated Syrian politics from his accession to the presidency in 1970 until his death in 2000.

KASSEM, NASSER, AND SADDAM

Nasser temporarily overshadowed the Ba'ath and briefly ruled both Egypt and Syria during the short-lived United Arab Republic (UAR) of 1958–61. He would have welcomed Iraq as a third member of the UAR, but he never trusted Kassem, who he believed was too dependent on the Iraqi Communists. Kassem's deputy, Abdel Salim Aref, however, was a devoted disciple of Nasser. He would gladly have seen Iraq incorporated into an expanded UAR. However, neither Nasser nor Kassem would compromise. Kassem knew he could not compete with Nasser's vast popularity in the Arab world and he did not wish to play second fiddle to the Egyptian leader.

Strongly influenced by the Syrian Michel Aflaq, who appeared in Baghdad only days after the July 1958 revolution to promote Ba'athism as a cure for all of Iraq's ills, Kassem embarked on soapbox speaking tours of Iraq. Aflaq preached about Arab unity and Nasser as a great leader and "liberator," and soon began demanding that Iraq should join the UAR under Nasser's leadership. This alarmed Kassem and his entourage. They realized that a tripartite UAR would be seen as a major threat by Israel and by the Shah's Iran, both of which were actively backing the Iraqi Kurdish separatists under Barzani.

Kassem and his Communist allies decided to face down and defeat Aref and his Ba'athist and Nasserite supporters. On September 11, 1958, they fired Aref from his post as deputy army commander-in-chief. Two weeks later Kassem removed him as deputy prime minister and interior minister. Aref, who had been advocating nationalization of Iraq's foreign-controlled oil industry, as well as merger with the UAR, was arrested on November 4 and charged with "conspiracy against the motherland": tantamount to treason.

Reaction among Aref's supporters boiled up in March 1959. A pro-Aref army colonel and brigadier general, whom Cairo Radio called "pan-Arab patriots" (in other words, Nasserites), attempted a coup which Kassem's troops quickly crushed. In the ensuing radio war, Cairo broadcasts incited Iraqis to "topple the tyrant," while Baghdad's radio countered with denunciations of "foreign interference." Colonel al-Madahwi, president of the People's Court that had sentenced Aref to death, added insult to injury by proclaiming in open court that "the Arab caravan is unaffected by barking dogs, even if some of them claim to be Arabs."

At this point, a 22-year-old Ba'athist gunman named Saddam Hussein al-Tikriti began to carve himself the niche he coveted in history. He was part of a Ba'athist assassination squad that opened fire on Kassem and his bodyguards in October 1959. Kassem was seriously wounded but survived. Saddam escaped with a bullet in his leg which, according to a Ba'athist legend, he extracted himself with a penknife and without anesthesia; then he absconded by swimming across the Tigris. The Communists tried to help Kassem's loyalists by mobilizing mobs in the streets and by sending Communist officers and soldiers to occupy key defense and communications points, hoping to win Kassem's gratitude.

Instead, Kassem behaved like an Arab nationalist of the Nasser type. He turned against the Communists and organized a split in the Communist party between pro and anti-Kassem factions. But he also continued to promote some genuine reforms. He began to undermine the power of wealthy, mainly absentee, landlords by restricting ownership of farmland. He raised tax rates for the rich from 40 to 60 percent on incomes over 20,000 dinars. He also introduced various new taxes, and both rent and price controls. Working hours were regulated, and Iraqi employers were legally obliged to build homes for their workers. Iraq's first social insurance provisions were instituted. A huge new quarter of workers' housing was built in a Baghdad suburb, first called Thawra (Revolution) City but later re-named Saddam City. It included 10,000 homes with electricity, water, new roads, clinics, schools, and public baths.

Despite Kassem's efforts to curtail the power and high profile of the Communists in society, they boldly demonstrated and on May 1, 1959, demanded at huge public rallies to be included in the government. Israeli observers and their supporters in the United States watched with consternation as the British government resumed its long-suspended arms deliveries to Iraq, hoping that Kassem could contain his own Reds and thus keep the Soviets at bay.[2]

Saddam Hussein's most knowledgeable biographer, Said Aburish, records that Saddam often visited the U.S. Embassy in Cairo during the period 1958–61. Egyptian intelligence, which kept a close watch on politically active Arab students and others, apparently knew of these visits and approved them, because the Nasser regime was also highly suspicious of Kassem's presumed aspirations to hegemony in the Middle East. As Aburish observes, "the Americans were so determined to overthrow Kassem," who had toppled the Iraqi monarchy and ended the era of Nuri al-Said's pro-Western orientation in July 1958, and who was suspected of dark anti-Israel and pro-Soviet intentions, "that they opened their doors [of their Cairo Embassy] to everyone in sight."

There were also contacts between U.S. officials and the many anti-Kassem Iraqi exiles in Beirut. Aburish recalls that some of them openly expressed both their opposition to Kassem and their connections with the CIA. He remembers meeting one Iraqi who boasted that he had the direct telephone number of CIA director Allen Dulles. There was a strong community of interest between the new Ba'ath party and the Americans. Liaison with the Ba'athist underground in Baghdad was apparently handled by William Lakeland, whose assignment (or cover) was as a military-political attaché at the American Embassy. In Cairo, where Saddam pursued desultory university studies, the senior CIA officer for the Middle East, coordinating anti-Kassem efforts with Nasser's intelligence services, was James Critchfield.

JAMES CRITCHFIELD: COLD WARRIOR PAR EXCELLENCE

Because of Critchfield's part in both the ultimately unsuccessful Ba'athist coup of 1963 and his later, if lesser, role in the successful Ba'athist takeover of power in 1968 that launched Saddam Hussein on his career of domination and tyranny, it is worthwhile to take a close look at Critchfield.

After a career as a World War II combat soldier, CIA Cold Warrior in post-war Europe and then in the Middle East, and finally as a consultant, soldier of fortune, and entrepreneur, James H. Critchfield died of pancreatic cancer at the age of 86 in his family home in Williamsburg, Virginia, on April 22, 2003. The U.S.-led military operation to topple Saddam Hussein, who Critchfield had helped to power, was well under way. His official obituary, published on the website of Arlington National Cemetery where he received a war hero's burial, quotes Timothy Naftali, an intelligence historian:

> Critchfield's talents as a spymaster, soldier and diplomat put him at the heart of a half-century of historic moments. ... What happened in Jim's lifetime was staggering. Fighting the Nazis, then seeing a new global conflict emerge and fighting in that, then seeing that conflict move to the Third World and becoming a general in that.

Critchfield was born in Hunter, North Dakota, the son of a school-teacher and a country doctor. After graduating from North Dakota State University, where he served in the ROTC program, he joined the Army and became one of the youngest colonels in World War II. He commanded the 2nd Battalion of the 141st Infantry of the 36th Division, pushing through France, Germany, and finally Austria. He was highly decorated for his wartime deeds, which included leading an infantry assault battalion against the Germans in Alsace-Lorraine on December 12, 1944. He emerged from the war as a full colonel, joined the CIA in 1948, and served the agency for 26 years.

One of the CIA officers who served under Critchfield remembers him as a sturdy, handsome, and outgoing man, who radiated a kind of ruthless charm but would not brook fools or insubordination. His intelligence contemporaries still remember him, not so much for his help to Saddam Hussein and the Ba'ath as for his earlier work in CIA liaison with what came to be known as the Gehlen Organization after World War II. This was a group of Third Reich military and intelligence personnel, commanded by Rheinhard Gehlen, one of the stars of Hitler's intelligence network working against the Soviet Union, who was especially adept at recruiting agents and in deception tactics. In post-war Germany, the U.S. Army recruited Gehlen personnel for Cold War operations because of their expertise in the affairs of Stalin's USSR. Although the organization soon revealed itself to be shot through with "fabricators, double agents and war criminals," as Critchfield's obituary puts it, it played an important role in founding West Germany's external intelligence service, the Bundesnachrichtendienst (BND), which became part of the NATO security network.

Before moving to the Middle East arena, Critchfield boasted that he had "covered everything from Greece to Burma." At various times he headed the East European Division and the Near East and South Asia Division of the CIA. His assignment included working with Tibetan guerrillas against Communist China's occupation, heading a CIA task force during the Cuban missile crisis, and anti-Soviet operations in Eastern Europe.[3]

Critchfield probably first identified Saddam as an up-and-coming Iraqi dissident who could help destroy Communism in Iraq through reports from the CIA station in Cairo, while Saddam was living there in exile. From Cairo, Saddam kept in touch with the Ba'athist plotters in Baghdad. So did Critchfield and William Lakeland. Historian Hanna Batatu writes that some of the Iraqi Ba'athists "were maintaining surreptitious contacts with representatives of American power." King Hussein, who was himself on the CIA payroll at the time, supplied the important detail that on February 8, 1963, a secret radio station in Kuwait beamed to the Ba'athist plotters in Baghdad a list of the Communists there so that they could be arrested and executed.[4]

Kassem's policies and Communist support had raised great alarm in Washington. CIA director Allen Dulles had earlier termed the situation in Iraq "the most dangerous in the world." Washington's Israeli partners in Jerusalem shared that concern. Kassem had withdrawn Iraq from the 1958 pro-Western Baghdad Pact, made many friendly overtures to Moscow, and revoked and nationalized the oil exploration rights of some of the foreign components of the Iraq Petroleum Company (IPC).

THE FIRST BA'ATHIST COUP

A successful and well-prepared Ba'athist coup, which James Critchfield later hailed as "a great victory," erupted at 8:30 a.m. on February 8, 1963 with the murder of the Communist Iraqi Air Force chief, Brigadier General Jalal al-Awqati, gunned down as he visited a bakery and sweets store with his small child. Next, a Ba'athist air force Major, Mundhir al-Windawi, led an air attack by two Hawker-Hunter jets. They dive-bombed the Rashid airbase near Baghdad, ruining the runway. Minutes later, Windawi led a series of bombing and strafing attacks by Hawker-Hunters and MIG-17s firing rockets and cannon on Kassem's Defense Ministry. Ba'athist ground forces, including elements of the Fourth Tank Regiment and the predominantly Ba'athist National Guard, attacked and secured the Al-Rashid base. Another tank unit, including Colonels Abdel Salam Aref and Ahmed Hassan al-Baqr, moved on the Abu Ghraib radio station and the Defense Ministry. The Ba'athist plotters then issued the first of a series of radio pronunciamentos They called themselves "the National Council of the Revolutionary Command," using non-pan-Arab language in order to please and propitiate the Kurds.

Kassem and his Communist allies tried to organize resistance. They were hampered by the fact that Kassem refused to arm the mobs of poor people pouring into Baghdad's streets, many armed only with sticks and canes. There was some fighting at two army camps outside Baghdad, As-Sa'd and Al-Washash. By 3 p.m. on the afternoon of February 8, the Ba'athist rebels had begun their main assault on Kassem's headquarters in the Defense Ministry, defended by about 1,000 able-bodied troops. The Ministry was finally captured and occupied on the morning of February 9. In the meantime, Kassem, hearing Aref proclaimed as provisional new president on the rebel radio, phoned Aref to tell him, "I am your brother, and will never forget the bread and salt that we ate together" (an Arab method of friendship bonding). Aref's reply was that the Revolutionary Council had decided that Kassem should surrender at the main gate of his headquarters with his hands in the air and no military rank showing on his uniform. Kassem pleaded vainly for his life and permission to leave the country, but was arrested with three aides at midday on February 9. Within an hour a drumhead court condemned him and his three aides to death. A firing squad killed them immediately. Iraqi historical tradition remembers Kassem as the most genuinely popular president Iraq has ever had.

Kassem's Communist allies, both Sunnis and Shias, continued resistance for several days, notably in Basra where they held out until February 12. The Arefs and the Ba'athists backing them, however, gradually rounded up the Communists in relentless camp-to-camp, village-to-village, and house-to-house searches. The lists of the Ba'ath's Communist opponents radioed from Kuwait were supplied by Critchfield's men, including a CIA operative who operated under cover of a *TIME* magazine correspondent in *TIME*'s Beirut bureau. The names were disseminated throughout Iraq and well over 1,000 of them were executed, many after torture. This was in addition to the 5,000 people the Communists estimated were killed in the fighting.[5]

Saddam Hussein heard the news on the radio in Cairo and rushed back to Baghdad in one of the first flights to land after the airport reopened. Said Aburish records that Saddam after his return was "personally involved in the torture of [anti-Ba'ath] Leftists in the separate detention centers for fellaheen (peasants) and the *Muthaqafeen* or educated classes."

Critchfield later acknowledged to the Associated Press that the CIA knew that the coup would happen about six months beforehand. "We came to power on a CIA train," according to the Ba'ath secretary general, Ali Saleh al-Sa'di, who was in charge of the mass executions of Kassem's supporters. Defensively, Critchfield insisted that Saddam Hussein, despite his unsuccessful assassination attempt against Kassem in 1959, was only a minor and peripheral figure in the Ba'ath party in 1963. "You have to understand the context of the time and the scope of the threat we were facing," Critchfield added. "That's what I say to people who say, 'You guys in the CIA created Saddam Hussein.'"[6]

ANGLO-AMERICAN COOPERATION

Critchfield had been less defensive in candid remarks he made in London to Sir Dick White, the chief of Britain's MI-6 external spy service. He had met White while en route to Beirut for a regional intelligence conference on Soviet activities in the region at the end of November 1962, when the Ba'athist coup in Baghdad, viewed in London as well as Washington as an anti-Communist and hence an anti-Soviet coup, was being planned. Critchfield told White: "The Russians are waging war across Arabia. We've got to stop them. Their influence is everywhere and it's spreading down to the Gulf." At the time, the CIA was apparently urging the Eisenhower administration to end its approval of another old anti-Communist friend, President Nasser of Egypt, who had inspired Kassem in Iraq.

The Agency was turning its attention to Nasser's support for the military men in Yemen who had proclaimed a republic in that ancient kingdom, whose royal family was supported by Saudi Arabia, Britain, and America. In 1963, following documented reports of Egyptian air force chemical bomb attacks against pro-royalist Yemeni villages—much later, in January 1967, I trekked through Yemen with a group of colleagues and verified one of these gas attacks—Critchfield visited White again. He argued that the "West" could not afford to "lose" Yemen (meaning the feudal royalist regime of the Imam of Yemen), and that the CIA should combat Nasser, regardless of President Eisenhower's policies. He told White that intercepts by the U.S. National Security Agency (NSA) showed that Russian pilots were flying TU-16 bombers with Egyptian markings from Cairo to Yemen. He proposed to bypass the more cautious British Foreign Office and State Department to institute closer MI-6/CIA relations in the Middle East. Although White apparently demurred at first, he came under pressure to comply with CIA wishes from Prime Minister Harold Macmillan. He was won over when James Fees, a CIA operative posted in Yemen under humanitarian agency cover, provided MI-6 with a copy of the Yemeni republican army's order of battle. Closer British–U.S. cooperation developed out of this and from a visit to London by the CIA's deputy chief for plans, Richard Helms (who later became Director of the Agency and then Ambassador to the Shah's Iran).[7] Although Critchfield pretty much ran the CIA's Middle East operations until his retirement in 1974, less is known about his role in Saddam Hussein's successful ousting of the Aref clan in the second and triumphant Ba'athist coup of 1968.

The importance of Middle Eastern oil in Western energy imports and consumption was growing. As the Iraqi regimes of the Aref brothers, followed by that of the Ba'ath from 1968, prepared for the final nationalization of the Western-owned Iraq Petroleum Company in 1973,

Critchfield operated in Washington in the late 1960s and early 1970s as the CIA's national intelligence officer for oil policy.

Later he became an energy planner in the Nixon White House. After his retirement from the CIA in 1974, he became a consultant on oil and related matters in the Gulf Kingdom of Oman. He founded a business and consulting firm called Tetratech and for a time, fronted a dummy CIA corporation in the region known as Basic Resources. This was used to provide intelligence to the Nixon administration on the OPEC oil cartel, of which Iraq was a founding and key member.[8]

SADDAM'S SWAY BEGINS

The purges and oppression which followed the 1963 Ba'athist coup in Iraq in many ways set a pattern for the way the Ba'ath behaved later, when Saddam held the party, government, and people under his absolute sway. Although the Ba'athists had assured the CIA that those detained would be given fair trials, the Ba'athist National Guard, wearing green armbands and carrying submachine guns, perpetrated what *Daily Telegraph* journalist Con Coughlin in his biography of Saddam terms "an orgy of violence." Sports clubs, cinemas, and many private houses were taken over and used as interrogation centers, torture chambers, and places of execution. Coughlin compares the liquidation of the Iraqi Communists with the anti-Leftist purges that would later occur in the Chile of Salvador Allende and Augusto Pinochet, who overthrew Allende with CIA aid, and with actions of the colonels' junta which ruled Argentina until they were overthrown after their defeat by Britain (this time with the CIA supporting Prime Minister Margaret Thatcher's Britain and opposing the Argentine junta) in the war for the Falkland Islands in early 1982. Saddam's elite Republican Guards were to behave in similar ways when they invaded Kuwait in August 1990, turning government offices and palaces into interrogation and torture centers.

Iraqi survivors of Saddam's tyranny have described one of the principal torture chambers in the so-called Palace of the End (Qasr al-Nihaya), so named because the monarchy was liquidated there during the July revolution of 1958. A sadistic Shia man named Nadhim Kazzar became chief torturer there, apt preparation for later becoming Saddam's chief of national security. Kazzar had joined the Iraqi Ba'ath soon after its inception in the 1950s and soon established his brutal reputation by leading the torture of the Communists held after Kassem's fall. A persistent story about him was that during interrogations, he extinguished cigarettes on the eyeballs of his victims.[9]

Hanna Batatu discovered in files of the Saddam regime that in the cellars of the Palace of the End were "all sorts of loathsome instruments of torture, including electric wires with pincers, pointed iron stakes on which prisoners were made to sit, and a machine which still bore traces of chopped-off fingers."[10]

The United States contacted the Ba'athist-led rebels only hours after the coup and promised them recognition. James Akins, a former U.S. Ambassador to Saudi Arabia who at the time of the 1963 coup was an attaché at the U.S. Embassy in Baghdad, told American author Robert Kaplan, "On account of the coup we enjoyed better relations with Iraq." The Americans expected, and received, something in return for their help. Said Aburish relates that according to Hani Fkaiki, a key participant in the coup, William Lakeland received several Soviet-built MIG-21s, T-54 tanks and SAM missiles, which the United States used to check their specifications and effectiveness. To the consternation of the Israelis, who as we saw favored Barzani's Kurds, in April 1963 the United States flew arms from Turkey and Iran to Baghdad government forces fighting against the Kurds in the Kirkuk region. The United States also advised Jalal Talabani to end the rebellion, which had begun in 1961—despite the Kurds having been informed in advance of the anti-Kassem coup, and having offered their tacit cooperation.

At the same time, what would eventually become a honeymoon between Saddam and American firms was kicked off. The U.S. firms of Parsons, Bechtel, and Mobil Oil were among those receiving important contracts and concessions from the Ba'athists. Robert Anderson, a former U.S. Treasury Secretary during the Eisenhower administration, took the lead in many of the new commercial ventures.

Saddam is said to have visited Damascus and returned to Baghdad with secret instructions from Michel Aflaq. This apparently enhanced Saddam's prestige with his fellow Iraqi Ba'athists and enabled him to move upwards in the hierarchy more rapidly.

The regime of the Aref brothers and their allies, from 1963 to 1966 was followed by a turbulent period of military coups and Iraq's participation in the 1967 war, leading finally to the Ba'ath's permanent seizure of power in 1968. During the period, 1963–79, Israel and the United States played at times seemingly contradictory political games. To be sure, as we saw, they both cooperated with the Shah of Iran to support the Kurdish movements against Baghdad, until the Shah suddenly dropped the Kurds in his 1975 deal with Saddam Hussein. However, Jerusalem and Washington sometimes seemed to be working at cross-purposes in their overt diplomacy, while working more or less together on the covert front.

When Abdel Salem Aref and his Ba'athist allies seized power in November 1963 with U.S. help, there were almost no vestiges left in Baghdad of representative or parliamentary institutions. Power in Iraq truly came out of the barrel of a gun. The military, as the British historians Marion and Peter Sluglett remind us, held a total monopoly of the means of coercion that kept them in power. From February to November 1963, rival nationalist and Ba'athist militias had contended with each other. Between November 1963 and Abdel Salem Aref's April 1966 death in a helicopter crash, the Republican Guard was created from the regular army's 20th infantry division. It soon became the regime's elite corps. After Saddam took total power in 1979, it became the military component of his praetorian guard. It was never totally defeated nor crushed in the two wars with the U.S.-led coalitions in 1991 and 2003. By the end of 1964, the militant Baqr–Saddam Hussein wing of the Ba'ath had been temporarily pushed out of power. According to Saddam Hussein's own account, Saddam was even briefly imprisoned. Aref was relying on other, non-Ba'athist allies, notably Nasserist officers, and was in some ways trying to emulate Nasser's so-called "Arab socialism."

On the sixth anniversary of the Iraqi revolution, July 14, 1964, Aref announced the nationalization of all banks and insurance companies, and of over 30 major business and industrial firms. Like most nationalizations everywhere, the Aref measures resulted in a general loss of efficiency and decline of most of the enterprises.[11] It was about this time, as Ahmed Chalabi once explained to me, that his father packed in his own banking institution in Baghdad and moved it to Beirut, where Ahmed himself became a student and then a professor of mathematics at the American University.

Feuding between the various Ba'athist and nationalist/Nasserist factions gave Saddam Hussein, then in his late twenties, a chance to exercise his gangster-like tendencies. The "civilian" wing of the Ba'ath, headed by the equally, if not more thuggish, Ali Saleh al-Sa'adi, took extreme stands. Abroad, this included pushing an old Iraqi claim to its neighbor Kuwait; a claim frustrated by a British show of force following Kuwait's accession to independence from Britain in 1961. Saddam and Baqr's "military" wing of the Ba'ath supported the concept that Kuwait rightfully belonged to Iraq. Baghdad policy until Saddam's invasion of Kuwait in the summer of 1990 was grudgingly to recognize the wealthy emirate as an independent country, while extracting generous financial aid from the frightened Kuwaitis. However, Baghdad stubbornly refused to demarcate or recognize any *de jure* frontier with Kuwait.

Early in 1964 Saddam fled to Syria, where Michel Aflaq named him the commander of a new Ba'ath Regional Command in Iraq. Saddam returned to Iraq and went underground with a group of Tikriti clans-men and other companions. They tried to organize Aref's assassination and to attack his palace with home-made bombs. Saddam was captured and confined again in the Public Security building in Bagh-dad. His sympathetic Arab biographers and Saddam's own book, *The Long Days*, claim that he endured solitary confinement and various "physical pressures" (the term Western, Israeli, and other jailers prefer to use for "mild" forms of torture). None of these "pressures" proba-bly ever remotely approached the hideous tortures Saddam would soon be imposing on his real or imagined adversaries. Saddam's wife Sadija was apparently allowed to visit him and bring him books to read. According to Saddam, she often carried messages wrapped in the baby clothes of their son Uday, then a few months old—destined, after a long and bloody career to be killed with his brother Qusay by U.S. forces in Iraq in the early summer of 2003. The only witness to Saddam's confinement was apparently his prison companion Abdel Karim Shaikhaly, who Saddam called "my twin." Saddam killed him, or had him killed, in 1972. By the end of 1965 Aflaq had made Saddam's mentor and ally, Baqr, the secretary-general of the Ba'ath's Iraqi branch, and Saddam deputy secretary-general. Shortly after this, Saddam escaped, or was allowed to escape.[12]

IRAQ'S STRATEGIC THREAT TO ISRAEL

On February 23, 1966, I was among correspondents in Beirut who covered a successful coup in Syria by the left wing of the Syrian Ba'ath, ending the control of Aflaq and his co-founder, Salah Bitar from the "National" or pan-Arab command of the party. The "neo-Ba'athists" ousted President Amine al-Hafez and his old-style Ba'athist supporters in three days of bloody fighting in Damascus, Aleppo, and elsewhere. The neo-Ba'athist Syrian rulers, younger men, immediately adopted an activist policy against Israel. The Syrian army had been sporadically skirmishing with Israeli forces throughout the 1950s and 1960s along the Syrian–Israel armistice lines of 1949 and between the Golan Heights and the Sea of Galilee (Lake Tiberias). The neo-Ba'athists cultivated rela-tions with Yassir Arafat's Al-Fatah guerrilla organization, which had taken over leadership of the "armed struggle" wing of the Palestine Liberation Organization (PLO). Together, Syria and the PLO militants continued attacks, beginning on New Years' Eve of 1965 with an aborted assault on Israel's irrigation system mounted from Syrian terri-tory. This, and disputes and armed clashes between regular Syrian and

Israeli armed forces over diversion of the Jordan river water system and demarcation of the 1949 demilitarized zones (DMZs), were proximate causes of the war Israel fought with the Arabs in June 1967.

Iraq's involvement in the 1967 war and the reactions of Israel and its American partner to that involvement were key factors in Saddam Hussein's slow but methodical rise to absolute power. To understand why, it is useful to look through an Israeli lens. Israeli academic and intelligence analysts who have made a careful study of the Iraqi–Israel relationships over the years stress the differences, as well as the historical continuities, between Iraq's involvement in the various Arab–Israel wars.

In Israel's war of independence in 1947–49, as we saw in previous chapters, the Iraqi monarchy of King Faisal II and Nuri al-Said played an important role. This role began in the summer of 1946, as the Arab League, just created with the blessing of Great Britain, began to plan military action against the *Yishuv*, the future Jewish state in Palestine. The League's predominantly Egyptian leadership appointed senior Iraqi officers to plan an Arab offensive to begin as soon as the British withdrew from Palestine. Israeli analysts believe that Iraq was prompted by two main concerns: to secure a position of leadership in the Arab world, and to secure control of the old pre-1948 British-built pipeline carrying Iraqi oil from the Kirkuk-Mosul areas to Haifa, thus giving it easy access to the Mediterranean and to world markets.

There had been clashes in 1952 between Ben-Gurion's Israel and the Jordan of the young and newly enthroned King Hussein (who as a boy of 16 had witnessed in the previous year the assassination of his grandfather, King Abdallah, on the steps of the Al-Aqsa Mosque in Jerusalem by a Palestinian gunman who resented Abdallah's contacts with Golda Meier and other Israeli leaders). Jordan sought, and apparently obtained, at least token military support from Iraq. King Hussein repeated the request in June 1956, as clashes increased between Israel and two other neighbors, Egypt and Syria. Jordan and Iraq formed a joint defense committee, along with a military council and a joint headquarters in Amman. During the run-up to the Suez War of 1956, one complete Iraqi division, about a third of Iraq's then existing ground forces, deployed in western Iraq, facing Jordan. This was the area where Saddam Hussein deployed many of the launchers for the 39 Scud missiles it launched against Israel during the 1991 Gulf War.

Shortly before it began the Suez War, in September 1956 these moves led Ben-Gurion's government to declare a policy which, like Iraq's "No, no, never" to armistice or peace with Israel, was to reiterate the traditional Israeli warning: introduction of Iraqi forces into Jordan would be regarded as a *casus belli*, causing Israel to send troops into the West Bank, then under King Hussein's rule. In September and October, during skirmishes between Israeli and Jordanian forces which were a kind of offstage overture to the main Suez War further south, Britain warned Israel that if it continued military action against Jordan, Britain would be obliged to fulfill its defense commitment to the Hashemite Kingdom. London also warned Jerusalem to desist from any military response if Iraqi troops entered Jordan. Ben-Gurion's government, was deeply unhappy over what appeared to be growing military cooperation between Jordan, Iraq, and Britain. On October 15, 1956 (during the final secret Israeli–British–French preparations to attack Nasser and occupy the zone around the Suez Canal, which Nasser had wrested from its Western shareholders/owners during the summer) it declared that any violation of the military or territorial status quo would lead to a military response by Israel. During this same period, Jordanian parliamentary elections in October resulted in a strong victory for Nasser's Jordanian supporters. President Nasser then let it be known that he would send military aid to Jordan, if needed. Jordanian–Iraqi relations, however, were cooling. When Britain, France, and Israel, with strong U.S. disapproval, began their air and ground assault against Egypt on October 29 neither Jordan, Iraq, nor any other Arab neighbor joined battle.

In 1967, the situation was decidedly different from that of 1948 in both Iraq and Israel. Ben-Gurion was living in retirement, and a rather indecisive Levi Eshbol was Israeli prime minister. In Iraq, President Adel Raman Aref was trying to hold his own against the rising power of Baqr and Saddam Hussein. When Aref visited Nasser in February 1967, he found the Egyptian president rather downbeat on the subject of any early pan-Arab military campaign against Israel. "[W]e cannot handle the Palestine question," said Nasser, assuring the Iraqi leader that the issue could only be settled by "continuous planning in a series of phases." As the mounting hysteria in the Arab world during the coming weeks would show, this was the exact opposite of what happened.

IRAQ IN THE 1967 WAR

In mid-May 1967 the hitherto slowly rising tension between Israel on the one hand and Egypt and Syria on the other began to reach boiling point. During these weeks I watched from Cairo the approach of war. President Nasser ordered UN peacekeeping forces out of Sinai, mobilized the Egyptian army, and announced the closure of the Straits of Tiran between the Red Sea and the Gulf of Aqaba to Israeli shipping.

Israeli briefings to foreign correspondents in Tel Aviv and Jerusalem warned of danger from Syria, whose ground and air forces had been clashing with Israel and where PLO forces were operating across the armistice lines against Israel. In Baghdad, Iraq joined the general Arab propaganda bluster against the Jewish state and began preparations for the looming conflict. On May 19, Baghdad placed the Iraqi army on high alert. An Iraqi delegation visited Damascus to coordinate military assistance, offering air support that would operate from H-3 base in Western Iraq.

What historians often overlook is that shortly before the Israeli onslaughts on Syria and the outbreak of Israel–Jordanian fighting in Jerusalem on June 5, Iraq flew an infantry battalion into Egypt. I have found no accounts of its involvement in the six-day conflict that followed. On the diplomatic front, the Aref government in Iraq, in vain, invited the non-Arab Muslim neighbors Iran and Turkey, in the name of Muslim solidarity to join the pan-Arab effort. Before King Hussein's May 30 flight to Cairo to sign a defense pact with Nasser, the Iraqi propaganda machine chided Hussein and his government for dragging their feet about joining the pan-Arab war effort. However, when a Joint Arab Military Command was established and Egyptian General Abdel Moneim Riyad set up the Unified Arab Command headquarters in Amman, comprising Iraqi as well as Syrian, Jordanian, and Egyptian officers, Iraq quickly sent spare parts and other military aid to Jordan (but not to its neo-Ba'athist-ruled rival, Syria), and signed a defense pact with Egypt.[13]

When the war was over, as Israel and much of the Western world celebrated Israel's crushing victory over the Arab coalition, the Arab world collectively mourned the loss of Sinai, East Jerusalem, the West Bank, and the Golan Heights to Israel's victorious armies. Nasser, chastened by defeat but still defiant, organized in August an Arab summit in Khartoum. Some of the more rhetorical Arab media called it a "summit of destiny." King Hussein, Aref, and Algeria's President Houari Boumedienne faced a Nasser who argued that perhaps they should think about a political settlement with Israel. Syria's neo-Ba'athist bosses flew home in disgust. Iraq's delegation was joined by Algeria's leaders in demands that the oil embargo on the West imposed at the war's outbreak should continue. The PLO's Egyptian-imposed leader Ahmed Shukairy, Yassir Arafat's predecessor, raved about kindling Palestinian guerrilla action and uprisings in the occupied territories. However, Nasser's views, a mixture of a continued hard line on Palestine and political realism about the dim prospects for any successful armed revanche in the near future, prevailed. The final communiqué vetoed the idea of accepting U.S. and Soviet plans for promoting peace treaties with Israel. It called for pan-Arab "political action" to recover territory and realize Palestinian rights, but insisted on the famous "Three nos" that were to dominate most Arab policies until Nasser's death in 1970 and the subsequent peace efforts of his successor President Anwar al-Sadat: "No recognition of Israel, no peace and no negotiations," accompanied by "all steps necessary to consolidate military preparedness."[14]

Iraq's poor performance in the 1967 war was one of the causes of the internal discontent and political turmoil that led to Saddam's seizure of power with his senior partner Baqr in the definitive, and this time successful, Ba'athist coup of 1968. During the war, Aref had taken over the premiership as well as the presidency, because the incumbent Prime Minister, Naji Talib, had proven incapable of keeping down tribal and factional quarrels. After the war Aref gave the job to a more forceful officer, Tahir Yahya. Following the line of the "Three nos" of Khartoum and a more militantly anti-Zionist and anti-imperialist line, Yahya broke off diplomatic relations with Britain and the United States (which since June 5 had been formally accused by Nasser and even by King Hussein of actively intervening on Israel's side in the war). Two new laws promulgated in August and October of 1967 prepared the ground for total nationalization of Iraq's oil under the state National Oil Company (INOC). This acquired wider powers and exclusive rights to develop the vast underground riches of the North Rumaila oilfield, near the Kuwait border. The field's vast reserves had been known and proven for many years. However, the Western-owned IPC had been prevented from developing it under the provisions of Law 80 of 1961, in the time of Kassem.

The two new oil laws signaled the opening to France that French oil companies had long been waiting for, especially since losing control of Algeria's oil and natural gas resources after that country wrested its freedom from France in the 1954–62 war for Algerian independence. On November 24, 1967, INOC opened the door to what would soon develop into major French involvement in Iraq and especially with Saddam Hussein's 1979–2003 regime. INOC signed a service contract with the French oil consortium ERAP. Simultaneously, INOC announced it would seek Soviet aid in the development of North Rumaila and other fields. In these ways, the Yahya government prepared the way for Saddam Hussein's later militant oil policies by showing its determination to continue eroding the position of Western interests in the IPC. On April 10, 1968, it was announced that INOC should definitely develop North Rumaila without any input or help from the IPC.

It was left to the Baqr–Saddam regime to carry the process to its final conclusion by the Ba'athist nationalization of the IPC in 1972.[15] This was a symbolic but highly significant demonstration that the Ba'athists were now absolute masters of Iraq.

How Saddam Hussein finally won absolute power for himself permanently, once again with American approval, and how the United States, Britain and the other main regional actors, Israel and Iran, reacted are our next subjects.

7

Saddam's Reign (I): Business With the U.S.; Warfare With Israel

Historians are dangerous, and capable of turning everything topsy-turvy. They have to be watched.

(*Nikita Khruschev, 1956*)

Historians might well ask themselves: why did it take so long for the United States and Israel, once only partners, sometimes hesitant ones, to become close allies against Saddam Hussein?

Early on, the perceived interests of Israel and the United States in Iraq were largely conflicting. From Israel's birth, and more intensely from the 1958 Iraqi revolution onward, Israel's main concern about Iraq was Israeli national security; the need for defense against a dangerous strategic enemy. Early Ba'athist rule in the late 1960s and the 1970s increased this perception in Israel. Saddam and his clique proclaimed on every possible occasion their determination to "crush the curse of Zionism" and "liberate Palestine."

The United States, however, especially the oil and business interests which exert a strong influence on American administrations, saw great opportunities in Iraq's oil and other energy resources and its large and growing market for Western technology. But when Israel and the United States, in the 1990s, both began their efforts to depose Saddam and to remake Iraq into a country more friendly to the West (and, if possible, to Israel), the commercial calculus in American thinking, linked to the role of American firms in Iraq's post-2003 reconstruction, was matched by hegemonic and strategic considerations—which well suited America's Israeli partner, now becoming a full ally.

U.S. BUSINESS AND SADDAM'S TRIUMPH

The record on U.S. support for the 1968 Ba'athist coup is much murkier than for the one of 1963. In published accounts of the period there is one American name that often appears: Robert B. Anderson. He was an oilman from Texas as well as a former secretary of the U.S. Treasury. In 1956, before the Suez War, President Eisenhower and Secretary of State

John Foster Dulles sent Anderson to try to persuade David Ben-Gurion and Gamal Abdel Nasser to make a deal. Another war seemed to be looming. Eisenhower and Dulles had withdrawn an offer of American aid for Egypt's Aswan High Dam, in retribution for Nasser's nationalization of the Suez Canal and his decision to buy arms from the Soviet bloc. According to Israeli historian Michael Oren, Ben-Gurion was willing to meet and talk to Nasser but would not consider any territorial concessions. Nasser, however, believed he could only lose from such a meeting.[1] It never took place.

Anderson experienced another setback in his efforts to bring about peace through commerce, this time on behalf of his fellow Texan, President Lyndon B. Johnson, during the prelude to the war of June 1967. On May 24 of that year, Johnson talked on the phone with Anderson about the gathering crisis between the Arabs and Israel. Johnson proposed to send Anderson on another secret mission to Cairo, apparently without the prior knowledge of newly-appointed U.S. Ambassador Dick Nolte. Anderson arrived in Cairo on May 30. This was only hours after King Hussein had visited and signed the defense pact with Nasser, an act making war highly probable. Anderson believed that business interests could repair the Middle East's chronic political problems. He suggested to Nasser that Egyptian Vice-President Abdel Hakim Amer should visit the United States. Anderson apparently believed that deliveries to Egypt of needed American wheat might be exchanged for a backdown by Nasser on his demands against Israel. Nasser insisted that Israel was massing troops to attack Syria and assured Anderson that Egypt was prepared to strike back at Israel. He suggested that another Vice-President, Zakkariya Muhieddin, like Amer an old friend and army companion of Nasser, should travel to the United States instead. This was agreed, but the entire hastily built scaffolding for possible peacemaking soon collapsed. Israel launched its well-prepared surprise attacks on June 5.[2]

Later, Washington again cast Anderson in a key role, this time in Iraq, in the years immediately preceding the Ba'ath's decisive 1968 coup. There are strong suggestions that U.S. interests were involved, this time for commercial advantage. Iraq's National Oil Company (INOC) had offered an oil concession to the French consortium ERAP in 1966. INOC had also invited the Soviets to develop the vast Rumaila oilfield, straddling the Iraq–Kuwait border. Both the French and the Soviets were having some success with marketing Iraqi oil. This raised competitive concerns in Washington, and in Texas and the other U.S. oil states. At the same time, the price of industrial sulfur had risen on the world market. This made sulfur mining in the Mishaaq region of northern Iraq look economically desirable. President Abdel Rahman Aref's government wanted to grant this concession to the French, whose ERAP firm was courting the Baghdad regime for more concessions.

A group of U.S. entrepreneurs, certainly with the blessings of Washington, which was anxious to offset its growing difficulties in the Indo-China wars with some successes, undertook to stem the pro-French and pro-Soviet tide in Iraq. Paul Parker, an adventurous American banker with strong ties to the U.S. Treasury's intelligence operations and an acquaintance of mine and other newsmen in Beirut, approached the Iraqi ambassador in Beirut, Nasser al-Hani and Lutfi Obeidi, an Iraqi lawyer with good Ba'ath party contacts. Parker, according to Said Aburish, made a tentative agreement with Carl Ludwig, an oil tanker tycoon, to ship Iraqi oil to world markets. At the same time, Robert Anderson began to shuttle between Baghdad and the United States with what Aburish terms "open-ended offers" for the oil, and also bearing purchase offers from Pan American Sulfur Co. and Gulf Sulfur Co.

By 1967, however, demonstrators in Baghdad were expressing the Ba'ath's distaste by shouting "Go back home, Anderson!" Neither Anderson nor Parker took heed. They began more active wooing of Iraqi officialdom and business circles. At one point, President Aref accused his intelligence chief, Abdel Razzaq al-Nayef, of working for the West's oil interests. Parker and Obeidi apparently arranged a meeting between Anderson and Saddam Hussein's mentor and the future Ba'athist president, General Ahmed Hassan al-Baqr, to discuss oil and sulfur, with no visible results.

THE JULY BA'ATHIST TAKEOVER

The "July revolution," as Saddam and his supporters chose to call their July 1968 coup, involved long and patient preparations. The Baqr–Saddam-led conspirators worked to win over several of President Aref's key military supporters, especially three colonels who controlled key troop units. Saddam insisted that some non-military Ba'athists should join the army and put on uniforms for the occasion to impress Aref with the size of the plotters' military backing. Saddam himself, and several others, including his half-brother, Barzan al-Tikriti (captured by U.S. forces before Saddam during the invasion in 2003), donned the uniforms of army lieutenants. They rode on tanks toward Aref's palace on the early morning of July 17, 1968. Sa'adun Ghaydan, who headed the presidential guard, took Baqr, Colonel Ahardane al-Tikriti, and other Ba'athist officers with him in the takeover of the 10th Armored Brigade's buildings. Others seized key points, including the Ministry of Defense. There was almost no real resistance or fighting, although Baghdadis were awakened by small-arms and machine-gun fire. Ahardane al-Takriti entered Aref's palace with his band of Ba'athist officers and summoned Aref to resign and go into exile. Aref answered with only mild remonstrances and a request that his wife be allowed to join him abroad. Ahardane drove Aref home, made him coffee and urged him to lie down and rest before flying out of Baghdad, which he then did.

Within hours, as pre-arranged, Baqr, Saddam, and their co-conspirators dissolved the old Aref revolutionary council and set up their own Revolutionary Command Council (RCC), under Baqr's chairmanship. When the Baghdad populace realized that this time there was no bloody repression of the Communists, Shia, or others, it largely accepted the Ba'athist takeover. Baqr was proclaimed president, but the premiership went to Colonel Nayef, a non-Ba'athist. Nassr al-Hani, who had been dealing with Robert Anderson and Paul Parker as ambassador in Lebanon, was promoted to Foreign Minister. Only six of the 24-member cabinet were Ba'athists. The Ba'athist second in rank and power to Baqr was General Ahardane al-Tikriti. He became Army Chief of Staff (and eventually a vice-president, defense minister, and commander of the Iraqi troop presence in Jordan). Ahardane's ally, General Saleh Mehdi Ammash, became Interior Minister.

Saddam Hussein's assignment was to head a new Ba'athist security service. It gave him total control of Iraq's internal security, a key to total power he kept from then on. The Ba'ath party's old internal security organization, Jihaz Hunein, had acquired such a bad name during the bloodshed and tortures following the 1963 coup that it was abolished. A new, harmless-sounding name was found for Saddam's new creation: the Office of General Relations. This would soon become one of the most sinister and oppressive security organizations in the Arab world.

Saddam took over an office next door to Baqr's. He virtually glued himself to the older man and had constant direct access to him. Only two weeks after the coup, Saddam got rid of two rivals in brutal fashion. Daoud, the Defense Minister, had been sent off to Jordan to inspect the Iraqi troop contingent stationed there since the June 1967 war with Israel. He was now dismissed and exiled to Saudi Arabia. Saddam personally ousted Nayef as prime minister by striding into Baqr's office, gun in hand, while Baqr was lunching with Nayef. He told Nayef, who pleaded for his life and that of his four children, that he was arresting him for "usurping" the revolution. Saddam drove with Nayef to the airport, ordering him, as he jabbed a gun in Nayef's ribs, to act normally and salute roadside soldiers. Nayef was flown to Rabat, Morocco, where he served briefly as Iraqi ambassador. Foreign Minister Nasser Hani was later dismissed and allowed to live at home until November 1968; then he was kidnapped, murdered, and his body dumped into the Tigris river, probably by Saddam's thugs.

Baqr denounced Nayef for "plotting" with foreign firms and individuals against Iraq's national interests, proclaiming that the revolution was now "complete," and that he, Baqr, would be his own prime minister and supreme armed forces commander. A film of Baqr's radio speech shows Saddam standing behind him holding a submachine gun across his chest, in the manner of soldiers in Communist-bloc states during military parades. As Aburish observes, "[T]he Leninist father figure, Baqr, was being guarded by the one member of the party who had no problems with using violence to achieve his aims."[3]

Israeli and Western analysts took note that this July 30 update (Nayef's ouster and Baqr's speech) of the July 17 coup was accompanied by strident declarations that "Zionism" would be crushed and that Palestine would be liberated "immediately." Baqr and Saddam made conciliatory gestures toward both Barzani's Kurds and the Communists. Instead of being massacred by the hundreds or thousands as in 1963, thanks to the lists provided by the CIA, they were offered three cabinet posts. They refused, demanding restoration of full civil liberties, legalization of political parties, and democratic elections. There was no Ba'athist response. Overtures to Barzani collapsed because of the obvious bias of the new regime in favor of Barzani's rival, Jalal Talabani. Barzani's two Kurdish supporters in the new cabinet resigned in August 1968 over the continuing presence in the cabinet of Talabani's man, Taha Muhieddin Maaruf.

PROGRAMS AND POWER STRUGGLES

In September the new regime issued a provisional constitution setting forth three main principles: Islam was to be the state religion; 'socialism" was to be the basis of the economy; and the RCC (chaired by Baqr and Saddam) would be the supreme authority, to which the cabinet and national assembly were subordinate. Once the new constitution was published, the regime added a hefty stick to the carrots it had tried to blandish to the Communists and Kurds. Communists, Nasserists, pro-Syrian Ba'athists, former senior officials and, last but not least, "spies" were culled in nation-wide security sweeps by Saddam's Ba'athist security service.

We saw in Chapter 3 what happened to the 'spies," including the Jewish ones, tried and hanged in January 1969. The next arrests included several hundred officers and about 40 businessmen, mostly Iraqis who had consorted with the likes of Anderson, Parker, or other Westerners. Former ministers and civil servants, like former Prime Minister Bazzaz, were rounded up too. This new reign of terror recalled to ordinary Iraqis the dark days of 1963.

An internal power struggle now developed within the Ba'ath between Baqr, backed by Saddam Hussein, and Colonels Saleh Mehdi Ammash and Ahardane al-Tikriti. These gentlemen had followings in the armed forces, and so were potential threats to their rivals. The Ministries of Interior (Ammash) and Defense (Ahardane al-Tikriti) both tried to build up rival security services to fortify their own power. Baqr and Saddam countered by increasing the muscle of Saddam's innocuous-sounding but deadly Office of General Relations.

Early in 1969, a new Regional Command of the Ba'ath Party was announced. Except for Baqr and Ammash, none of the new command group (including Saddam) had genuine military backgrounds. All of them came from the 'sunni triangle," made notorious during the American invasion and occupation in 2003 and 2004 as the seat of the toughest resistance to the U.S.-led coalition's occupation forces. The "Triangle" was, and is, bounded roughly by Baghdad, Mosul, and Tikrit, on the Tigris river; and the small Euphrates river towns of Ana, Rawa, Haditha, and Falluja. All of these cities and towns, since Ottoman and British colonial times, have been washed by strong currents of Arab nationalist sentiment flowing from Syria. Most of the new command group were Sunnis. At the same time, Baqr and Saddam "Ba'athized" the armed forces by replacing hundreds of officers they did not trust with loyal Ba'athists or sympathizers.

During this period Saddam Hussein ruthlessly grabbed control of all of the remaining state security organs. These included the RCC's National Security Bureau (*maktaba al-amn al-qawmi*), the personal security service of the presidency, dealing mainly with collecting intelligence on political and religious opposition. Saddam had overall supervision of the older and pre-Ba'athist "official" state security service, (*al-amn al-amn*). His immediate underling here was Nazim Kazzar, who would later be accused and executed in a bizarre plot which recalled the epoch of secret police chief Lavrenti Beria in Joseph Stalin's Soviet Union. Saddam was also head of the Ba'ath party militia, the National Guard. These arrangements left Baqr to secure support of the regular armed forces and to isolate Ammash and Ahardane al-Tikriti.

By May 1969, the Special Revolutionary Court had condemned another group of businessmen and others for alleged links with the same CIA that had earlier helped Saddam take power. Next, in June 1969, the deceased former hero, General Abdel Salem Aref, was named as a former CIA agent; former Interior Minister Rashid Muslih himself confessed to working for the CIA and Zaki Abdel Wahab, former Iraqi manager of the Coca-Cola company, admitted that he had been working for Britain's MI-6 since 1956. Repression of the Communist leadership, the party's "Central Command," headed by Azziz al-Haj which had defected from the Iraqi Communist party's main body in September 1967, was especially savage. Al-Haj's interrogators and torturers broke him. He appeared on state television with his "confession" and condemnations of himself and fellow party members for a campaign of sabotage against the regime. Al-Haj called on the Kurds to abandon Mullah Mustafa Barzani. Later, Baghdad radio broadcast what it said was a long letter signed by al-Haj and 70 other Communists in support of the regime's decision to recognize Communist East Germany. As it tightened links with the Soviet bloc, the Saddam–Baqr duo was trying to show that it could outdo the tired old Communist Party and prove that their Ba'ath was the authentic Left.[4]

Saddam was already attracting Western admirers. In November 1969, the British Ambassador to Baghdad cabled to the Foreign Office in London an assessment of Saddam, who he perceptively recognized had emerged "into the limelight" as "the recognized heir-apparent to the President [Baqr]." After a meeting with Saddam, the ambassador found him, as a conversationalist, although shy at first, later speaking "with great warmth and what certainly seemed as a mastery of various subjects." Saddam insisted, the ambassador reported, that "Iraq's relationship with the Soviet bloc" was "founded on the central problem of Palestine," and Saddam revealed an apparently "earnest" desire for improved ties with Britain—"and with America too for that matter." The British envoy described him as "young," with an "engaging smile" and as "a formidable, single-minded and hard-headed member of the Iraqi hierarchy, but with whom, if only one could see more of him," it would be useful to do business."[5]

Saddam also charmed several American diplomats. American and European businessmen would soon flock to Baghdad to "do business" with the ascendant dictator.

ISRAEL'S COVERT WAR ON SADDAM

Saddam's rise did not charm Israel's leadership, nor please its intelligence services, who sensed that Iraq's threat to the Jewish state was growing in intensity. They believed that from being just one part of the general Arab strategic threat to Israel, Iraq's acquisition of advanced Western technology, through the vast purchasing power potentially stemming from its huge oil income might soon put it in a position to challenge Israel's very existence with weapons of mass destruction. So, nearly half a century before the validity of received intelligence about such weapons became such crucial issues for President George W. Bush and Prime Minister Tony Blair in planning their 2003 war, Israel had begun to learn all it could about Iraq's weapons technology and its foreign suppliers. It began to move actively to deprive Iraq of the WMDs (especially the nuclear ones) it wanted or already had.

Two major Israeli successes of this period were its successful seizure of an Iraqi MIG-21 fighter-bomber in 1966 and, more importantly, the destruction of Iraq's potential to build nuclear weapons with Israel's long-range air attack on the Osirak nuclear reactor outside Baghdad in 1981.

On a crisp and cloudy winter afternoon in early 2004, a knowledgeable and talkative Israeli taxi driver drove me from my Tel Aviv hotel to the palatial home of retired IDF colonel, former senior Mossad officer, and multi-millionaire arms dealer, business tycoon, and real-estate magnate, Yaacov Nimrodi. A self-avowed architect of the MIG-21 and Osirak operations and many others, Nimrodi had agreed on the telephone to meet me, after I told him that I had been a frequent visitor to Tehran and to the Shah before 1979. Nimrodi had been a kind of personal Israeli liaison officer with the Shah and his generals for 25 years of long, eventful, and largely clandestine links between Tehran and Jerusalem; links which became highly profitable for him.

Driving to Nimrodi's home in suburban Sabion, down palm-fringed boulevards past mansions which reminded me of La Jolla, near San Diego, California, we passed Ora Yehuda. This is a close-knit community, composed predominantly of Iraqi-born Jews, founded by Mordecai Ben-Porat and other survivors of Operation Ezra and Nehemiah. Luxury cars, guard dogs, and a couple of burly private security guards at his villa were a few of the outer signs of the elevated status of Nimrodi, the owner of *Maariv* newspaper and its publishing house (his son Oren was editor of the paper in 2004).

Nimrodi, fit, rotund, and almost jovial, gave to me his weighty and amply illustrated two-volume memoirs in Hebrew, entitled *My Life's Journey*. He expressed the wish that I could find a translator to compensate for my admitted ignorance of Hebrew. He recalled to me how he was born in Iraq in 1926, and carried to Jerusalem when he was only ten days old.[6] One of eleven children, brought up in a family which spoke both Arabic and Hebrew, he had to live a double life as a school pupil and child worker, in order to help support his family. When he was 16 he was drafted into the militia of the pre-state *Yishuv*. Because of his fluency in Arabic and adventurous spirit, Nimrodi by his early twenties was already a member of the elite Palmach forces and was being sent into combat and on covert missions—for which he apparently never lost his taste—to Egypt, Syria, Lebanon, and other enemy or neutral territories. After independence in May 1948, he became an officer in Aman, the Israeli military intelligence service. In 1955 Nimrodi and his wife Rivka were sent to Tehran as representatives of the Jewish Agency, to assist in the continued immigration of Iranian Jews to Israel. In the summer of 1958, as alarm bells rang after the violent end of the Iraqi monarchy, Nimrodi returned to Israel for a short visit. During this period the Shah's interest in close ties with Israel, which Nimrodi had already been promoting in Tehran, began to bear fruit. General Ali Kia, the chief Iranian military intelligence, visited Israel and Nimrodi hosted him. Kia suggested that Israel should send a "liaison officer," later to become military attaché, to Tehran. Ben-Gurion eventually named Nimrodi to be the IDF's representative in Iran. During a decade of activity, including Iranian and Israeli operations on behalf of the Iraqi Kurds and other covert ventures against successive Iraqi regimes, Nimrodi also used his considerable social skills. He brought together nearly all of the chiefs of staff and other senior officers of both the Israeli and Iranian armies. In the words of Israeli author Samuel Segev, a close follower of Nimrodi's fortunes, up to and through the epoch of his key role in the Iran–Contra affair "the Iranian market opened to the Israeli arms industry." One of Nimrodi's achievements in Israel's semi-covert war against Baghdad was to serve as the main human channel for the transfer of Soviet arms Israel had captured in the June 1967 war to Barzani's Kurds.[7]

Nimrodi returned to Israel in 1970, and understood that he would be appointed as Israeli coordinator of the occupied West Bank. When this fell through, Nimrodi resigned from the IDF and entered business. "The State of Israel's decision made me a millionaire," he joked to me.

Nimrodi's status as an arms dealer again attracted the IDF command. Major General Zvi Tzur, an aide to the minister of defense, got him sent back to Tehran for the third time, this time to represent Israeli arms manufacturers. Nimrodi renewed and nurtured his old high-level contacts, this time with the royal family, especially the uncle of the Shah's Queen, Farah Diba. Nimrodi orchestrated many a major deal, including supplying Iran with 50 water desalination plants, as well as sales of Israeli weapons that created hundreds of jobs in Israel.

THE MIG-21 CAPER

However, Nimrodi's proudest achievement was his role in the acquisition of an Iraqi air force MIG-21, the most advanced fighter plane that the Soviet Union had supplied to Arab states. Granting U.S. intelligence access to the MIG, once Israel had secured it, was one of the most significant early steps in cementing the close U.S.–Israel military partnership, which, by the 1990s, would become a firm alliance.

During the summer of 1963, Israel airforce commander Ezer Weizman made a "flippant" remark to Meier Amit, who had just replaced Isser Harel as director of the Mossad: "If you bring me a MIG-21, you will have done a good day's work."

Earlier efforts had failed. An Egyptian-born Armenian using the name of Jean Thomas had been operating in Egypt since the late 1950s. Thomas had left Egypt after Nasser's 1952 revolution. Mossad seems to have recruited him in West Germany, perhaps under a "false flag" (which in intelligence parlance means he did not know which state or regime was really recruiting him). His Mossad *katsa* or case officer was Jo Ra'anan, who operated for Isser Harel in Europe. The going price Mossad was offering to any Egyptian pilot who would fly a MIG-21 to Israel was supposed to be $1 million. When Thomas and accomplices tried to hire helpers, an Egyptian air force officer named Adib Hanna exposed them, leading to the capture of Thomas and five others in January 1961. Thomas and two accomplices were hanged by Nasser's regime in December 1962; others involved got prison terms. A second attempt to steal a MIG for Israel also failed. Two Iraqi pilots, one training in the United States and the other in Baghdad, were roughed up by Mossad agents after they refused to be recruited.

The more carefully planned third attempt began in late 1964. "Yosef," or Joseph, a diabetic in his sixties with Iraqi underworld connections, made contact with Yaacov Nimrodi in Tehran and other Israeli officials in Europe. The sister of his girlfriend, he told them, was married to a Catholic Iraqi air force pilot named Munir Radfa (in some accounts he is Munir Rofa). Radfa was the highly skilled and experienced deputy commander of an Iraqi MIG-21 squadron, based near Kirkuk and operating against Barzani's men in Kurdistan. Yosef's story was that Radfa was disaffected. He had been passed over for promotion and was refused when he requested transfer to a base near his home in

Baghdad. Furthermore, he was allowed to fly only short missions with small fuel tanks, which cut down his air time. He was mistrusted because he was a Christian in an otherwise overwhelmingly Muslim force. Yosef said he was ready to defect to Israel with his plane, if Israel could help. The intelligence supremos enthusiastically assigned a senior pilot and an officer of Israeli airforce (IAF) intelligence to the operation. Radfa was persuaded to meet Israeli representatives at a safe house in Europe. Attending were Radfa, the IAF intelligence officer, Yosef, and his girlfriend. Meier Amit, the Mossad chief, watched secretly from an adjoining room through a peephole. Radfa insisted that his parents, wife, children, and some other relatives should be smuggled safely out of Iraq just prior to his flight to Israel. This was agreed, as was a payment to Radfa of over $1 million on successful completion of his mission.

The next step was to get Radfa transferred to an air base closer to Israel, to minimize the length of the hazardous flight. An elite Mossad team settled in Baghdad, to monitor the operation and prepare the family's exodus. In mid-1966 Radfa was transferred to Rashid air base, outside Baghdad. By stages, Mossad began sending his family members out of Iraq, one as a tourist, another for medical treatment in Europe. Radfa was invited to Israel to see the airfield where he was to land his MIG. He managed to secure leave and he flew to Paris in the company of an attractive female Mossad agent, whom some sources described as an attractive and wealthy American woman, never publicly identified. In Paris Radfa obtained false travel documents and then flew to Israel, where he met IAF commander General Mordecai Hod, who gave him assurances about protection of his planned flight path and safe extraction of his family. By early August Radfa knew that he would soon be allowed enough fuel for a 900-kilometer flight, long enough to reach Israel.

His successful MIG flight to Israel took place on August 16, 1966. The news stunned us members of the foreign press contingent in Beirut and made good copy. Jordanian radar tracked a jet aircraft streaking at top speed across northern Jordan. King Hussein was notified. The Jordanians asked the Syrian air force, then commanded by future Syrian president General Hafez al-Assad, what they knew. The reply was that the plane was probably a Syrian bomber that had been flying a practice run in the area. By the time this erroneous report had percolated up to the top leadership in Amman and Baghdad, Radfa had successfully landed his MIG in Israel.

Unable to avoid public gloating over this unprecedented intelligence coup, the Israeli Defense Ministry took the wraps off the operation with a rare public news conference for Munir Radfa. He related how two IAF Mirage fighters had met him as he approached Israeli air space. As prearranged, he dipped the MIG's wings and lowered its landing gear, before landing at an Israeli air base "on his last drops of fuel." On the same morning, Mossad agents in two hired vans picked up Radfa's remaining family members outside Baghdad, where they had gone on the pretext given their neighbors of a picnic. Nimrodi's services in Tehran had helped to arrange a crossing of the Iranian border, assisted by SAVAK and Kurdish guerrillas. Once inside Iran, they were flown to Israel for a happy and relieved reunion with Radfa.

Once the Israelis had thoroughly checked out and recorded for future IAF staff planning the details of this state-of-the-art combat jet, including its armament, fuel capacity and range, its turn-around servicing time, its avionics, and electronic counter-measures—knowledge which largely contributed to the IAF's overwhelming successes in the June 1967 war— Israel loaned the MIG-21 to the United States. The Pentagon gave it what was possibly an even more rigorous going-over, providing the U.S. Air Force and NATO with precious data on a principal weapon of their Soviet adversary.

Such data helped Israel to prepare its surprise attack of June 5, 1967, on Egypt and Syria, which virtually annihilated their air forces. It also crippled Iraq's western air bases, following the early success of a couple of Iraqi bombers in penetrating Israeli air space. A few days earlier, on May 24, a U.S. National Security Council meeting was convened in Washington. CIA director Richard Helms responded to Defense Secretary Robert McNamara's negative estimate of Israeli air force capabilities. He told the meeting that Israel had subjected Radfa's MIG to exacting test maneuvers, and showed "in the April 7 air battle with Syria that they had learned their lessons well." French-made Dassault Mirage IIIc interceptors had shot six Syrian MIG-21s out of the sky with no Israeli losses, a kind of overture to the IAF performance against the Arab air forces in the coming war.[8]

The next major Arab–Israel conflict was the Yom Kippur or Ramadan war (depending upon whose side you were on) of 1973. The intelligence failures of Israel, the United States, and Britain before the 2003 Iraq war had a momentous prelude in 1973 Israel. Golda Meier's government was left in uncertainty over Arab intentions by a complacent military intelligence service until just before the Arab assaults. Some of its senior commanders ignored early signals of enemy intentions, because of the false "Concept," as Israeli commentators later came to call it, that the Arabs lacked the will, or were unable, to start and wage a real war. The evidence that this was untrue caused serious Israeli soul-searching, leading in turn to more caution and a greater willingness to let other states, such as the Shah's Iran and eventually the United States, fight battles that Israel considered furthered its own interests.

SADDAM'S REAL AND IMAGINED FOES

The Ba'athists in Iraq, during the run-up to the October 1973 war, were dealing, like a paranoid Stalinist-type regime, with real and imagined conspiracies from a variety of sources. No sooner had Communist and "Zionist" plots been met with new waves of massive repression, torture, and executions, than Baqr and Saddam perceived a major strategic threat to Iraq from Israel's ally and Iraq's eastern neighbor, Shah Muhammad Reza Pahlevi of Iran. The Shah's Shia clerical foes, including the Ayatollah Ruhollah Khomeini, had taken refuge in Iraq. Despite this, Baqr and Saddam viewed the restless and oppressed Shia majority in Iraq—the same Shia majority whose leaders and doctrines were destined to make life so agonizingly difficult for the Anglo-American occupation authorities in their proclaimed efforts to prepare post-Saddam Iraq for "democracy" in 2004—as adjuncts of the sinister designs of the Shah, Israel, and the United States.

Saddam's goons, despite protests by the United Nations and human rights groups at the January 1969 hangings of the Jewish "spies," continued their witch-hunts. Show trials were often televised. Executions mostly took place in Basra, chief city of the Iraqi Shia, and near Iran's border.

The Shah now made a drastic move which humiliated Iraq, and which Saddam Hussein never forgot nor forgave. In April 1969 the imperial Iranian government suddenly declared null and void a 1937 treaty concluded between the then Iraqi and Iranian monarchies. This had given Iraq de facto hegemony on the crucial Shatt al-Arab river boundary and strategic waterway, situated at the head of the Gulf and separating the two countries. It had extended effective Iraqi control of the Shatt all the way across to the Iranian bank. All vessels, including Iranian ones, were obliged to fly Iraqi flags and obey Iraqi traffic orders when they navigated between Iran's big river port and oil city of Abadan and the Gulf. What Tehran now proclaimed was that the border was henceforth no longer on the Iranian side, but in mid-river. Soon afterward, the Iranian Information Ministry followed this up by inviting this reporter and several others to a boat ride on an Iranian naval cutter. (In charge aboard was a certain Ali Akhbar Tabatabai, who as press attaché in the last Embassy of imperial Iran in Washington in 1979 was assassinated at home by agents of Khomeini disguised as parcel couriers.)

Our boat chugged downstream from Abadan, flaunting a huge red, white, and green Iranian flag with its imperial symbols of the Persian lion and sun. We navigated provocatively close to the palm-lined Iraqi riverbank under the eyes of Iraqi sentries. Meanwhile the Shah moved Iranian troop reinforcements to the Iraqi borders and sandbagged government buildings in Tehran against any sneak attacks by land or air.

The tension came to a head with events that constituted a prelude to the big Iran–Iraq war of 1980–88. In January 1970, Saddam Hussein was able to discover and expose a conspiracy by a group of Iranian-backed officers, most of them Shia, to overthrow his regime. On January 20, retired colonel Mehdi Saleh al-Samarrai and about 50 men, under the orders of a former associate of the two Aref brothers, headed for the Presidential Palace, intending to seize it. Several other "hit squads" were supposed simultaneously to attack and capture other key installations. Samarrai and his men were lured inside the presidential palace by a Ba'athist activist crony of Saddam, then wiped out there in a gun battle with Saddam's security men.

With his usual speed and ruthlessness, Saddam a few hours later convened a special security court which convicted and executed 44 of the plotters, including Samarrai. Exiled former Prime Minister Nayef was condemned to death in absentia and later assassinated in London. The Iranian ambassador was given 24 hours to leave Iraq, and the Iranian consulates in Baghdad, Basra, and Karbala were closed. Many Iranian residents of Iraq were expelled. Publicity for the government's success against the plotters emphasized that it was a victory for Saddam Hussein. The motive for the coup, the government said, was not only the Shatt al-Arab affair, but was also part of a larger conspiracy to return Iraq to "Anglo-American imperialist control" and to weaken the country in the continuing conflict with Israel.[9]

SADDAM AND THE PALESTINIANS

In Jordan, the 1970 crisis and civil war between King Hussein's royal troops and the forces of the Palestine Liberation Organization (PLO) would soon undermine the arguments of Iraq's Ba'athist leadership that it would fight harder than the previous regime for the Palestinian cause. It did support various Palestinian guerrilla groups, and gave cash, homes, and special consideration to refugee Palestinian intellectuals, artists, and writers. Many of the guerrilla groups were active as terrorists on the international scene: Abu Nidal's Fatah Revolutionary Council, Mahmoud Abas' Palestine Liberation Front, George Habbash's Popular Front for the Liberation of Palestine (PFLP) and its splinter offshoots like Wadi Haddad's terrorist faction and Abu Ibrahim's May 15 faction, as well as Syria's creation, Ahmed Jibril's Popular Front for the Liberation of Palestine-General Command (PFLP-GC), were involved in numerous aircraft hijackings and other attacks inside and outside the Middle East. These groups often used offices and base facilities in Iraq, and sometimes direct Iraqi logistical support in operations abroad. Later, during the second half of the 1980s, when Saddam urgently needed (and got) U.S. and other Western support for his war with Khomeini's Islamist Iran, Saddam cut back this support.

In 1970, Palestinian organizations in Jordan, where at least half of the population at the time was Palestinian, were forcing a major confrontation with King Hussein. Some of them, especially the PFLP, sought to overthrow the King and turn Jordan into a huge political and guerrilla base against Israel. The Iraqi military forces left behind in Jordan after the defeat by Israel in 1967 were assumed by many Israeli and Western analysts to be potential allies of the Palestinians in any confrontation with the royal Jordanian forces.

Israel's security services, chiefly the "domestic" service Shin Beth, were waging ruthless war against Al-Fatah and other PLO (and non-PLO) Palestinian groups, which were striving to increase guerrilla resistance to the Israeli occupation of the West Bank and the Gaza Strip. It was therefore a source of satisfaction in Israel to see the onset of clashes between the royal Jordan army and the Palestinian fedayeen in November 1968, when 28 Palestinians and four Jordanians were killed.[10]

There followed many other such clashes and some apparent Palestinian assassination attempts against King Hussein. In June 1970 came a hostage crisis. Myself and my new Greek wife, Vania, were on a working honeymoon in Amman when George Habbash's fedayeen held 90 foreigners, including ourselves, in two Amman hotels for four days in order (successfully) to extract concessions from King Hussein. Army–fedayeen skirmishes raged throughout Amman during those four days when we were cooped up in Amman's old Hotel Philadelphia. Concessions to the fedayeen included the dismissal of Hussein's uncle, Major General Sharif bin Jamil, of non-Palestinian Bedouin stock, as army commander-in-chief. Brigadier General Mashrour Haditha, whom Arafat and the other Palestinian leaders trusted, was named chief of staff. This won Jordan a brief summer respite from the brewing civil war.

BLACK SEPTEMBER IN JORDAN

Early in September, events began to unfold that were sorely to test Iraq's role in the Arab–Israel conflict. A ceasefire in the Egypt–Israel "War of Attrition," negotiated by U.S. Secretary of State William R. Rogers, had taken hold when President Nasser and the Israeli government had both accepted it. This caused great anger in the so-called "rejectionist" Arab regimes, especially in Baghdad and Damascus. The Rogers Plan, as it was called, required Nasser to curb PLO activities based in Egypt. Nasser struck a heavy blow at the PLO by closing its two Cairo broadcasting stations, "The Voice of al-Assifa" (Al-Fatah's armed guerrilla and terrorist wing) and "The Voice of Palestine," which diffused Palestinian propaganda throughout the Middle East. Corresponding PLO broadcasts from Syria and Iraq were not affected. However, Arafat was able to use all the stations, including those in Cairo, to transmit operational orders in code, as well as propaganda and information.

Arafat, whom I interviewed a number of times during this period and later on, with his perennial conspiratorial mentality, believed in a plot hatched in Washington, London, Amman, and Jerusalem, to trap the whole guerrilla movement. "We see it this way," a Palestinian university student in Beirut told me, "if we take on Hussein and lose, it will be a catastrophe. If we take him on and win, we would have to take over Jordan and run it." This would have suited Israeli extremists, including then Colonel Ariel Sharon, whose slogan was that "Jordan is (or should be) Palestine," implying the desirability of expelling the entire West Bank and Gaza Palestinian population to Jordan, "the true Palestinian state," in order to permit Israel to be purely Jewish.

In the absence of their leader, George Habbash, who was in Beijing at the time, and apparently acting against the wishes of Arafat and the PLO's central command, PFLP guerrillas hijacked four Western airliners: a British BOAC plane to Cairo international airport, and TWA, Swissair, and Air France airliners to an isolated desert airfield near Zarqa in Jordan, near the bases of the Iraqi army contingent. The fedayeen released the hostages aboard in Cairo, but held those in the planes in Jordan for a week before releasing some, moving others to one of their camps, then blowing up the three empty planes.

For King Hussein the hijacking was the last straw. Late on September 15, the King named Field Marshal Habes al-Majali, a tough Bedouin officer, as martial law commander in charge of a new military regime.[11] A Pakistani military officer who served in Jordan narrates in detail the operation to "free Jordan from the presence of the PRM" [Palestinian resistance movement], as he calls it. Hussein ordered his staff first to liberate Amman, a city sprawling over seven hills and constructed of solid stone buildings, "devilishly hard to attack," as one involved Jordanian officer told me later, "and extremely easy [for the entrenched Palestinians] to defend." Once the fedayeen were beaten in Amman, a large Palestinian contingent in control of the northern city of Irbid had to be defeated. The smaller cities and towns of Zarqa, Ramtha, Jerash, Ajlun, and Es-Salt had also to be neutralized or recaptured by the army.

For King Hussein's military chiefs, and for the carefully watching Israelis, Americans, and British, a major question mark was the Iraqi expeditionary force, concentrated in a rough triangle between Zarqa, Mafraq, and Ramtha, the latter on the Syrian border. It consisted of three brigades of Iraq's 3rd Armored Division, and two brigades of the 9th (Logistic) Division: in all, about 12,000 fighting men plus another 1,000 or so support troops. Two Jordanian air force Hawker-Hunter fighter squadrons were assigned on September 16 to the King Hussein Air Force Base at Mafraq, and a squadron of U.S.-supplied F-104 interceptors was based at Prince Hassan Air Force Base at the site called H-5, in eastern Jordan. If the Iraqi artillery were to open fire in support of the PLO, the Mafraq air base, especially vulnerable to shelling, could be knocked out.

Just before 5 a.m. on September 16, the Jordanian assault on the Palestinians began. Jordanian tanks and armored cars simultaneously moved against PLO positions in all of the affected cities and towns. Majali imposed a 24-hour curfew and ordered anyone on the street to be shot at once. Tactics earlier used by the British in Palestine, refined by its Israeli occupiers and adopted later by the Americans in Iraq in 2003, were applied ruthlessly: artillery fire destroyed any house from which fire or sniping came. Arafat was holed up in a private house with Nayef Hawatmeh, leader of the Marxist-inclined Popular Democratic Front for the Liberation of Palestine (PDFLP). He radioed to the central committee, in another hiding place, to call for help from the Iraqis. Arafat, who had visited Baghdad in August, believed that Baqr and Saddam had promised him help if needed.

Arafat narrowly escaped death several times during the coming days. Unlike three of his top aides, including Salah Khalef, known as Abu Iyad, he managed to evade Jordanian capture. In a recorded radio message to President Nasser, Arafat appealed, "Intervene! Intervene by any possible means to prevent the bloodshed in Jordan. The situation is extremely serious. They have launched their general attack simultaneously against our positions in Amman and Zarqa." A team of Palestinians moved into the studios of Damascus Radio and broadcast coded operational messages: "The grapes are ripe. Gift delivered. Thank you." Baghdad Radio made similar coded broadcasts.

To discourage the Iraqis, King Hussein ordered his 9th Armored Brigade and the headquarters troops of his 3rd Armored Division to move into deterrent positions with loaded weapons near Zarqa. The borders with Iraq and Syria were ordered closed. Troops of the Royal Jordanian Air Force headquarters regiment, reinforced by two infantry companies, secured the Amman international civil airport at Marka and its adjoining air force base. This was Jordan's sole link with the outside world in case of airborne Israeli or U.S. intervention—the Pentagon had orders from the Nixon administration to preserve Hussein's throne by force if necessary, and had already alerted American forces.

President Nixon, Henry Kissinger, and other advisers in Washington wondered: should they immediately mount a "limited" intervention to rescue trapped Americans in Amman? U.S. Ambassador Dean Brown, who in less dangerous times had been known to drive around Amman in a jeep or armored car, and was reputed to pack a six-shooter, was blocked in the downtown Embassy with his staff, just across from the besieged Intercontinental Hotel. U.S. troop units were alerted from Fort Bragg, North Carolina to Ramstein, Germany and Incirlik, Turkey. The U.S. 82nd Airborne Division was made ready. Israeli Prime Minister Golda Meier, visiting Washington, was consulted. Israeli forces were readied on the Jordan border. Israeli intelligence outposts in the occupied Golan Heights watched Syrian preparations for intervention on the side of the PLO. Israeli signals intelligence monitored Iraqi communications for any sign that Baghdad would move. In Washington, Henry Kissinger, in close touch with Israeli Ambassador Yitzhak Rabin, argued to his colleagues that Israel should be encouraged to come to King Hussein's aid if either the Syrians or the Iraqis used their forces. In the meantime, some fresh U.S. military supplies should be sent to bolster Jordan.

President Nixon was immersed with advisors in the latest difficulties with Castro's Cuba and suspected Soviet naval designs there, and with fighting the Vietnamese Communists while conducting tortuous peace negotiations with them. He could not focus fully on the Middle East. He made it clear to Kissinger, in an angry note he scribbled on a written summary of a crisis meeting Kissinger gave him, that he, Nixon, was opposed to aiding King Hussein against the PLO, and even to encouraging Israel to do so. Nixon, despite contrary advice from Kissinger and others, preferred that if military action to save the Hashemite throne was unavoidable, then it should be unilateral American action.

Early on September 19, while diplomats and some journalists in Amman were calling Arafat the prospective Kerensky of the Palestinian revolution, with the absent Habbash as the would-be Lenin, some elements of the Syrian army invaded Lebanon. My friend and colleague Andrew Borowiec of the *Washington Evening Star* managed to enter Syria and make his way southward to Ramtha, just inside the Jordanian border. He spotted tanks freshly painted with the red, black, and green emblems of the PLO's "conventional" military wing, the Palestine Liberation Army (PLA). The tanks were speeding into Jordan to attack Jordanian tanks between the border and Irbid, which was under control of fedayeen. As time went on, it became clear that this was a maverick Syrian political operation ordered by the neo-Ba'ath politicians in Damascus. Crucially, Lieutenant General Hafez al-Assad, former Syrian air force commander and Syrian Defense Minister, disapproved. Assad refused to authorize Syrian air cover for the operation He realized correctly that Israeli (and possibly U.S.) intervention and a general Middle Eastern war might erupt if Syrian jets attacked Jordanian forces in a fratricidal inter-Arab war. The Syrian ground unit involved was the 28th Armored Brigade of Syria's 5th Armored Division, commanded by Brigadier General Muhammad Deiry, acting on orders from Major General Salah Jadid, one of the Syrian neo-Ba'ath party's "armchair generals."

In Washington on September 20, a new crisis meeting rejected President Nixon's choice of last-resort unilateral U.S. action. Instead it adopted Kissinger's policy preference, because Israel was better placed to act immediately and Israeli action was less likely to provoke Soviet involvement. Secretary of State William Rogers and Defense Secretary Melvyn Laird favored this view too: both hated the idea of committing U.S. troops to the bloody fray in the Middle East. The final recommendation on that fateful evening was that the United States should encourage Israeli air strikes against the Syrian tanks, while doing some saber-rattling in the form of more U.S. troop and naval alerts in and around the Eastern Mediterranean.

SYRIA REPULSED; IRAQ WITHDRAWS

King Hussein's skillful tank commanders and the pilots of his outdated but sturdy Hawker-Hunter fighter-bombers removed any need for either Israeli or American action. As the street and hillside battles raged on in Amman, with the fedayeen in stubborn rearguard actions and slow retreat, the Jordanian garrison in Zarqa, mostly very young soldiers in their teens, fought the PLO guerrillas to a standstill. However, on the morning of September 20, the two battalions of the Iraqi-commanded Palestine Liberation Army brigade opened fire on the Jordanians, apparently to boost either the Palestinians' morale or their own. At this point, an armored brigade of the regular Jordanian army's 3rd Armored Division deployed themselves between the combatants, so that the regular Iraqi troops were dissuaded from any further interference. Fighting ended in that region with a general ceasefire arranged by an Arab League delegation in Jordan on September 25.

Another Iraqi armored brigade was located north of Jarash. I had seen their dug-in tanks near the main highway toward the Syrian border. Early on September 19, the Iraqi field commander notified Jordanian headquarters that the Iraqis would move eastward, apparently to get out of the way of the invading Syrians. The half-buried Iraqi tanks lurched out of their earthwork positions and moved off.

Soon the Soviet-made Syrian T-54 and T-55 tanks that had entered Jordan in force after midnight moved into the positions the withdrawing Iraqis had left behind. At Ramtha, the Syrians knocked out several of Jordan's British-made Centurion tanks. But then the Hawker-Hunter squadrons, unopposed by any Syrian air assets, went into action. They strafed, bombed, and rocketed the Syrian armor in relays of eight aircraft each, with half-hour intervals between sorties. In a very large tank battle at Wadi Swallah, east of the Ramtha crossroads, some 30 Jordanian tanks advanced and destroyed about a third of a massed force of about 100 Syrian attackers. The Jordanians prepared for a limited counter-offensive to chase the Syrian remnants, but this proved unnecessary. After dusk on September 22, the Syrians began a hasty retreat back across the border. At dawn on September 23, the Ramtha valley was emptied of Syrian tanks and infantry. During the three-day battle, the Syrian armored brigade had lost 62 tanks, 60 APCs, and over 600 men killed and wounded, including 450 Palestinians. A Jordanian armored brigade reoccupied Ramtha and positions along the Syrian border.

By this time, President Nasser in Cairo had rallied senior leaders of the Arab League states in an effort to secure a ceasefire, which would save face for both the Palestinians and King Hussein's victorious but bloodied (and, in the Arab world, bitterly criticized) forces. Egyptian army Chief of Staff General Muhammad Saddeq flew in to see Hussein and managed after several attempts to track down Arafat. Neither Hussein nor Arafat would agree to attend a summit conference in Cairo, as Nasser wanted. One was finally held without them. On September 22 it sent to Amman a four-man peacekeeping team composed of senior Sudanese, Tunisians, and Kuwaitis, and General Saddeq. King Hussein and Sudan's Major General Jafaar al-Nimeiry made a joint radio appeal for a ceasefire: both guerrillas and army should move out of Jordan's cities. The guerrillas should withdraw to bases exclusively near the Israeli border. Only the official PLO (including Al-Fatah) and no other maverick organizations should henceforth be recognized as "representing the Palestinian people" (Habbash and Hawatmeh had already been outlawed in Jordan and rewards of $12,000 each placed on their heads). The guerrillas should obey Jordanian laws and recognize Jordanian sovereignty. Some of Arafat's associates objected, insisting that the fight should go on. Under pressure from emissaries of Nasser, who were negotiating with the PFLP for liberation of the airline hostages still held in Amman's Wahdat neighborhood, they finally agreed that Arafat should accept the ceasefire and join the Arab delegation to Cairo for a full-scale Arab summit.

Arafat flew to Cairo. At a stormy meeting in the Cairo Hilton with Nasser, he and eight other Arab leaders, including Iraq's President Baqr with Saddam Hussein at his side, debated the slaughters and the ceasefire, which was gradually taking hold in Jordan. Hussein's troops had freed the airline hostages in Amman. At noon on September 27, King Hussein arrived in Cairo and faced Arafat and the other Arab leaders at the Nile Hilton. Both ostentatiously wore revolvers, but their Arab colleagues were able to cool the atmosphere sufficiently to avoid any guns being drawn.

The Jordan crisis finished off an exhausted and ailing President Nasser. Yassir Arafat last saw the Egyptian leader and one-time idol of the Arab world alive in Cairo just before noon on September 28, 1970. Suffering and in pain from chronic diabetes aggravated by extreme fatigue, Nasser shook hands with Arafat one last time, and Arafat flew back to Jordan in a military plane. After seeing off the Emir of Kuwait, Nasser returned home, telling his family he needed a long rest. Soon a fatal blood clot stopped his heart. He died at 6:15 that evening. His funeral on September 30 brought Arafat and nearly all of the Arab kings and presidents back to Cairo. It was probably one of the most extraordinary displays of mass grief ever seen—certainly this author and colleagues who watched the funeral procession from a rooftop on the Nile corniche had never witnessed anything like it. Millions of mourning Egyptians watched the flag-draped gun carriage move slowly by, assailed by women whom police beat back with bamboo canes and whips when they tried to snatch away the body of their beloved leader before it was taken to the mosque for burial.

Back in Amman, the superior Jordanian armor, artillery, and troop discipline prevailed over the PLO. When most of the fighting ceased on September 25, there were thousands of military and civilian casualties. Many neighborhoods of Amman looked as though an earthquake had struck them. There, as in northern Jordan, neither of the PLO's ostensible allies, Syria or Iraq, had been able to dent King Hussein's victory. Gradually the surviving guerrillas moved into the mountains around Ajloun, north of Amman. Many crossed into "enemy" Israel, where they sought asylum and protection from the IDF. By July of 1971, King Hussein's army had surrounded, trapped, and killed or captured a remnant of 800 or so fedayeen in their last mountain refuges.[12]

The repercussions of the Iraqi withdrawal, which soon led to an Iraqi troop pullout from Jordan, mainly fell upon General Ahardane al-Tikriti, a distant cousin of Saddam. The Black September crisis also strengthened Saddam's overall power position. With Nasser's death, the pressures on the Iraqi Ba'ath to either join in an Arab union with Egypt (as Syria had done from 1958 to 1961) or join a military pact aimed at eventually fighting Israel again, were gone. Relieved of these pressures, Saddam could consolidate his domestic power and return to urgent matters, such as oil and the Kurds. Regardless of who had ordered the retreat of the Iraqi army in Jordan, Saddam blamed this on others, mainly Ahardane al-Tikriti. He turned this blame to his own advantage in a campaign to purge the army of real or suspected enemies, as for example during the pro-Iranian conspiracy of January 1970.

Saddam moved against Ahardane al-Tikriti, whom he regarded as a possible dangerous rival, firing him on October 15 and exiling him as Ambassador to Algeria. Saddam replaced him with another man from Tikrit, General Hamid Shehab. However, the Algerian military government under President Houari Boumedienne wished no involvement in Iraq's intrigues and refused to accept Tikriti, who moved to Kuwait. According to Said Aburish, Tikriti settled in there to conspire against Saddam. In May 1971, Saddam's gunmen killed him in Kuwait City.[13]

The breathing space that both Saddam and his Israeli foes had gained in their strategic conflict was relatively short. In Cairo, Nasser's chosen successor was President Anwar al-Sadat. In Iraq's neighbor Syria, General Hafez al-Assad evicted the neo-Ba'athist politicians who had bungled both the 1967 war and the Jordan–Palestinian conflict. Assad became President in a non-violent coup in October 1970, partly because of his astute avoidance of U.S.–Israeli intervention in Jordan.

Both Sadat and Assad would soon be planning a new war against the Jewish state, with the connivance and support of King Faisal of Saudi Arabia. Baghdad was destined to be drawn into this war to a greater degree than in previous Arab–Israel conflicts, with serious consequences for both Iraq and Israel. That war and its repercussions, including the cementing of the U.S.–Israeli alliance in the Middle East, are our next subjects.

8
Saddam's Reign (II): Power Plays and War, 1970–80

Nationalism is that "revolt against history" which seeks to close what cannot any longer be closed. To fence in what should be frontierless.

(Salman Rushdie, 1997)

It has long been clear that in the war and occupation of Iraq in 2003 and 2004, the U.S.-led coalition attacked on the basis of false intelligence that Saddam Hussein threatened neighbors and the world in 2003 with the chemical and biological weapons he had used in the 1980s, and was seeking to develop nuclear arms as well. It became equally clear after the report of an Israeli parliamentary investigation in spring of 2004 that not only had the intelligence gathered and analyzed by the United States and its loyal junior partner Britain seriously erred, but that Israeli information had been wrong as well.

One Israeli specialist on Iraq, Tel Aviv University Professor Ofra Bengio, published in 1998 a thoughtful analysis of Iraq's "unique stance" in the Arab–Israeli conflict and its large impact on the entire region. She expertly charts Saddam's real and rhetorical strategies, using open and published sources. Although Iraq lacks a common border with Israel, Professor Bengio reminds us, it has behaved in major Arab–Israeli wars since 1948 like a "confrontation state," and unlike the others, it has always refused to sign peace or even an armistice with Israel.[1] This will be a tradition which the wishful planners of a probably chimerical "democracy" in post-Saddam Iraq will have great difficulty in overcoming, as they try to realize the probably impossible dream of "normalization" of Israeli–Iraqi relations.

One of the historical landmarks of this tradition was Iraq's participation in the 1973 Arab–Israel war. The war was planned by Egypt's Sadat and Syria's Assad with the support of King Faisal of Saudi Arabia. The Arab purpose was to recover, if possible, Arab territory and honor lost in 1967, and to draw the United States into active peacemaking. Unlike Egypt, Syria, and Jordan, Iraq had lost no territory to Israel in 1967. However, Saddam Hussein was anxious to efface memories of his failure to help the Palestinians in Jordan, and to restore Iraq, if he could, to some kind of leading role in the struggle to "liberate Palestine." A bonus of Iraq's role in the war was its emergence as an important player in the political games connected to the brandishing and use of the so-called Arab "oil weapon."

THE REASSURANCE OF U.S. AID

United States cooperation with Israel, in particular military aid sent during the Kennedy administration in 1961–63, continued by Lyndon B. Johnson, and dramatically increased by Richard Nixon in the early 1970s, had added to Israel's sense of security in 1973. It fortified Israeli complacency about Arab capabilities in any new war. On September 17, 1970, the very day that King Hussein's army moved forward to crush the PLO in Jordan, the Nixon administration had agreed to increase military aid to Israel by $500 million, and to accelerate delivery schedules of McDonnell-Douglas Phantom F-4 fighter-bombers under earlier agreements. In the next three years, the U.S. Congress granted more money to Israel than the total sent since Israel's creation in 1948, a publicly reported total of $1.608 billion as compared to $1.581 billion in the whole earlier period .

Annual aid, measured in dollar totals and in the readiness of the U.S. Treasury to forgive loans, has generally increased since then. American largesse has ensured that Israel's people enjoyed a much higher standard of living than their neighbors. It enabled, for instance, Jewish settlers (many of them American Jewish immigrants) to commute from new homes in the occupied Jordan West Bank, Gaza, and the Golan Heights to jobs and other homes in Tel Aviv, Jerusalem, Haifa, or elsewhere. Since 1970, huge chunks of U.S. taxpayers' cash have cemented links between the Israeli and U.S. military–industrial complexes and economies. In 1971, when Sadat's Egypt was struggling with the various curbs Moscow imposed on the USSR's considerable loans and military deliveries, American subsidies enabled Israel to spend fully 20 percent of its gross national product (GNP) on defense, a large part of which was accounted for by purchases of American arms.

Under an accord signed in December 1970, with the grandiose title of Master Defense Development Data Exchange Agreement, Israel steadily obtained technical data allowing it to manufacture or maintain military technology developed in the United States. In 1971 another accord authorized Israel to build U.S.-designed weapons. Some that were soon put to use included an Israel-produced heat-seeking air-to-air missile called the

Shafrir, assembled from U.S. designs (very similar to the U.S. Air Force's Sidewinder missile) by the Israel government's Raphael Armament Development Authority. Washington also gave Israel permission to manufacture the U.S. J-79 jet aircraft engine for use in Israel's Kfir fighter-bomber, which Israel Aircraft Industries developed from the French Mirage 5, which France sold to Israel (following a hiatus of some years in the earlier lavish French military aid, a hiatus caused by President Charles de Gaulle's angry decree embargoing French arms shipments to Israel after the 1967 war). Later, France sold the Mirage 5 to Saddam Hussein's Iraq as well.

There was a belief in Washington and Jerusalem that Israel, strengthened by its military victories and by Washington's generosity, was not an attractive target for any Arab attempts at a military revanche. However, just as the more experienced analysts in the U.S. State Department and CIA tried to warn President George W. Bush's neoconservative and pro-Israel advisers in 2003 that occupying and "democratizing" Iraq would not be a pushover, warnings not to misjudge Arab military efficacy were coming from experienced U.S. Middle Eastern hands in 1973. Archibald Roosevelt, for example, had been a CIA operative for almost a whole generation among the Arabs of North Africa and the Middle East. He observed that the Israelis underestimated their Arab adversaries, finding that they were "alien, threatening, hateful and inferior ... a people with whom they have nothing in common. Hence their [Israeli] intelligence failures."[2]

SADAT PLANS FOR WAR

President Sadat began planning for the new war shortly after he took power following Nasser's death in October 1970. He soon began consultations with Syria's President Assad. They agreed that neither Iraq's President Baqr, Libya's Qaddafi, nor any other Arab leaders were to be trusted with the war planning, which should be done in great secrecy. In 1971 Cairo and Damascus launched an extensive information campaign, focused on the UN General Assembly, over the injustice of Israel's 1967 territorial conquests. In November 1971, Sadat held a long and candid discussion with the chief Soviet military adviser in Egypt, General V. V. Okunev. Moscow from then on reiterated that, while it would continue to aid Egypt in every way possible, it opposed launching war against Israel. Sadat proclaimed 1972 to be a "Year of Decision" and in July 1972 suddenly, to the delight of Washington and Jerusalem, expelled from Egypt most of the 21,000 Soviet military personnel—instructors, technicians, air crews, missile and anti-aircraft crews, from the generals down to the privates.

In December he began secret joint meetings with the senior Syrian military to plan a "limited" war. The idea was to recover as much occupied territory as possible and to draw the attention, and if possible the diplomatic intervention, of the United States and the international community. Sadat's Defense Minister, General Muhammad Saddeq, was fired when he advocated a total war, aimed not only at recovering territory lost in 1967, but also at destroying the Israeli armed forces (and by implication the state) as well.

Saddeq's replacement was General (later promoted to Marshal) Ahmed Ismail Ali. On August 29, 1973, Sadat's personal envoy Hassan Sabri al-Khouli and Syrian Defense Minister Mustafa Tlas visited Amman to offer peace and reconciliation to King Hussein. Jordan's monarch had been to a great degree isolated and ostracized in the Arab world since the Black September of 1970. Hussein heard a vague description, without details or timing, of Operation Badr, the Arab war plan. The King was asked to prepare a defensive deployment of Jordan's armed forces to protect Syria's exposed northern flank against any Israeli envelopment, once war broke out. Hussein apparently agreed with Sadat and Assad, whom he met at an Arab summit in Cairo on September 12, 1973, not to inform Baghdad. He also agreed to Jordan's defensive deployment, and said he would join more actively if Syria succeeded in liberating the Golan Heights and securing the east bank of the Jordan River, north of the Sea of Galilee.

Two senior PLO operatives, Saleh Khalaf (Abu Iyad) and Farouk al-Khaddoumi (Abu Lutf) were summoned to Cairo October 1, briefed vaguely on the Syro–Egyptian plans, and asked to launch simultaneous PLO guerrilla warfare in the Sinai and Golan.[3]

Final planning took place on October 3 in Damascus. Marshal Ahmed Ismail Ali, acting for Sadat, obtained President Assad's approval for D-Day and H-Hour of the Arab attack on Yom Kippur, the holy Jewish Day of Atonement, when transport, radio, and other public services in Israel were at a minimum, rendering fast mobilization more difficult. The Jordanians were given a vague "heads-up," which Jordanians told me referred to Israeli mobilization plans and the possibility of a limited Israeli offensive against Syria. King Hussein declared a state of alert and awaited developments.[4]

ISRAEL'S "CONCEPT"

There were ample signs of Arab intentions, including likely Iraqi involvement. However, Israel's ruling politicians and some of the senior military men had a kind of psychological mind-set that Israeli military commentators call "the Concept." The Arabs were thought to be too cowed by Israel's proven military superiority to attack. Investigations by Israel's post-war Agranat Commission concluded that Prime Minister Golda Meier's government and the IDF bosses misjudged the situation. The basic fault, the investigation found, was misplaced confidence in Defense Minister Moshe Dayan's outdated ideas about the prevailing strength of Israeli deterrence, based in part on the theories of General Israel Tal, hero of the 1967 Sinai campaign. Tal, who fathered the Merkava (Chariot), Israel's own battle tank, believed that strategy and tactics should be built almost entirely around tank warfare, somewhat in the manner of Germany's successful *Panzerkrieg* of World War II against the Allied forces in France and the Low Countries in May and June of 1940.[5]

There were telltale signs of Arab war preparations from April 1973. In that month, Saddam Hussein and his nominal boss, President Baqr, sent a squadron of 16 Iraqi Hunter jets and a squadron of the much newer Mirage fighters purchased from France to beef up the Egyptian air arm. Israeli intelligence agents in Egypt signaled that the Arab command had set May 15, 1973, as D-Day for five divisions to attack across the Suez Canal. The IDF began mobilizing some reserve units and bolstering fortifications, tank traps, and minefields. The preparations were code-named "Kahol-Lavan" (blue and white). However, General David Elazar, the Israeli Chief of Staff, was skeptical. At a General Staff meeting on April 6 he scoffed that Sadat had predicted war in 1971, and was again promising liberation of the occupied territories in 1973. General Eli Zeira, chief of military intelligence, argued at meetings on April 12 and 15 that war was a "low probability." He also pooh-poohed the idea of a simultaneous two-front war by Syria and Egypt, theorizing that the Syrians would join any war only after Egyptian success, because they feared the Israel Air Force too much. The prospect of Iraq offering any effective support seems to have been ignored.

Mossad chief General Zvi Zamir was more cautious. At the April 15 meeting, he conceded that Sadat's war preparations were worrying. Divisions capable of crossing the Suez Canal had a protective anti-aircraft umbrella of missiles and bridging equipment. There were effective anti-aircraft defenses for the Nile Valley, and behind the front lines for Cairo and other cities. Moshe Dayan concurred. He cited Arab frustration over the continuing military and political stalemate as the basis for possible conflict.

At a new Israeli leadership meeting on May 9 in Tel Aviv's Defense Ministry, Zeira continued to downplay the possibility of war. Zeira kept reassuring the General Staff and the cabinet that military intelligence could provide a "five to six-day" advance warning of war, and that a minimum "48-hour warning" was feasible in a "worst-case" or catastrophic situation. Nothing much happened throughout the early summer, and Zeira's complacent theories were generally accepted. This remained true even in August, when the normally careful Syrians began deploying heavy forces near the ceasefire lines, protected by a thick anti-aircraft missile network covering airspace over both Syrian and Israeli forces on both sides of the lines.

U.S. COMPLACENCY AND THE "OIL WEAPON"

During this period, the United States also largely ignored political signs of the coming storm. On the petroleum front, Muammar Qaddafi's Libya assumed control of most of the Western oil operations in the country. There was growing talk of an Arab oil embargo. On July 4, 1973 myself for the *Christian Science Monitor* and the *Washington Post*'s Jim Hoagland together interviewed Saudi Arabian King Faisal in Taief, the Saudi summer capital, then met with Oil Minister Ahmed Zaki Yamani. He analyzed the sermon given us by the King, warning the kingdom's oil customers not to aid Israel "in the event of a new war" (which Faisal, alone among other Arab leaders, knew that Sadat and Assad were brewing). "If war comes," Yamani cautioned us over a family lunch with his wife and his two daughters, just returned from schools in the United States, "we'll have to shut down [oil] wells and curb exports. If we don't, not even the entire Saudi army or the [U.S.-trained] National Guard could protect them from sabotage" by people fuelled by anti-American wrath.[6]

When we relayed this message to the U.S. Ambassador at a Fourth of July afternoon reception at the consulate-general in Jeddah, he scoffed, "Aw, the Saudis have been talking like that for months now. We don't give it any credence." America's Israeli allies reacted similarly to the Saudi warnings. According to historians Black and Morris, a senior Israeli military intelligence officer said of the Saudi kingdom: "On top there is just sand, with some backward people, and underneath there is oil."[7]

An air battle added to Israeli complacency. On September 13, 1970, Syrian MIGs tried to ambush Israeli jets on a reconnaissance mission over Syria. The Israeli jets also drew ground fire in the area around Latakia, not far from Hafez al-Assad's native village of Khardaia.[8] Twelve Syrian fighters and one Israeli jet were shot down in the ensuring dogfight. The battle added to Israeli complacency and helped to cover Arab war preparations. Israeli military intelligence wrongly evaluated new alerts in the Arab air forces as purely defensive moves caused by the air battle.

As late as September 21, IDF's General Zeira was assuring the Israeli leadership that the Arabs were incapable of an attack because of Israel's overwhelming air superiority, proven again in the September 13 battle. On September 24 and 25, Egyptian troops began to move from their Nile bases toward the Suez Canal. Boats were put in positions on the Canal banks. Egyptian army leaves were cancelled. Promotion exams for Egyptian officers were postponed from October to November. However, General Zeira's services dismissed all of this and the gradual Egyptian mobilization as preparations for an Egyptian maneuver codenamed "Tahrir [Liberation] 41" due to begin on October 1.

In Langley, Virginia, later CIA estimates were less sanguine. On September 24 a combined U.S. intelligence estimate by the CIA, the NSA, and the DIA (the Pentagon's Defense Intelligence Agency) was sent to their Israeli allies. Apparently based on communications intelligence intercepts, it asserted that a combined Egyptian–Syrian attack was possible. The response of Zeira's service was to downplay the threat.

However, on September 26 Dayan, with the concurrence of the IDF's Northern Command commander, General Yitzhak Hoffi, reinforced the under-strength Golan defenses by deploying the entire 7th Armored Brigade to the Heights. On October 1 Israel received a warning from agents in place in Egypt that Egypt and Syria would turn Egyptian "maneuvers" into a full-scale Egyptian–Syrian attack across the Canal and into the Golan. However, Zeira again insisted to a staff meeting that "the situation is completely normal ... and there is no intention of turning it into a war."

Multiple warning signs finally began to make an impression in Tel Aviv on Thursday, October 4. Zvi Zamir and Zeira met, and Zamir bet Zeira that war was coming. Zeira agreed with Zamir's decision to meet a top Mossad source in Europe who had warned of an imminent Arab attack. Egyptian army units had been ordered to break off their Ramadan fast. Flares on Egypt's Gulf of Sinai oil wells had been turned off to lower vulnerability to enemy air raids. A fleet of Aeroflot planes left the Soviet Union to pick up and evacuate families of Soviet officials in Egypt. Eleven of the Russian transports arrived at Damascus airport the next day for the same purpose; four new Boeing airliners of Egypt Air's fleet were flown to Jeddah for safekeeping, and Soviet merchant ships hastened abruptly out of Alexandria and Port Said harbors. Despite these and many other signs, Zeira still gave Golda Meier and her cabinet a "low probability" assessment of the chances for war. It was not until 5 p.m. on October 5 that a foreign message was intercepted predicting an imminent war on both Israel's Western and Eastern fronts. Confirmation came from Zamir of the earlier Mossad warning from Europe. Zamir phoned key leaders and convened a 6 a.m. meeting on October 6 in General David Elazar's office to discuss the enemy war plans and Israeli defenses.

On the previous evening in Washington (it was already early morning in Israel), Ray Cline, chief of the State Department's INR (Intelligence and Research) division, also concluded that war was probably imminent, but reportedly did not immediately inform Secretary of State Henry Kissinger.

ISRAELI INTELLIGENCE FAILURE

Coordinated Egyptian–Syrian attacks began with massive artillery bombardments and air strikes at 1:55 p.m. on October 6, while the Israeli cabinet was still in emergency meetings and trying hastily to prepare a tardy general mobilization for the war, which was expected four hours later, at 6 p.m. The outnumbered, and at first unreinforced, Israeli troops were pushed back. The Egyptians, after battering down the Israeli sand walls on the Canal's east bank with high-pressure fire hoses, crossed the Canal at several points and established bridgeheads in Sinai. Five Syrian divisions with 1,400 tanks and over 1,000 artillery pieces simultaneously knifed into Israeli defenses on the Golan.

Israel's Agranat Commission investigators heavily criticized the performance of the IDF's military intelligence during the early hours and days of the war. It had failed adequately to report or to disseminate information about new Soviet-made weapons in Arab hands, such as the Egyptian infantry's Sagger anti-tank missile and the RPG-7 rocket-propelled grenade used by Syrian commando units. Worse, the Israeli spooks had wrongly predicted that the massive, Soviet-supported anti-aircraft missile screens in Egypt and Syria could be destroyed within hours. An attack by two armored divisions commanded by Ariel Sharon and Avraham Adan against the Egyptians in Sinai was repulsed with heavy losses to Adan's units.

The tardy but crucial Iraqi involvement in the war was at first overlooked. Astonishingly, Israel failed to appreciate the size, purposes, and at times, it seemed, even the existence of the Iraqi military effort.[9]

Inside Iraq, the position of President Ahmed Hassan al-Baqr and his powerful sidekick, Saddam Hussein, from the time Iraqi oil was nationalized in June 1972 until the Algiers agreement with the Shah of Iran in March 1975, was somewhat shaky. The Ba'ath needed the support or at least neutrality of the Communist opposition on the political Left, and needed also to bring the northern Kurds under control. In order to convince their own people and the larger Arab world that they meant what they said about fighting imperialism and "liberating Palestine," Baqr and Saddam ordered the Iraqi armed forces to join the 1973 war with Israel, and to at least hold the line against any Kurdish offensive. Saddam and his military colleagues chose General Salim Shaker, a close and loyal companion of Saddam during the Ba'ath's rise to power in the 1960s, for a key command in the Iraqi expeditionary force. This consisted of two Iraqi armored divisions, the 3rd and the 6th, equipped with about 500 tanks, 700 armored personnel carriers (APCs), and a total of 30,000 troops. These were dispatched in increments from bases west of Baghdad, beginning on October 6. Israeli air reconnaissance failed to detect the movement of the Iraqis from their bases to south-central Syria's Hauran area, a distance of about 400 miles, during which they had very sparse air cover from the Iraqi air force.

The initial Syrian offensive lasted only about 42 hours, from midday on October 6 to the morning of October 8. By midnight of October 7, while Nixon, Kissinger, and their advisers in Washington were still dithering about how and in what quantities to respond to Israel's urgent pleas for emergency military aid to stem the Arab tide, the momentum for the Syrian thrust had carried advance Syrian units through the Golan plateau almost to the borders of northern Israel itself. The hard-pressed Israeli forces switched from local tactical containment to a two-stage counterattack. Early on October 11, General Yitzhak Hoffi's Northern Command forces moved across the 1967 ceasefire line and into Syria proper. This removed the "existential threat," as Israeli commentators later called it, to Israel itself. Despite the heavy Arab attacks and massive tank battles, which followed, the Israelis from this time on were essentially on the offensive, halting only with the UN-imposed ceasefire of October 22. For several days—until Iraqi intervention—it looked as though the Israelis, who reached Syrian villages within artillery range of Damascus, might go on to capture the Syrian capital itself.

Although Sadat's forces were still gaining ground in newly liberated portions of Sinai—the Israeli counter-offensive to the west bank of the Suez Canal, that trapped the Egyptian 3rd Army in a pocket along the Canal and the Great Bitter Lake had not yet materialized—the Israeli breakthrough on the Golan on October 11 gave rise to optimism in Tel

Aviv. Moshe Dayan proclaimed that the "back of the Syrian army had been broken" and the "way to Damascus was now clear." General David Elazar flashed a message to Hoffi's command reading "Good hunting, gentlemen!" At 11:00 a.m. on October 11, the Israeli 7th Armored and Barak brigades pushed across the old ceasefire line and found themselves in bitter fighting with a tough Moroccan expeditionary force, airlifted to Damascus across North Africa and the Mediterranean, and with elements of the 7th Syrian Division, one of whose brigades withdrew without orders, facilitating the Israeli advance. By sundown on October 12, General Rafael Eytan's troops had captured Syrian villages and tactically important crossroads along the main Kuneitra–Damascus highway. The Syrians lost a fierce tank battle on the Leja lava plain. Israel's elite Golani infantry brigade took the place of the armored units in the most forward Israeli positions.

At 1 p.m. on October 11, General Dan Lanner's 240th Israeli Division cracked the main Syrian defense positions astride the Kuneitra–Damascus road. Other Israeli units captured a crossroads five miles east of Kuneitra and the villages of Jeba and Tel Esh Shar. The Israeli air force had managed to destroy many of the deadly SAM anti-aircraft missile sites, and the Syrian army was suffering serious losses from the Israeli air and land assaults. The 19th and 17th Israeli brigades drove toward Kanakir, ten miles south of the big Syrian military base of Kiswe (one of the sites from which many coups had been launched against Damascus regimes). The Israeli aim was to outflank and eventually capture the hamlet of Saasa on the main highway to Damascus, only 22 miles to the southwest of the Syrian capital. From here, Israeli artillery would be able to pummel the Mazza airport and military base and other targets in and around Damascus, which had already suffered Israeli air attacks, including one that hit the Soviet Embassy.

IRAQ TO THE RESCUE OF SYRIA

This moment near Saasa was the high watermark of Iraq's efforts to influence the conflict. While the leading Israeli tanks were moving fast forward just south of Kanakir, a village near Saasa, General Dan Lanner, peering through binoculars from his Tel Esh Shar forward command post, spotted around 150 tanks forming up to the east. They belonged to the Iraqi 3rd Tank Division, which had arrived in the battle area on October 11. It was commanded by Saddam Hussein's old crony Salim Shaker, and would be reinforced by an additional Iraqi tank brigade on October 13. The main mission that the Syrian High Command gave to the Iraqis was to counterattack the southern flank of the growing Israeli salient in one sector of the Syrian 9th Infantry Division's defense zone. The first Iraqi assault was repulsed by Israel's 79th Brigade, with substantial losses of men and tanks on both sides. However, the Arabs could count the encounter a tactical success. It had halted the advance of the Israeli 17th and 19th Brigades toward Damascus, forcing them back to an area behind Saasa. North of there, Rafael Eytan's division beat off dogged Arab attacks around the Damascus–Kuneitra highway, but could not advance much farther until the final ceasefire on October 22. By the evening of October 12, despite the earlier boasts of Moshe Dayan and David Elazar, the Syrians and Iraqis together had blocked any Israeli drive on Damascus.

Arab commentators acknowledge that although the Iraqis fought bravely, their adherence to the rigid Soviet doctrines taught by Russian instructors led them into a trap laid by Israeli General Dan Lanner on the night of October 12 to 13. Lanner arranged his four brigades in a box formation. The corners were formed by four Syrian villages, where each of the four Israeli brigades was deployed. At 3 a.m. on October 13, the Iraqi 3rd Tank Division, reinforced by the newly-arrived 6th Tank Brigade, launched an orthodox (according to Soviet practice) and anticipated drive on a four-mile front through the open end of Lanner's box-trap. The trapped Iraqis fought stubbornly but lost hundreds of men and 80 tanks before the survivors could extricate themselves. Casualties and battle fatigue halted most action by the weary Israeli and Arab forces until the Jordanian 40th Armored Brigade, which had entered Syria on October 1 in an unpublicized deployment to back up Syrian defenses, attacked Israeli forces on October 16, in loose coordination with the Syrians and Iraqis, along a wide front from Um Butneh in the west to Tel Antar and Tel Al Alakieh in the east. The Syrian High Command coordinated the operation badly: the Jordanians found themselves without needed Syrian backup, while the Iraqi 3rd Tank Division failed when it was confronted by a surprise Israeli counterattack on their northern flank, which the Iraqis wrongly thought Syrian units were protecting. Still following Soviet tactics, the Iraqis moved forward on a narrow frontage and withdrew as soon as the Israelis threatened their flanks. This exposed the Jordanians, who had counted on Iraqi support and who, to add insult to injury, found themselves being shelled by Iraqi "friendly fire." Profiting by the disarray in Arab command and control, General Musa Peled, who had relieved the exhausted Dan Lanner, sent Israel's 31st Paratroop Brigade to capture Syrian positions at Um Butneh in a night battle that cost them heavy losses.

In one last hurrah, the Iraqi 3rd Tank Division and Jordan's 40th Armored Brigade together hit forward Israeli positions. The Iraqis led with a head-on assault comprising over 130 tanks and 100 APCs, covered by concentrated artillery fire. At one point they almost managed to overwhelm the Israelis, but at nightfall they broke off the attack and withdrew, leaving about half of their tanks and APCs strewn over the hillsides. At 10 a.m. on October 18, the Jordanians made their last move against the Israelis, but the general lack of coordination with their Arab allies, including more Iraqi artillery fire, made the Jordanians lose the day and retire by evening.

Despite Israel's tactical successes on October 18, most Arab and Israeli historians seem to agree that the combined Iraqi–Jordanian counterattack on that day had prevented any final Israeli drive on Damascus—if such was intended by Defense Minister Dayan and the rest of the Israeli cabinet. Not only did the Arabs recapture Saasa, but the Israelis had to withdraw to the jumping-off positions they had occupied by October 16. This gave rise to President Assad's confident prediction that any long-drawn-out war of attrition on Syrian home ground would prove too costly and therefore untenable for the Israeli invaders. Assad's arguments could not dissuade President Sadat, whose over-extended armies were now trapped on both sides of the Suez Canal, from signing a UN-brokered ceasefire on October 22. King Hussein, relieved that his military commanders had acquitted themselves honorably in a battle to defend an Arab homeland, soon withdrew his troops without taking any formal part in the ceasefire agreements.

SADDAM GETS A BREATHER

In Baghdad, Saddam and Baqr, after assessing Iraqi losses, were able to declare to their people that they had helped to save "Sister Syria" from the Israeli enemy. They withdrew their surviving troops and equipment, and soon resumed playing politics with the *après-guerre* situation. The Ba'athists sought to curb the Kurds while holding the Kurds' allies, the Shah and newly victorious Israel, at bay. Saddam hoped his oil wealth and growing arsenal would give him leadership of the Middle East, and ultimately the wherewithal to confront the Israeli enemy again on something like an equal footing. The Algiers agreement with the Shah, with the consequent immediate cessation of Iranian military pressure, was accompanied by more favorable commercial and political attitudes on the part of the Shah's Western allies, especially the United States. Due to the world oil price increases and production cuts that followed the 1973

Arab–Israel war, Iraq's oil revenues jumped from $575 million in 1972 to $1.84 billion in 1973 and to $5.7 billion in 1974. The Ba'athists were able to boast correctly that they were launching huge and ambitious new programs in infrastructure, education, public housing, health, and welfare, which stretched onward into the 1980s and would continue despite the ravages of the 1980–88 war with Iran. Oil wealth also helped nudge Iraq into greater integration with world trade markets and to reduce its need for Soviet economic aid, although Soviet military aid continued.

With the United States, attacked almost daily in the Iraqi media as the perfidious and imperialistic ally of Israel, Iraq had entertained no diplomatic relations since the 1967 Arab–Israel war; commerce and business nevertheless began to prosper. U.S.–Iraqi trade in both directions grew from a paltry $32 million in 1971 to $284 million in 1974. Trade with Japan, and especially with West Germany, whose more adventurous traders, manufacturers, and engineers soon began to work with Iraq's weapons programs, also expanded dramatically.

Internally, the regime got a closer and closer grip on the economy. More than any previous regime since Ottoman times, it could hand out patronage and what would be called in Washington "pork barrel" goodies in the form of contracts and concessions to favorite businessmen, domestic and foreign, speculators, and contractors of all sorts. This new Ba'athist-oriented middle class benefited from social welfare programs, subsidies on essential foodstuffs like bread, cooking oil, and sugar, wage increases, and new jobs created in the expanding defense and other manufacturing sectors. Later, many of these developments would have damaging consequences. Farm production would fall, largely because of rural to urban population movements, and the uneven and often unfair land distribution that formed part of such programs as the "Arabization" of the Kurdish north. As the Ba'athist surveillance and repression of people built gradually up toward Orwellian proportions, industrial managers and civil servants at all levels grew more and more timid about taking decisions not backed by higher authority. However, few of these abuses seemed acute until later, in the 1980s and 1990s.[10]

SADDAM CLAMPS DOWN—AND SEEKS TOTAL POWER

Politically, despite the strife with the Kurds and troubles with the Shias and the Communists, Saddam was able to conduct his march toward absolute power against the background of a fairly stable internal situation. The regular armed forces, commanded by General Adnan Khairallah, the son-in-law of Baqr and brother-in-law of Saddam, were under total control. Political commissars placed all the way down to platoon level assured military loyalty to the Ba'ath Party.

The Soviet KGB and East Germany's STASI trained Iraqi security forces. A new Office of National Security (*maktab al amn al qawmi*), with Saddam at its head, began operations in 1974, running most of the civilian and military intelligence and security services. Russian-style Ba'athist political commissars, chosen from those of the million or so party members deemed most loyal, were placed in overseas embassies to spy on and oversee, Russian-style, the career Iraqi diplomats.

Izzat Ibrahim Douri, the faithful, red-haired Saddam disciple who was still being hunted by the occupying coalition forces in late 2004, was in charge of an expanding Popular Army. It was given sophisticated weapons and replaced the regular army as the main source of armed political power behind the regime.

The patriarchal figure of Baqr, the President, who signed papers that Saddam put on his desk and delegated nearly all except purely protocol-type tasks to Saddam, was nevertheless a symbolic limitation on Saddam's absolute power.

Both domestic and foreign factors favored Saddam's successful final grab for total power in 1979. Traditional opponents of the Ba'ath, including the Kurds, Shia clergy, and Communists, still opposed the Ba'ath and the RCC in whatever ways they could, despite the military and police repression intended to subdue them. However, all of these groups had been weakened by emergence of the growingly prosperous and politically docile middle class that Saddam had taken pains to create.

Outside Iraq, the United States and Israel, following the lead of Iran's Shah, had greatly reduced their support for the Kurds, whose charismatic chief Mullah Mustafa Barzani was slowly dying of cancer in the United States. The Shah was unwilling to use military force against the growing tide of religious opposition in Iran. Saddam's relations with the Shah and his Pahlevi family had grown so warm in the wake of the 1975 Algiers accord that Empress Farah of Iran made the unprecedented gesture of visiting the Shia holy places in Iraq, demoralizing Shia opponents of Saddam. As was true for other Arab Communist parties, Moscow's support for the Iraqi Communists had dwindled. This process accelerated when Saddam publicly opposed the Soviet invasion of Afghanistan in December 1979. Sadat's Egypt, which in 1978 and 1979 was busy negotiating permanent peace with

Israel at Camp David and Washington under the benevolent eye of U.S. President Jimmy Carter, was no longer a power factor able to influence events in Iraq, as it had been in the time of Nasser. Wealthy Saudi Arabia and Kuwait in the late 1970s found Saddam to be a "good neighbor" (the historical Iraqi claim to Kuwait would resurge only a decade later). Poor countries like Somalia and Sudan were enjoying Iraqi financial aid. Yassir Arafat and his mainstream PLO, as well as marginal Palestinian or pseudo-Palestinian terrorist groups, were getting support in Baghdad. Arafat was willing to burnish Saddam's prestige in the Arab world by publicizing this support.

Saddam's careful cultivation of his own garden and avoidance of high-profile foreign adventures during this period ensured Western political acquiescence in his rule. The Iraqi market for Western products grew, especially for weapons and dual-use products like cars, trucks, helicopters, and fixed-wing aircraft. In his strategy toward the perennial enemy, Israel, Saddam was circumspect during and immediately after his seizure of total power in 1979. Israeli analysts, in view of the 1967 and 1973 experiences, and facing terrorist threats from Baghdad-based Palestinian groups, viewed Saddam's Iraq, as always, as a long-term strategic threat. In public pronouncements about Israel, however, Saddam and his underlings took care not to use language more extreme than that used by Sadat, King Hussein, and other "moderate" Arab statesmen. Iraqi diplomats also understood, as one of them told me in 1979, that the Carter administration, despite its successful peace negotiations with Sadat and Israeli Prime Minister Menachem Begin, did not appreciate Begin's often belligerent statements about other Arab states. The Carter administration wanted to draw Saddam into comprehensive peace talks with Israel, and so wished to promote better relations with Baghdad for political, as well as commercial, reasons.[11]

THE DOWNFALL OF BAQR

Ironically, it was Baqr himself who precipitated his own final political eclipse by challenging his "deputy," Saddam. Baqr did this by proposing a union of Syria and Iraq, run by separate factions of the Ba'ath party under a central Ba'athist leadership. Sadat's defection from the common Arab front against Israel had left what Israel called its "Eastern Front"— Jordan, Syria, and Iraq—more exposed, as the Arabs saw it, to their Zionist enemy. A union of the two Ba'athist states, even if it could not include Jordan's monarchy, would, in the opinion of many ordinary Arabs, strengthen Arab unity against Israel.

On October 1, 1978, Baqr on his own took the initiative of offering
to send Iraqi troops back to Syria again, this time not in a shooting war
as in 1973, but as part of an open-ended proposal for a political merger
between Iraq and Syria. Accordingly, President Hafez al-Assad visited
Baghdad on October 26 for a summit meeting with Baqr and Saddam.
They announced a condemnation of Sadat's peacemaking with Israel and
a "Charter for Joint National Action" to coordinate anti-Israel policies.
Baqr proposed an immediate Iraqi–Syrian union with himself as president and Assad as vice-president, leaving Saddam, as it were, out in the
cold. Assad, realizing that Saddam was already too powerful to acqui-
esce in this, backtracked. He said there was no need for Iraqi troops in
Syria just then. It would be better to space out the steps toward total
union over a period of several years.

Baqr tried to persuade Assad to accept his concept. He visited Damascus in January 1979, reducing his demands to a merger of the two
branches of the Ba'ath Party as an initial step. Assad temporized.
Saddam, uneasy with the whole process, decided to end it.

The Iranian revolution, with the departure of the Shah and the return
of Khomeini from exile on February 12, 1979, to take power in Tehran
helped Saddam. It ended the good relations he had entertained with the
Shah's Iran. Baqr was rebuffed when he congratulated Khomeini in a
cable. The Ba'ath was far too secular for the taste of the now ascendant
Iranian clergy. Syrians, however, reacted favorably to the Iranian political earthquake, realizing that it gave the Arabs a new ally against Israel.
As Damascus–Tehran relations warmed up, those between Tehran and
Baghdad chilled to the freezing point. Within a week of his assumption
of power, Khomeini let it be known that he "wanted Najaf," one of
Iraq's Shia holy cities. Saddam replied with the insult that Khomeini was
"a Shah in clerical disguise."

Saddam now began to install Tikriti clansmen and allies at all levels
of authority to prepare for a showdown with Baqr. He further under-
mined the idea of union with Syria, and consequently Baqr's remaining authority, by sending Assad an ultimatum: accept union right now,
or forget the whole thing. When Assad failed to respond, Saddam
began liquidating the joint committees supposed to be discussing the
merger. In order to secure Baqr's resignation, Saddam in early July
visited Jordan and Saudi Arabia. He persuaded King Hussein, and
apparently renewed his old contacts with the CIA in Amman; then
wooed the Saudi royal family. Jordan, Saudi Arabia, and the United
States (and, of course, especially Israel) hated the idea of an
Iraqi–Syrian union. Saddam offered all three his guarantee to bury the

union plans in return for their non-intervention in his coming ousting of Baqr. The Carter administration in Washington already considered Khomeini to be a threat, and, like Iraq, the Saudis, and the Jordanians, believed that he had to be stopped. (This was before the Iranian seizure of the American Embassy and its staff in November 1979 and the protracted hostage crisis which followed, punctuated by the abortive American military mission to rescue the hostages in 1980 and resolved only through outside mediation, especially by Algeria.)

Feeling secure from outside interference, Saddam perpetrated an internal coup in the Ba'ath Party to remove Baqr. The latter went on Iraqi television on July 16 and announced his retirement for "personal reasons." This was later elaborated as failing health, to which Saddam later added Baqr's supposed despondency over the deaths of his wife, son, and son-in-law during the previous two years. But the real reasons why Saddam forced Baqr out of his office and sent him home under guard soon appeared—and were even recorded on an official film that Saddam ordered to be made. Saddam instigated a series of denunciations and trials in a Communist-style "people's court," followed by a bloody, Stalinist-type purge. It involved murders of a number of alleged pro-Syrian conspirators, some of them Saddam's closest associates and friends, in the RCC, the armed forces, the Ba'ath party structure, and trade union and professional associations.

Saddam began the purge before Baqr's removal by dismissing Abdel Hussein Mashadi, Secretary General of the RCC, who was arrested, tortured, and forced to denounce Ba'athist colleagues. Then, on July 18, 1979, a meeting of 400 of the top Ba'athist leaders from the regions of Iraq was convened and the proceedings recorded on video. Mashadi was forced to recite a carefully rehearsed expose of the supposed conspiracy against Saddam, naming names, dates, and details, and referring to the accused as traitors. As he mentioned each name, security goons were filmed escorting the person out of the hall, never to be seen again. Protesters were shouted down by Saddam, who at the end appeared, at least for the camera, to be weeping with emotion, especially after he had fingered his close friend and aide, Adnan Hamdani. Saddam claimed that the conspirators had plotted to divide him from Baqr and sully the name of the Ba'ath Party.

Naim Haddad, a Shi'ite member of the RCC headed a special, secret court. During two weeks, 22 Ba'athist functionaries, including Mashadi and Hamdani, were convicted and executed and over 40 others sent to prison. Among these victims were all of the advocates of union with Syria. Abdel Khaliq Samarrai, another former close associate of Saddam who had been in prison since 1973, was executed with the others. Saddam on television invited anyone to denounce "suspicious" or "subversive" activity. Hundreds did so, often settling personal scores or exercising petty grudges. Saddam insisted that the firing squad be composed of top Ba'athist loyalists, to whom he issued handguns. Joining the shooters, he doubly ensured their future loyalty and subservience by making them kill their associates. Tribal custom in Iraq would normally require that the relatives of the victims would have demanded the right to shed the blood of their executioners. In this case, however, Saddam saw to it that the executioners were himself and close associates, protected by the massive Ba'athist security apparatus.

In public, Saddam began to conduct himself like a combination of Stalin, all of whose works he collected for his private library, and an Oriental potentate—the new Nebuchadnezzar, as propaganda posters portrayed him. He appeared often, sometimes daily, on television, with hour-long lectures and admonitions, playing the role of a benevolent but menacing father figure who knew what was best in all walks of life for his people. Saddam, dressed in any one of his hundreds of uniforms, suits, or other outfits, liked to go on public walkabouts, when supposedly adoring people would cluster to get a glimpse of him and be filmed while doing so. However, the new President's security guards began to carry sticks and electric cattle prods, like those used by American police (and apparently obtained from the United States). The guards would administer blows or shocks to anyone who got too close or tried to touch Saddam.[12]

In defense and foreign affairs, Saddam speeded up the retooling of his armed forces for what was beginning to look more and more like a major confrontation looming with Khomeini. He had begun shifting from Soviet to Western sources for his military establishment years before his ouster of Baqr. Before the Algiers agreement with the Shah in 1975, it had been nearly impossible for Iraq to purchase and deploy major Western weapons systems. As we saw, Soviet military doctrine and Soviet equipment were the rule in Iraq's contribution to the 1973 war with Israel. It would not have been feasible to train the Iraqi armed forces to use other than Soviet equipment when they were either fighting the Kurds or Israel, or in a state of permanent alert. More important, the West could not consider offering large-scale military supplies to Iraq while analysts in Washington and elsewhere considered it to be something of a Soviet 'satellite."

The first major Iraqi arms purchase from the West came in September 1976, when the France of President Georges Pompidou, the successor of

President Charles de Gaulle, agreed to sell Iraq between 60 and 80 Mirage F-1 fighters. This was followed by an order for 200 French AMX 30 tanks in 1977. Brazil supplied 200 Cascavel APCs in 1978 and Italy kicked in with small and sophisticated naval vessels for Iraq's Gulf patrols. All three—France, Italy, and Brazil—were among the main importers of Iraqi oil in the 1970s. These and other Western arms deals tended to be tied in with oil deals. However, despite this diversification, the USSR, also a big importer of Iraqi oil, remained until the end of the 1980s Iraq's major supplier of tanks, artillery, and military aircraft, since the West would not replace Iraq's Soviet equipment with its own (as the United States did with Sadat's Egypt after the 1979 peace treaty with Israel) without greater control. Also, Saddam wished, in cultivating his populist appeal inherent in his public slogans about the liberation of Palestine, not to appear to be "selling out" to the United States, as he accused Sadat of doing.[13]

A "CYNICAL EMBRACE"

As he groomed his growing war machine for the coming battle with Khomeini's Iran, Saddam's de facto rapprochement with the United States—Aburish rightly calls it "a cynical embrace, the results of which remain to this day"—was encouraged by two main events. One was the Soviet invasion of Afghanistan in December 1979, which Saddam at least passively opposed. The other was the rise of militant Islamism in Khomeini's Iran, and Tehran's announced intention to export its Shia revolution wherever it could. Saddam's internal foes were encouraged. Kurdish leaders cabled their congratulations to Khomeini soon after his elevation to power. More serious for Saddam than the Kurdish attitude was the Iranian revolution's effect on the Iraqi Shia majority. Tehran's strident calls to them to overthrow the "non-Muslim" [read "Sunni"] Ba'ath were matched and amplified by appeals against "tyrannical" rule in Baghdad launched by the Ayatollah Muhammad Bakr al-Sadr, the religious leader of the Shi'ite Iraqis. Tehran found that it was able to foment riots, not only in Iraq, but wherever in the Gulf there were Shia minorities—Saudi Arabia's Eastern oil province, Bahrain, and even Sunni-ruled Kuwait.

Saddam at first used carrot tactics with the Iraqi Shia, by flooding their areas with goods like TV sets and refrigerators. But Sadr, although he had been arrested five times since 1972, kept up his agitation and his public calls for fealty to Khomeini. Saddam cracked down hard, not on Sadr, but with arrests and executions of hundreds of others. The repression was stepped up after April 1, 1980, when partisans of Sadr's Dawa (Islamic Call) Party tried to assassinate Tarik Azziz, only wounding him slightly but killing a number of others at a student conference at Mustansiriya University. On April 5 Dawa hit squads killed more people at the funeral for the university victims. Saddam's special forces entered the Shia holy city of Najaf on April 9, arresting Sadr and his sister Amina, apparently torturing both, and definitely killing them in Baghdad on the same day. Riots in southern Iraq and skirmishes on the border with Iranian troops followed.

Saddam's envoys began to tour Saudi Arabia and other Sunni-ruled Arab states to garner support for his coming assault on Khomeini's Iran. At the same time, he stepped up denunciation of Soviet actions. According to Aburish, Saddam traveled to Amman in July 1980 during the presence there of three CIA operatives. Whether a direct Saddam–CIA meeting took place or not, both sides met with King Hussein and all of the parties discussed the Iranian threat to the Arab Middle East and Western interests, and what could be done about it. Saddam extended a friendly hand to President Ronald Reagan's administration and the Boeing Aircraft Corp by asking to purchase five Boeing 747s, a deal approved by Washington in 1981. At the same time, the Reagan administration approved the sale to Iraq of General Electric engines for the Italian-built warships the Iraqi Navy was getting. U.S. business magazines began publicizing the business opportunities in the Iraqi market.

SADDAM ATTACKS IRAN

On August 5, 1980, after a short stopover in Jordan, Saddam landed in Saudi Arabia, wearing one of his military uniforms and packing a gun. In a ten-hour meeting with Crown Prince Fahd (later King Fahd, but already in 1980 the strongman of the regime), Saddam discussed his plans to attack Iran. Some Arab commentators claim Fahd promised Saddam billions of dollars of Saudi aid and use of the Saudi Red Sea port of Jeddah in the event of Basra being incapacitated by war, as it subsequently was. As border clashes increased, Saddam on September 17 abrogated the Algiers agreement that had granted Iran control of its own half of the Shatt al-Arab waterway.[14]

At dawn on September 22, 1980, Saddam's air force tried to duplicate the 1967 Israeli knockout of the Arab air forces, by striking without warning at ten Iranian air bases, including the military base at Tehran International Airport. The object was to knock out the U.S.-supplied air assets Khomeini had inherited from the Shah and prepare the way for a massive land invasion by Iraq. After suffering considerable damage, the

Iranians sent their own U.S.-made Phantom F-4s against two Iraqi airfields, Iraqi missile boats in the Gulf, an Iraqi gas-processing plant, and various oil installations near the Iran–Iraq border. On the next day, six mechanized Iraqi divisions knifed into Iran. This was the start of one of the longest and most ruinous wars since World War II. When it ended in 1988 in a ceasefire which Iraq and its Western backers needed as badly as did the battered Iran of Khomeini, over a million people had been killed and the economies of both nations lay in ruins.

During this war, both America and Israel offered encouragement and material aid, first to one side and then another. It was a time when Israel stepped up its covert warfare against Saddam Hussein's Iraq, but also explored the remote possibility of a strategic accommodation with Saddam, based on Washington's own growing ties with the increasingly powerful dictator in Baghdad. Above all, it was a time when the maneuvers of both sides in the U.S.–Israeli alliance in the Middle East brought the two partners ever closer, setting the scene for the final showdown with Saddam, which both partners sought and prosecuted in the war of 2003. We must next examine these processes and their consequences.

9
Saddam's Reign (III): Defeat and Defiance, 1980–90

Mankind must put an end to war, or war will put an end to mankind.
(President John F. Kennedy, inaugural address, 1961)

The decade beginning with the Iran–Iraq war and ending with Saddam's disastrous adventure in Kuwait proved crucial for the Middle East and for the U.S.–Israeli alliance. Just as the 1973 war with the Arabs was costly for Israel because of Israel's intelligence failures before that war, the huge gaps in American intelligence about the Shah's Iran rendered the Shah's fall perilous for his avowed American ally, and extremely difficult for his more discreet Israeli one. Washington was reluctant to heed Israeli warnings that the Shah's regime had become shaky. The huge American military and diplomatic missions in Iran, devoted mainly to Cold War operations against the neighboring USSR, had largely ignored domestic developments under their noses in Iran. This was a U.S. intelligence failure of the first order. It greatly increased the shock of the Shah's fall, which knocked away a major pillar of American policy in the Middle East. One consequence was the Ayatollah Khomeini's determined efforts to export his Iranian Islamist revolution, destabilizing countries from Iraq and Saudi Arabia to Lebanon.

Israel's 1982 invasion of Lebanon was intended to smash the PLO forever and remove from its small, multi-sectarian neighbor what it considered to be a strategic threat. The invasion's consequences backfired on both Israel and the United States. With Syrian connivance, Iran sent its Revolutionary Guards who helped to found the Hizbollah (Party of God) militant Shia movement in Lebanon. The start of hostage taking and suicide bombing in Lebanon became features of this backlash. Another was the ill-considered and unsuccessful U.S. military intervention in Lebanon in 1983–84 and the Reagan administration's ensuing hasty retreat. Covert ties between the Reagan administration and an Iranian revolutionary regime, eventually seen by Israel as an even greater strategic enemy than Iraq, facilitated a secret triangle of U.S.–Israeli–Iranian collusion in the Irangate imbroglio, which so rocked Washington during the 1980s.

In a previous book, *Payback, America's Long War in the Middle East*,[1] I described the decade of the 1980s in the terms just mentioned. The intention here is to delve more into what happened behind the scenes, directly affecting relations inside the U.S.–Israel–Iraq triangle. The Iran–Iraq war of 1980–88 was a backdrop for turbulent events that had begun in 1979: Saddam's seizure of total power in Iraq, the Khomeini revolution and occupation of the U.S. Embassy in Tehran by his disciples, the revolt of radical Sunni Islamists in Saudi Arabia who seized the Great Mosque in Mecca, and the Soviet invasion of Afghanistan. There was continued internecine strife among Syrians, Israelis, and Palestinians in Lebanon, which had begun in 1975.

The world's response to the Iran–Iraq war included UN Security Council resolutions calling for a ceasefire. The Council enjoined all member states to refrain from actions intended to keep the war going. The Soviet Union was already tied down in Afghanistan, an adventure which would eventually finish it off once its defeated armies had left Afghanistan in 1989. Moscow opposed the Iran–Iraq war. At first it decreed a cut off of arms to both sides, only to resume weapons deliveries to Iraq in 1982. The massive American military sales to Iran had ended with the Shah's fall, and the Carter administration broke off U.S. diplomatic relations with Iran in 1980 because of the Tehran Embassy hostage crisis. Iraq had not renewed diplomatic relations with the United States since breaking them off in the 1967 Arab–Israel war.

The Carter administration proclaimed its official neutrality in the Iran–Iraq war. It claimed not to be arming either side, and proclaimed "Operation Staunch" to cut off the arms flow to both. Iran, however, depended totally on its American-made weapons and spare parts. It soon found that despite Khomeini's vitriolic demonization of Israel as a "viper state," and a satellite of "The Great Satan," America, back-channels and "private" Israeli operators like Yaacov Nimrodi could still provide those weapons and parts. Iran also turned to European, Asian, and South American countries for arms. Iraq began to deplete its big Soviet-supplied arsenal, and, as we saw, was using many channels to seek armaments from the West.

ISRAEL, IRANGATE, AND THE IRAN–IRAQ WAR

In September 1980, Saddam's six invading divisions at first drove quite a deep wedge into Iranian territory, but were soon halted and then driven back by fierce Iranian counterattacks. By the middle of 1982, Saddam's forces faced "human wave" attacks, often led by young Revolutionary

Guards, and even teenagers, callow youths called *baseej* who charged into certain death with symbolic plastic "keys to Paradise" dangling from their necks.

The new Reagan administration decided that an Iranian victory would not be in the American national interest. Accordingly, the slow upgrading of U.S.–Iraqi ties was speeded up. High-level official visits were exchanged. Executives of American and multinational oil companies, notably Exxon-Mobil, conscious that Iraq's reserves were second in the world only to Saudi Arabia's, quietly lobbied the Reagan administration to cozy up to Saddam. In February 1982, the U.S. State Department struck Iraq from its list of states supporting international terrorism, after Saddam made some cosmetic changes in his backing of Palestinian groups. On July 12, 1983, President Reagan signed National Security Decision Directive (NSDD) 99, classified Secret. It set forth U.S. regional interests and goals in the Middle East and South Asia, hinting strongly at a coming tilt toward Iraq in official American policy.[2]

Israel made hidden and open moves of its own. Even before the outbreak of the Iran–Iraq war, and shortly after the November 1979 takeover of the American Embassy in Tehran by Iranian "students" and Revolutionary Guards, Israeli Prime Minister Menachem Begin approved an Israeli shipment of tires for Iran's McDonnell-Douglas Phantom F-4 fighter-bombers, as well as of small arms and some heavy weapons for the Iranian army. President Carter rather angrily admonished Begin to ship no further military supplies to Tehran until the American Embassy hostages were released. However, after the election of Ronald Reagan and the instant release of the American hostages that followed his inauguration on January 19, 1981, neither Israel nor Western European states considered themselves still bound by the Carter administration's sanctions. An Israeli arms dealer (not Nimrodi), working through French intermediaries, negotiated in Lisbon with an Iranian arms merchant, Ahmed Khudari, who was acting under Iranian Defense Ministry instructions. Once again, the Iranian request was for tires for Phantom jets, and also, this time, communications gear, 106mm recoilless cannon, mortars, and ammunition, altogether worth $200 million. The only condition the Iranians made was that the deal be kept secret and publicly denied if news of it leaked.

Ahmed Khudari's greed proved stronger than his patriotism. An Israeli plane with 100 106 mm cannon flew to Lisbon, where the cargo was transferred to an Iran Air cargo aircraft. However, before another shipment could be made, Khudari absconded with the $56 million down payment in Iranian treasury funds.

The next phase of the clandestine Israeli arms shipments to revolutionary Iran publicly exposed the trade, but did not end it. A British arms agent chartered an Argentine cargo plane whose radio call sign was Yankee Romeo 224. After a night flight to Amsterdam, it arrived in Tel Aviv and loaded its arms cargo. On July 11, it began a circuitous route to Tehran in order to avoid hostile airspace, stopping at Larnaca airport in Cyprus to refuel. After being cleared for Turkish airspace, the pilot, Stuart MaCafferty, told the Ankara control tower that he was carrying "fruit and vegetables" to Iran. He completed that trip to Tehran and returned to Israel, then flew another shipment to Tehran. After MaCafferty took off on July 18 on his third weapons run, he strayed—or was forced by hostile aircraft (this mystery remains unsolved to my knowledge)—out of Turkish airspace, crashed and was killed in Soviet territory. Both Iran and Israel denied any knowledge of Yankee Romeo 224's missions.

By May 1982, at about the time the U.S. Secretary of State Alexander Haig was giving Israel his famous "green light" to invade Lebanon in order to smash the PLO based there, Israeli Defense Minister Ariel Sharon informed Haig and Defense Secretary Caspar Weinberger of another Israeli arms deal with Iran, this time for less than $100 million worth of 160mm mortars, 106mm cannon, and shells. The United States again asked Israel not to send Iran U.S. weapons or weapons with U.S.-made parts. Israel began to send arms from its immense stores of Soviet arms captured from Palestinian groups over the years.[3]

In September 1982, Iran's royalist opposition, loyal to the "baby Shah," the Shah's son and former crown prince, Reza Pahlevi, solicited new Israeli arms supplies—this time in order to overthrow Khomeini. Reza aimed to restore the Iranian monarchy. This would also ensure Israel and its ally the United States their regional predominance, and so frustrate Saddam. This operation was largely orchestrated by none other than Yaacov Nimrodi, Israel's former unofficial envoy to the Shah. In September 1982 Nimrodi and two ex-senior officers of the Shah's army, General Said Razvani and General Feridoun Jam (who back in May 1969 had written a personal letter to Israeli Chief of Staff General Haim Bar-Lev, appealing for extension of Nimrodi's term as military attaché in Tehran by another two years)[4] visited Ariel Sharon's office in Tel Aviv. To overthrow Khomeini, Razvani told Sharon, "We can raise $2 billion. We need arms and later—maybe—instructors as well. Are you willing to help us?" He added that the weapons could be transferred from Israel to Sudan, where President Jafaar Nimeiry would provide storage space on a Sudanese military base for the weapons and for training the counter-revolutionaries.

Earlier, in February 1982, Nimrodi told the BBC's *Panorama* program that the West ought to support Khomeini's ouster and begin training forces to restore the monarchy. Prince Reza phoned his thanks from Morocco. Reza had himself crowned as absentee Shah at a ceremony in the Kubbeh Palace in Cairo on October 31, 1980, on his twentieth birthday. Among those attending were his mother, Queen Farah Diba; the late Shah's twin sister, Princess Ashraf Pahlevi; and several loyal followers. Reza swore to depose Khomeini and reclaim Iran's Peacock Throne, as his father's disciples had christened it. Other plots had already failed, including one by Iranian Air Force officers who had planned to bomb the Ayatollah's home in Qom. The plot was unmasked and scores of officers, including pilots, were tried and executed.

Reza first tried to operate from Cairo, where he made some broadcasts under Sadat's watchful eye. Later he moved to Morocco, where Nimrodi visited him in 1982 along with his associate, the Israeli–American flier, adventurer, and arms dealer Al Schwimmer. After meetings with other Iranian exiles, Nimrodi and Schwimmer contacted the Saudi Arabian tycoon Adnan Kashoggi, a former middleman between American companies and the Saudi royal family. Kashoggi had personally met Presidents Nixon, Ford, and Carter. The Saudi Ambassador in Washington, Prince Bandar bin Sultan, introduced Kashoggi to Robert McFarlane, President Reagan's national security adviser. Kashoggi had also met David Kimche, former secretary-general of the Israeli Foreign Ministry, when Kimche was a senior figure in Mossad's European network, as well as Menachem Begin, Shimon Peres, and Ariel Sharon. Israeli technicians are said to have installed the security system of Kashoggi's famous cruising yacht, the *Nabila*.

Kashoggi joined Nimrodi and Schwimmer in their Iranian enterprise. Kashoggi enlisted the indirect support of King Fahd of Saudi Arabia, as well as that of Sudan's President Nimeiry. However, Sharon hesitated when Nimrodi and Schwimmer met him in Tel Aviv in September 1982. Israel had invaded Lebanon on June 6 of that year. Just before their September meeting, Israeli soldiers had watched while Lebanese Christian militiamen massacred hundreds of Palestinians in the Sabra and Chatila camps at Beirut. Sharon would later be blamed by an Israeli investigation as "indirectly responsible," causing his resignation as defense minister. He evidently did not believe in the prospects for the enterprise to restore Reza in Iran. He either seriously considered or approved, the conspirators' request to buy from Israel $800 million worth of captured Soviet-made Arab weapons, which the Israelis really did not want, but there was no further serious Israeli consideration of help to the Iranian supporters of the "Baby Shah." Israel reluctantly accepted revolutionary Iran as a fait accompli, and, as the Israeli writer Samuel Segev puts it, "tried with determination to find a way into the hearts of those elements likely to be Khomeini's successors."[5]

THE OSIRAK CAPER

During this period, Menachem Begin's formidable military and intelligence services launched their covert war aimed at blocking Saddam Hussein's plans to acquire nuclear weapons. This involved the murder of several key scientists and other figures connected with the Iraqi nuclear program. Then, at 5:34 p.m. on June 7, 1981, eight U.S.-made Israeli Air Force F-16 fighter-bombers, covered by F-15 interceptors, bombed Iraq's French-supplied Osirak nuclear reactor into rubble. The only apparent casualty was a lone French technician on weekend duty at the reactor. The attack came just at the time when Osirak was nearly complete and ready to "go hot," the process in which enriched uranium rods are inserted into the core to activate the reactor.

Although at least one key Iraqi scientist has insisted that Saddam never seriously planned to make nuclear weapons until after the destruction of Osirak, Begin and his advisors, like some (though by no means all) analysts in Washington and elsewhere, believed differently.[6]

Begin, who in 1979 had wearily completed the long-drawn-out but finally successful peace negotiations with Sadat, brokered by President Jimmy Carter, was always one of Saddam Hussein's most implacable foes. He considered Saddam to be nothing less than a new Adolf Hitler. Begin regarded Osirak as potentially the most sinister of all of Iraq's projects. The Israeli information offensive painted it as an invitation to world Armageddon and its intended removal as a favor to world civilization. Begin was much less tolerant of the publicly known nuclear relations between Iraq and France, then under the presidency of Valery Giscard d'Estaing, than his predecessors had been.

Shimon Peres, the Labor Party's Defense Minister in the 1950s, had been largely responsible for attracting the French technology and equipment that enabled Israel to build its own nuclear-weapons complex at Dimona, in the Negev desert. At one point Peres apparently believed that he could persuade the French to cut off their aid for the engineering and construction of Osirak. However, the Israeli Ambassador in Paris, Mordecai Gazit, reported that neither the persuasion of Peres nor the strictures of Begin were successful. The American administration of Jimmy Carter did not get involved.

The top military planners of the Jewish state began planning for the Israeli air attack in November 1979, according to historians Blackman and Morris. However, military intelligence chiefs and Mossad boss Yitzhak Hoffi were at first opposed. The reactor, they said, could not be a threat for some years to come. A strike might lead to full-scale war, halting or even destroying the ongoing peace process with Sadat's Egypt. However, they were assured by technical experts, apparently informed by Roger Richter of the UN's International Atomic Energy Agency (IAEA)—whose inspectors, led by Hans Blix of Sweden, were destined to play such an important part in the inspections of Iraq between the wars of 1991 and 2003—that Saddam's design was indeed a weapons program. The IAEA fired Richter after the Osirak bombing, following Iraqi complaints that he had given Israel and the United States classified inside information.

A series of sabotage operations followed against Saddam's presumed nuclear weapons program. On April 6, 1979, at about 3 a.m., a series of simultaneous explosions rocked the huge warehouses at La Seyne-sur-Mer, France, of the Constructions Navales et Industrielles de la Mediterranée (CNIM). Major structural and engineering parts for Osirak were stored there pending shipment to Iraq, dates and details of which were shrouded under France's top security classification, *Secret Defense*. The French police concluded that Israel was the main suspect. Next, in June 1980, Dr. Yahya al-Meshad, an Egyptian metallurgist working for Iraq's Atomic Energy Commission, was stabbed to death in his Paris hotel room while on a mission to arrange for shipment of French nuclear fuels to Iraq. Nothing was stolen, and police ruled out burglary as a motive. A prostitute who had met Meshad that evening and heard voices coming from his room was questioned by French police on July 1. Twelve days later, a hit-and-run driver ran over her and killed her.

Beginning on August 2, 1980, bombs damaged offices and residences of officials of key suppliers of Iraq in France and Italy: Techniaatome, SNIA-Techint, and Ansaldo Mercanico Nucleare. The three firms had contracted to supply Iraq with an experimental reactor and hot cells used in the uranium enrichment process. Their officers and workers had received threatening letters calling on them to suspend their work for Iraq. They complied. Israel's terror campaign was codenamed "Operation Sphinx." It reminded commentators of one carried out by Jerusalem in 1962–63 against West German scientists working on rocket programs for Nasser's Egypt. That one was codenamed Operation Damocles and involved kidnappings and letter bombs, killing at least five persons.

In September 1980, before the Israeli raid, world attention had been briefly on Osirak when two Iranian air raids caused minor damage to it, causing the French and Italian experts to leave the site and go home, to return only in February 1981. The wisdom of bombing the reactor was disputed among senior Israeli civilian and military leaders. However, the cabinet approved the attack in principle on October 28, 1980. The Israeli Air Force command gave the attack plan to the general staff.[7]

How Mossad penetrated the inner sanctum of the reactor and marked with pinpoint accuracy the best part of it to hit is the subject of a highly colored but possibly true tale, told by a man who claims to have performed this mission for Mossad.

A "Gerald Westerby," most probably a pseudonym, in 1998 published a book called *In Hostile Territory*. It purports to show how Westerners who want to learn aggressive business tactics should apply the methods Westerby used in various high-risk covert missions for Israel against several Arab states, including Iraq, using as a cover his real-life profession of financial consultant. His tale runs as follows: Israeli agents arranged for him to meet an Iraqi physicist, Dr. Ali Ragoub, at a London cocktail party. Ragoub was said to be the offspring of a Sunni mother of Tikriti origin (therefore tribally privileged), and a Shia father who had been disgraced and executed by the regime. Because of his Tikriti connections and exalted status as a nuclear scientist, Ragoub was allowed to travel abroad. Westerby was instructed by his current Mossad handler, whose cryptonym was "Gray Cell," to approach Ragoub and let him know that he was aware of the secret that Ragoub's father had been disgraced and executed on Saddam's orders.

In early summer 1980, runs the story, a woman case officer of Mossad named Daphna met Westerby in London. She briefed him on his next mission to Iraq: to renew contact with Dr. Ragoub, by now a key operative inside the nuclear program at Osirak. Westerby flew to Baghdad, rented a car and hired a government-approved tourist guide, inevitably an informer for Saddam's secret police. To allay suspicion and establish his bona fides as a tourist, he was first to visit a known tourist site in the guide's company. Mossad believed that Ragoub was ripe for turning, and would cooperate with the scheme to plant a homing device inside Osirak. This would guide the Israeli attackers to exactly the right target in the reactor complex. Westerby met Ragoub in Baghdad's Sheraton Hotel, under the watchful eye of all the usual spies. Inside a copy of the *Financial Times*, he handed Ragoub what looked like a standard international electricity converter kit with its protruding plugs, and a can of Flying Dutchman pipe tobacco. Westerby claims that Ragoub was happy to carry out Mossad's wishes, as revenge on the regime that had killed his father. He says he told Ragoub that the device was a sophisticated scientific recording instrument that would "enable us to decipher certain operational routines of the reactor." Westerby asked Ragoub to attach the device to a wall near the reactor core, and leave it there. He promised vaguely to return within weeks to retrieve it. He never did.

Westerby then flew to Israel, via Kuwait and London. He arrived at Tel Aviv airport on Israel's election day, June 7, 1980, several months before the active phase of attack planning. He does not claim to know for sure that Ragoub planted the device and that it did its job. He simply writes that after the attack, "Israel's air force had done its job, and for all I know, Ragoub had done his."[8]

Reactions to the attack were predictably totally different, depending on whether you were the average Arab or Muslim, or the average Westerner. Iraq issued aggrieved statements contending that the Osirak programs had been for strictly peaceful purposes. Donald Neff, an American historian not unsympathetic to Arab viewpoints, concluded that the raid was a kind of declaration of war against the Arab world's efforts to enter the nuclear age, demonstrating that only the Jewish state would be allowed to participate in advanced technology, while the Arabs would be consigned to low-tech weapons and second-class economies. There were, at first, some strong condemnations, especially in France, whose companies suffered major financial losses as a result. Following advice from the Carnegie Endowment for International Peace, the White House notified Congress that a "substantial" violation of the Arms Export Control Act prohibition against the use of U.S. weapons except in self-defense "may have occurred" in the Osirak attack. This was the third time the Act had been invoked against Israel, the first two during the Carter administration because of Israeli attacks on Lebanon, in one of which cluster bombs were used. However, as in the two previous cases, Israel's supporters in Congress were able to forestall any action. President Reagan found extenuating circumstances: "Israel might have sincerely believed it was a defensive move," he said. "It is difficult for me to envision Israel as being a threat to its neighbors." The United States did join in a rare unanimous UN Security Council resolution "strongly" condemning Israel, but made it clear it would, as usual, veto any resolution calling for sanctions against the Jewish state. So Council Resolution 487 had no teeth.

RETRIBUTION FOR INMAN

There was an important backlash in the American intelligence community, worth remembering in 2004, when the performance of the American, British, Israeli, and other intelligence services in Iraq have come under intense scrutiny. Bobby Inman, the deputy CIA director at the time, believed that the Israeli F-16s could not have hit Osirak without guidance from aerial imagery supplied by spy satellites. (It is possible, though not certain, that the CIA was unaware of Westerby's homing device caper.) Under a secret arrangement which CIA director William Casey, Inman's boss, had worked out with his friends and allies, Israel had been granted access to U.S. satellite intelligence. The agreement was supposed to limit such access to sites posing potential "direct threats" to Israel, as Inman said. When Inman discovered that Israel had used material on more distant areas, such as Iraq, Libya, and Pakistan, he gave orders to limit Israeli access to images of areas no farther than 250 miles from Israel's borders, thus restricting it to immediate neighbors.

Israel's supporters in Washington were furious. Their retribution against Inman came nearly 13 years later when President Bill Clinton nominated him to be secretary of defense in Clinton's first term. A campaign of bitter personal attacks against Inman, especially by the prominent pro-Israel columnist of *The New York Times*, William Safire (after the year 2000 one of the strongest supporters of George W. Bush's war against Iraq), caused Inman to conclude he could not run the Pentagon under such pressure. He declined the nomination,[9] and receded back into the privacy he had always cherished as one of the very top intelligence chiefs in the CIA and the National Security Agency (NSA).

TILTING TOWARD SADDAM

Despite the understandable rejoicing in Israel over Osirak's destruction and the lukewarm Reagan administration reaction, Washington's tilt toward Saddam was not derailed. Following a White House meeting that decided on the tenor of that reaction, Defense Secretary Caspar Weinberger let it be known to his Pentagon subordinates that he was furious with Israel and wanted to punish it. He persuaded President Reagan to delay scheduled delivery of four F-16s that Israel had purchased—the aircraft type used against Osirak. Secretary of State Al Haig, who had applauded the attack, complained bitterly to President Reagan when he found out about Weinberger's move. Weinberger viewed Iraq as the secret ally of the United States in the struggle against the Khomeini regime in Iran, and against potential dangers posed by the export of the Iranian Islamist revolution around the Gulf and in Lebanon. Weinberger, like President George H. W. Bush, would refer to the threat in terms of national security (as President George W. Bush and his neoconservative advisers nearly 20 years later referred to the threat from Saddam and his supposed weapons of mass destruction). However, what Weinberger really had in mind—and this was confirmed to me by a veteran and very senior American oil company executive whom the Reagan and other administrations often consulted—was that U.S. backing of Iraq would prevent Iran from interfering with navigation of oil tankers in the Gulf (where the United States would soon be flagging Kuwaiti tankers with the Stars and Stripes to protect them) and generally with U.S. access to Middle Eastern oil.

If Weinberger wanted to prop up Saddam in the Iran–Iraq war, another faction sought reconciliation with Khomeini's Iran. According to historian Alan Friedman, Reagan did little to control or adjudicate this internal dissension. A former White House official, writes Friedman, told him that "There was substantially no leadership. Reagan was sleeping through it all."

Shortly after the White House meeting about Osirak, Haig found that Jeane Kirkpatrick, the U.S. Ambassador to the United Nations, was cooperating with Iraq's then Foreign Minister, Saadoun Hamadi, and Saleh Omar al-Ali, the Iraqi UN envoy, in drafting a resolution condemning Israel for the attack. When Kirkpatrick signed the resolution and it passed, on June 19, 1981, Haig sought a meeting with Reagan at the Beverly Wilshire Hotel where Reagan was staying in Los Angeles. Reagan apparently ordered Haig not to cross Kirkpatrick, even though Kirkpatrick was actually Haig's subordinate in the State Department hierarchy.[10] The tension between them would continue, but would have no real effect on the continuing tilt toward Iraq. Already in March 1982, a few weeks after removing Iraq from the State Department's terrorist list, the Reagan White House in a new National Security Study Memorandum had encouraged this tilt. Haig by this time was preoccupied with Sharon's coming invasion of Lebanon to destroy the PLO.

By 1983, the war with Iran was costing Saddam Hussein hundreds of millions of dollars a year. Kuwait, Saudi Arabia, and the United Arab Emirates in the Gulf were giving Iraq massive loans and grants. Washington's own tilt toward Baghdad was expressed in many ways. Most of them neatly served the interests of American businesses, bankers, and farmers. The White House and State Department persuaded the Export–Import Bank to provide Iraq with financing. This improved its international credit rating, enabling Iraq to obtain loans from other institutions around the world. The U.S. Agriculture Department provided taxpayer-guaranteed loans for Iraqi purchases of American commodities, especially grain.[11] This helped Reagan's Republican Party and its sitting and aspirant congressmen to get needed votes in the Middle Western grain states.

Turning over crucial military supplies and intelligence to Saddam, at the same time that Israel was slipping covert military aid to Saddam's enemy Khomeini, had to be handled more delicately than the economic assistance. William Casey and other senior White House officials hit upon the idea of using King Hussein as middleman. Hussein was on close and friendly terms at the time with Saddam. Jordan depended heavily on oil from Iraq, partly paid for at below-market prices, or given as a free gift. In meetings with Casey and American diplomats, King Hussein advocated all possible assistance to Saddam. Like the Saudis, Kuwaitis, and other Arab rulers in the region, Hussein regarded Saddam's Sunni but secular Iraq as a shield against the Shia revolutionary threat from Tehran. Aqaba, Jordan's only port on the Red Sea, although under constant intelligence surveillance from its close next-door neighbor, Israel's Eilat, was a natural to receive cargoes that could then easily be shipped overland to Iraq.

As for intelligence, including satellite reconnaissance images of Iranian troop, air, and naval movements, this was at first, in late 1982, given personally to King Hussein to hand to the Iraqis in Baghdad, to make sure it did not go astray. Later, Iraqi liaison officers traveled by the desert road to Amman to pick up the material. U.S. intelligence officers made covert trips to Baghdad to help the Iraqis interpret the images and reports. The United States very quietly even put a high-tech building in Baghdad to provide Saddam with a downlink receiver for better reception and processing of the satellite signals. In the domain of intelligence, this was premium treatment for Saddam which surpassed what even Israel was getting from the United States—apparently one of the motivations for Israel's activation of its American spy, Jonathan Pollard, later convicted and imprisoned for selling top-secret defense secrets to Israel.

In February 1983, Iraqi envoy Saadoun Hamadi had his first meeting in Washington with Haig's successor as Secretary of State, George Schultz. Parallel with Iraq's widening circle of friends at upper levels of the U.S. oil and business community were certain diplomats, such as William Eagleton, head of the U.S. interests section (not yet a full embassy, in the absence of formal diplomatic relations) in Baghdad. In a cable in October 1983, perhaps mindful of Reagan's memorandum of the previous July 12 urging a policy opening toward Iraq, Eagleton argued for the lifting of "third-party transfers of U.S.-licensed military equipment to Iraq." Soon, covert shipments of military and dual-use supplies were moving to Iraq through Jordan, Egypt, and Kuwait. Public rapprochement between the Reagan administration and Saddam began toward the end of 1983, despite repeated intelligence reports, which

George Schultz's State Department often cited in briefings to the White House, of Saddam's use of chemical warfare against both recalcitrant Kurds and Iranian troops on the battlefields.

REAGAN, RUMSFELD, AND SADDAM

A prelude to presidential emissary Donald Rumsfeld's first trip to Baghdad to meet with Saddam came in a new presidential directive dated November 26, 1983. It called for "heightened regional military cooperation to defend oil facilities, and measures to improve U.S. military capabilities in the Persian Gulf." It did not mention chemical weapons. On December 17, 1983, Rumsfeld flew into Baghdad, bearing a personal handwritten letter from Reagan to Saddam Hussein. Rumsfeld had served in senior posts in both the Nixon and Ford administrations, including that of Defense Secretary under President Ford. At the time of his visit he was CEO of the multinational pharmaceutical firm of G. D. Searle and Company. In the letter Rumsfeld handed to Saddam, Reagan held out the prospect of renewing diplomatic relations and expansion of both commercial and military ties. Matters they discussed face-to-face, according to the record, included Syria's recent action to cut off a pipeline that had moved Iraqi oil through its territory to the Mediterranean, and U.S. efforts to find alternative routes to transport Iraq's oil to its export markets.

On the same visit, Rumsfeld also met with Tarik Azziz, then Iraqi Foreign Minister. Rumsfeld assured him of the Reagan administration's "willingness to do more" to help Iraq against Iran, but "made clear that our efforts to assist were inhibited by certain things that made it difficult for us, citing the use of chemical weapons, possible escalation in the Gulf, and human rights" (meaning treatment of Kurds, Shias, and political prisoners). Later, the U.S. interests section told Rumsfeld that Iraq's leadership was "extremely pleased" with the visit and that Azziz had "gone out of his way to praise Rumsfeld as a person."[12]

ISRAEL'S OIL CONCERNS

What followed in the economic and strategic domains contains important clues to one of Israel's goals (stated only sparsely in public), which it hoped the United States could accomplish for it in the 2003 overthrow of Saddam and occupation of Iraq. This was restoration of the old British colonial-era oil link between Israel and Iraq. In some ways, this goal paralleled the Reagan administration's own efforts to move more Iraqi oil out to Western markets.

The Israeli academic analyst Ofra Bengio in 1998 recalled Iraq's "geostrategic constraints" and how these affect Israel. As an oil country with only a tiny outlet to the sea (at best about 40 miles, when the Shatt al-Arab waterway from Basra to the Gulf was open), Iraq "has always felt a kind of economic strangulation," Bengio wrote. It tried to overcome this by building pipelines through neighboring countries: Turkey, Syria, Saudi Arabia, or Kuwait. From 1935 to 1948, British-ruled Iraq shipped oil to British-ruled Palestine through a Kirkuk/Mosul-to-Haifa pipeline.

This oil flow from Iraq to Palestine continued from 1932 until war closed it in 1948. Since then, every Iraqi regime sought channels back to the Mediterranean in order to export its oil to world regions like Europe and America, regions not quite so readily reachable from Iraq's Persian Gulf terminals.

Oil pipelines from Iraq to the Mediterranean, and Israel's interest in them, were on Donald Rumsfeld's agenda when, accompanied by Howard Teicher, a former National Security Council adviser (who later supplied information about the U.S.–Iraqi rapprochement), Rumsfeld returned to Baghdad in late March of 1984. Rumsfeld knew in advance that the "atmospherics" in Iraq had chilled a bit since his December visit because of Iranian military successes and a public U.S. condemnation on March 5 of Iraqi use of chemical weapons. Rumsfeld had been instructed in Washington to discuss with senior Iraqis the Reagan administration's hope that it could obtain Export–Import Bank credits for Iraq. These would include $500 million in loan guarantees, backed by American taxpayers, for construction of a new pipeline that could carry a million barrels of crude oil daily from the Kirkuk and Mosul areas to Jordan's Red Sea port of Aqaba. This would divert oil away from the Persian Gulf war zone, where Iraqi and Iranian tankers were being attacked and sunk by each other's air forces, and where Iran was threatening to close the Straits of Hormuz, at the Red Sea's entrance and outlet to the Indian Ocean. Such a pipeline would make it more difficult for Iran to disrupt Saddam Hussein's oil sales and therefore throttle him economically.

According to a later affidavit from Howard Teicher, another subject of discussion was a secret offer of aid to Saddam Hussein from Israel, which had found itself bereft of Persian Gulf oil since the 1967 Arab–Israel. Prior to that, the Shah's Iran since 1957 had been sending oil to Israel in tankers, which docked at Eilat. An eight-inch pipeline pumped the oil from Eilat to Beersheba. Later this was augmented by another Eilat–Ashdod pipeline that enabled Israel to export Persian Gulf oil. The Israeli offer in Rumsfeld's sales pitch was rejected, but the pipeline, to be built by U.S. firms and local contractors without Israeli investment, was eagerly discussed.[13]

The proposed contractor was the giant engineering and construction firm, the Bechtel Corporation of California, with a long history of projects in 135 countries, including many in the Arab world from Libya to Saudi Arabia. Both Casper Weinberger and George Schultz were alumni of senior executive jobs in Bechtel. Schultz had gone directly from Bechtel to his office as Secretary in Foggy Bottom, the legendary nickname of the Department.

Saddam, of course, liked the pipeline idea, but had one important reservation that proved fatal. To reach Aqaba, the Bechtel pipe had to cross Jordan, tantalizingly close to Israel and so making it an easy target for Israeli disruption. (It would probably also have irritated many senior Israelis to see the high-quality Iraqi crude oil passing so close to their own port of Eilat and not getting any of it, while having to import oil from some corners of the world at prices much higher than those for the premium Iraqi crude.) Saddam wanted an ironbound guarantee from the United States that its ally Israel would not attack the pipeline. Foreign Minister Tarik Azziz told old Middle Eastern hand Richard Murphy, the Assistant Secretary of State, that unless there were "direct U.S. involvement," Washington could "just forget" the project.

In Washington, however, the Reagan administration had to overcome the Eximbank's objection to extending loans to an embattled, cash-short government like Iraq. So Vice-President George Herbert Walker Bush, himself an old oil and Middle East hand, was asked to help. Shultz's office sent a confidential memo to Donald Gregg, a CIA veteran and Bush's close adviser. Bush was asked to explain to the chairman of Eximbank, William Draper, that the pipeline would cost $1 billion; that Iraq and Jordan had given Bechtel a June 25 deadline to enlist both official and private U.S. participation; and that Eximbank's support was crucial to U.S. objectives in the Middle East—including ensuring that neither Iran nor Iraq should win their war and dominate the region. Draper agreed with his old Yale schoolmate, Bush, and on June 25, 1984, reversed the bank's long-standing refusal and authorized the $500 loan for the pipeline.[14]

WESTERN ARMS FOR IRAQ

The next tricky subject on Iran–Iraq agendas was the arms exports to Saddam that had already begun covertly. Officially, supply of U.S. military equipment directly to Iraq was prohibited. However, in April

1984 the Baghdad U.S. interests section asked Washington to keep it informed about ongoing the negotiations of Bell Helicopter Textron with Iraqi purchasing agents to sell Iraq helicopters. These were supposed not to be "in any way configured for military use." The purchaser was the Iraqi Defense Ministry. Back in December 1982, Textron's Italian subsidiary, Augusta Bell, had informed the U.S. Embassy in Rome that it had refused Iraq's request to "militarize" recently purchased Augusta Bell helicopters. Another U.S. ally, South Korea, informed the State Department of a similar Iraqi request in June 1983. When a congressional staffer in Washington asked in March 1983 whether heavy trucks recently sent to Iraq were intended for military purposes, a State Department official responded that "we presumed that this was Iraq's intention, and had not asked."

In the spring of 1984, the Reagan administration was becoming involved with Israel in the devious groundwork and footwork for the later Irangate affair. (Yaacov Nimrodi and a picturesque Iranian arms dealer and adventurer named Manuchehr Ghorbanifar would deal with Israel and the United States to trade Israeli-controlled weapons for American hostages held by Shi'ite militants in Lebanon.)[15]

The National Security Archive documents show that the U.S. administration was then reconsidering its policy on the sale of dual-use equipment to Iraq's "nuclear entities." Although nuclear nonproliferation was never a top priority for the Reagan administration, a 1984 Defense Intelligence Agency (DIA) analysis concluded that once the war with Iran ended, Iraq was likely to "continue to develop its formidable conventional and chemical capability, and probably pursue nuclear weapons."[16] This, as the UN weapons inspectors who combed Iraq during the early 1990s were to learn, was indeed the case.

As the conflict with Iran dragged on, Saddam's commercial agents ranged far and wide in their quest for the sinews of war. True to form, the UK government of Prime Minister Thatcher authorized sales of "non-lethal" or defensive gear, like chemical warfare protection suits; then winked at Iraq's purchase of an elaborate electronic military command and control system worth about $600 million for the Iraqi Army. Several British companies became Saddam's main suppliers in the United Kingdom. In 1987, Iraq bought the machine tool manufacturer, Matrix-Churchill and Technical Development Corporation. These cooperated in procuring buying material and parts for Saddam's WMD programs, working through a subsidiary in the United States called Astra. Said Aburish, who knows because (as he candidly reports in his book *Saddam Hussein, the Politics of Revenge*) at one time he acted as

a middleman for Saddam's arms deals, says that the Matrix-
Churchill–Astra combo became "totally dependent" on Iraqi business.
The British government infiltrated them with its personnel to keep an
eye on their business. In America, the Iraqis used companies called
American Steel Export Co. and Al Haddad Trading, and a Chilean with
close CIA connections called Carlos Cardeon. He was to arrange for the
sale to Iraq of cluster bombs, a weapon prohibited by the laws of war.
The United States rapped Israel on the knuckles for using them in its
1978 incursion into south Lebanon. Together with front companies on
which Israel's Mossad kept close tabs, official government arms sales by
France and the USSR gave Saddam solid support from most of the
world's main arms suppliers.[17]

Business with Saddam was made easier for the Americans by the
formal re-establishment of U.S.–Iraqi diplomatic relations on November
26, 1984. President Ronald Reagan welcomed Iraqi Foreign Minister
Tarik Azziz to the White House. The Iraqi ambassador's residence was
the scene of a lavish reception for Azziz and the cream of Washington
diplomatic society. A State Department briefing paper dated a few days
earlier stated that Iraq had suspended using chemical weapons after U.S.
remonstrances in November 1983, but had started using them again in
February the following year. By this time, the Reagan administration
was treating Iraq's use of chemical warfare as a "potentially embarrass-
ing public relations problem" (as the National Security Archive analysis
puts it), which might impede continuing U.S. military and intelligence
aid. However, Saddam's cruel and repressive human rights abuses inside
Iraq were not mentioned in the presidential directives of the period.[18]
The United States was concerned almost solely with developing its growing military clout in the Middle East, keeping the oil flowing and, of
course, protecting the interests of its Israeli partner, even when that partner, as during the clandestine arms deals with Iran of the Irangate
period, was not always the perfect ally.

Officially and publicly, official U.S. aid to Iraq was supposed to be
used for buying food. The result, however, foreshadowed Saddam's
extensive abuse of the UN's Oil-for-Food program of the 1990s,
proposed by the United States to alleviate the human suffering caused by
the UN and Western sanctions against Iraq of that period. This was
allegedly riddled with corruption and kickback deals, which came under
investigation in 2004. In the same way the "food aid" freed other funds,
which Iraq used to buy weapons. By the mid-1980s, the Atlanta, Geor-
gia, branch of the Italian Banca Nazionale di Lavoro (BNL) had
extended credits to Saddam worth well over half a billion dollars. BNL's

local manager, Christopher Drogoul, began by offering Iraq loans under the U.S. government's Commodities Credit Corporation (CCC) guidelines, amounting to a U.S. federal guarantee of private bank loans. The unsecured loans which BNL also reportedly offered Iraq amounted to over $4 billion and made it possible for Saddam to continue the war until its final bitter end for both sides in 1988. All in all, by 1988 BNL had provided Iraq's war effort with about $5 billion. As Loretta Napoleoni, the author of an informative recent book on the financing of terror, *Modern Jihad*, points out, the U.S. taxpayer ended up reimbursing some of the loans, which Saddam, of course, never paid back but which the U.S. government had guaranteed.[19]

SADDAM'S LARGESS FOR PALESTINIANS

Saddam's ideological support for Palestinian guerrilla or terrorist groups harmed Israel's efforts to keep the lid on the Arab *intifada* in the 1990s. Saddam began paying the families of "martyrs" (successful suicide bombers) as much as $25,000 each (and lesser sums to unsuccessful ones and to Arab civilian victims wounded in the conflict). In the early 1970s, quarrels between Saddam and Yassir Arafat's mainstream PLO, which had little to offer Iraq in return for its help, became so serious that Saddam closed the Baghdad offices of Al-Fatah, Arafat's own controlling organization inside the PLO. Publicly the causes were Arafat's growing willingness to tacitly accept UN resolutions for a peaceful solution of the Arab–Israel conflict, and his attempts to reach an understanding with the United States.

To punish Arafat, Saddam threw Iraqi support to Abu Nidal (Sabry al-Banna), heading a breakaway faction of Al-Fatah, and a sworn enemy of Arafat. Saddam's men waged an Iraq–PLO war in the Middle East and Europe in 1976 through 1978, marked by targeted assassinations. PLO advocates of negotiated peace with Israel, like Said Hamami in London, were murdered by Abu Nidal's men or by direct agents of Saddam. On June 3, 1981, a Palestinian gunman apparently linked with Abu Nidal wounded the Israeli Ambassador to Britain, Shlomo Argov, in London. Israel blamed Arafat's mainstream PLO. This was an important trigger for the Israeli invasion of Lebanon a few days later.

By 1983, Saddam was showing his appreciation for American aid by toning down his anti-Israel rhetoric and initiating various secret but unsuccessful contacts to offer Israel an olive branch. Saddam tried to please the Reagan White House and such players as Weinberger and Richard Murphy, and to counter criticism from U.S. congressmen. He expelled Abu Nidal from Baghdad, and ordered other Palestinian groups based in Baghdad, including Iraq's own homegrown creation, the Palestine Liberation Front, to halt their activities.

Abu Nidal, at various other times sheltered by Syria and Libya, had received, as a reward for his hostility to Arafat and willingness to carry out hits for Saddam, $4 million of Al-Fatah's assets, about $15 million in arms and a bonus of $5 million after Al-Fatah formally passed a death sentence against him. During his sojourn in Baghdad, Abu Nidal brokered weapons and services between Iraq and other armed groups. Shortly after the outset of the Iran–Iraq war, he had offered to supply Iraq with Soviet-made Polish T-72 tanks. Saddam authorized a down payment of $11 million to Abu Nidal, which he immediately deposited in a Swiss bank account. When the Iraqis decided to cancel the tank deal and asked him to procure artillery instead, Abu Nidal could not deliver—but kept the down payment. This was one of the mistakes that led to his expulsion to Syria, where he continued to make profitable arms deals with both sides in the Iran–Iraq war. [20]

GOOD COP, BAD COP

Israeli analyst Ofra Bengio has thoroughly analyzed the ambiguity that Saddam displayed toward Israel during the long war with Iraq, and Washington's parallel flirtation with Saddam. The destruction of Osirak had been a grave "moral, military and political blow for Iraq," she wrote in 1998. It had opened a "strategic account" between Baghdad and Jerusalem, damaging the Ba'athist regime's prestige and its symbol of power projection outside Iraq, the Iraqi armed forces, which had been powerless to prevent the attack. (She might have added that it was also decisive in crippling the Iraqi armed forces' hopes for obtaining a nuclear option in the future.) In 1948, 1967, and 1973, Iraq had taken the military initiative in joining the Arab wars against the Jewish state. However, the Osirak attack had given the initiative back to Israel. Saddam was made to understand, if he had not realized it earlier, that Israel was a real strategic threat to Iraq. At the same time, Israel was more or less openly, with American approval, selling arms to Iran, while Israeli leaders were declaring publicly that they supported prolonging the Iran–Iraq war so that both these adversaries would be seriously, if not fatally, weakened.

At the same time, there was a parallel, more cautious line in Saddam's policies. The prolonged conflict with Iran had compelled him to seek all the support he could find inside and outside Iraq. It had diverted his energies away from the Arab–Israel conflict. Saddam now realized that a less strident tone toward Israel was part of the price he must pay for better relations with the United States. He possibly hoped to discourage Israeli arms sales to Iran, and to receive the necessary tacit agreement of Israel to the projected oil pipeline from northern Iraq to Aqaba (which, despite the wheeling and dealing described above, had to be dropped as Bechtel and other interested private companies decided that it was too much of a risk). "Israelis," as people (not the state of Israel, as some media mistranslated Saddam's words) were entitled, he said on January 7, 1983 to "conditions of security" (*wad' min al-aman*). This statement was made to visiting U.S. congressman Stephen Solarz, highly influential in the American foreign-policy establishment at the time. Foreign Minister Tarik Azziz and Iraqi Ambassador to the United States Nizar Hamdoun stated that Iraq would not oppose a peaceful settlement to the Palestinian problem and did not want a new Arab–Israel war. Later, there were rumors of secret contacts between Iraq and Israel, especially in 1987. Reports of these contacts came from Hussein Kamel Hassan, Saddam Hussein's cousin and son-in-law, who defected to Jordan in August 1995. Kamel Hassan asserted that the first such (unsuccessful) Iraqi approach to Israel had been made as early as 1978.

Uncertainty about Saddam's attitude toward Israel during the final years and months of the Iran–Iraq war in 1987 and 1988 caused some senior Israeli leaders, notably Shimon Peres, then a deputy prime minister, to reassess Israel's policy. Peres and those who thought like him argued that Prime Minister David Ben-Gurion's early policy of the 1950s of cementing alliances where possible with non-Arab regional countries, like Turkey, Ethiopia, or the Shah's Iran, had become anachronistic. Despite the covert dealings of Nimrodi and figures in the Reagan administration like Colonel Oliver North and Admiral John Poindexter, who had promoted the "arms for hostages" deals through Israeli middlemen (and later directly) with revolutionary Iran, Iran's hostility to Israel had not lessened. A more pro-Iraqi stance, they speculated, might help the Arab–Israel peace process. The first Palestinian *intifada*, which had begun in Gaza in 1987, was drawing more world attention to this process. Gestures toward Iraq during its growing exhaustion from the war might move Saddam, Peres believed, to reciprocate by a more conciliatory stance toward Israel. The meager signals of possible conciliation from Baghdad, they argued, might be the first signs of such a stance.

Saddam's own words and above all his actions soon gave the lie to this Israeli theory. Nevertheless, the lingering hope among some Israelis that Saddam might be someone "whom you could do business with" was a cause for the shock suffered by these wishful thinkers when Saddam hit Israel with missiles during Operation Desert Storm in 1991.

Signs of Saddam's true intentions toward Israel had rarely been lacking. Right after the Israeli raid on the Osirak nuclear reactor in June 1981, Saddam Hussein blustered that Iraq would not be discouraged by the attack. Instead, he said, it would "transform lessons into programs." He openly called on other countries to help the Arabs to acquire "atomic bombs." Broadcasts by Baghdad Radio, which I was able to follow during my months of research that summer at the Carnegie Endowment in Washington, quoted Saddam as asserting that Iraq had already approached "friendly" countries. (These probably included Pakistan, Brazil, and Argentina; the latter was already cooperating with Iraq in trying to develop the long-range Condor missile.) It had asked for their help in acquiring a "kind of weapon that would make Israel hesitant to implement a strike."

Eight years later, with the war with Iran well behind him, Saddam was snarling at Israel again. Official Iraqi newspapers on March 14 and March 29, 1989, boasted that Iraq already possessed "long-range missiles capable of reaching the Zionist entity and destroying it in its strategic depth." One such commentary predicted that Israel would no longer exist by the end of the twentieth century.

A year later, in the run-up to his August 1990 invasion of Kuwait, Saddam hardened his threatening rhetoric to such a degree that resulting alarm bells ringing in Jerusalem were loud enough to echo in Washington. If Israel made any hostile moves against Iraq, Saddam said in April 1990, Iraq would make "the fire [from its chemical weapons] eat up half of Israel."[21]

The new decade would see the start of Saddam's decline and fall. This, and the tighter-than-ever lacing of the military, political, and ideological bonds between the United States and Israel in the Middle East, are our next concerns.

10

From Jerusalem to Washington:
An Alliance Strengthened and Confirmed

*And this is the writing that was inscribed: MENE, MENE, TEKEL
and PARSIN ... God has numbered the days of your kingdom and
brought it to an end; you have been weighed in the balances and
found wanting; your kingdom is divided and given to the Medes and
the Persians.*

*(The Jewish prophet Daniel to King Belshazzar of Babylon;
the Book of Daniel 6:24–28)*

Once the Iran–Iraq war had ended with both countries greatly weakened, Western strategic planners breathed a sigh of relief. In Israel, the
relief was qualified. The Israeli intelligence establishment believed that
in any new wider Arab–Israel war, Iraq would again send an expeditionary force and, this time, also provide WMD for an Arab "Eastern
Front," allied with Syria and Jordan. Such an Iraqi force was seen as
hypothetically more dangerous than those of 1948, 1967, or even 1973.
Iraq, like Iran, had suffered well over a half million dead and disabled.
But at least on paper, it still had sizeable forces. It could field ten or more
armored or mechanized divisions and a serious striking force of missiles
and aircraft, all, the Israeli analysts believed, armed with chemical and
biological weapons.

Another Israeli concern was that an Iraqi–Jordanian alliance could
emerge and bring a massive Iraqi troop deployment into Jordan. By the
first half of 1989, Israeli intelligence, doubtless aided by American satellite surveillance, was spotting visits by senior Iraqi officers along the
Jordan–Iraqi frontier, intelligence cooperation between Amman and Baghdad, and Jordanian fighters escorting Iraqi air force photo-reconnaissance
missions.

Top military commanders such as Reserve Major General Avraham
Tamir, former IDF Planning Branch director, had been suggesting that
Israel should give up the Iranian part of its old doctrine of using "periph-
eral" allies and stop backing Iran in its war with Iraq. Iran, they
believed, was henceforth a bigger threat to Israel than Iraq. Some senior
Israelis, probably including Shimon Peres, wishfully thought that

Saddam could be weaned away from the Arab "rejectionists," and won over to the concept of a comprehensive Arab–Israel peace settlement. General Tamir reportedly took part in secret talks in 1988 and 1989 with Iraqi Foreign Minister Tarik Azziz, Deputy Prime Minister Saadoun Hammadi, deputy foreign minister Nizar Hamdoun and a fourth senior Iraqi, probably Saddam's half-brother, Barzan al-Tikriti, in private homes of "friends" in New York and Europe. (Kurdish sources, without other confirmation, reported that Barzan, as Iraqi delegate to the United Nations in Geneva, was a channel of communication between U.S. President George Herbert Walker Bush and Saddam in 1991, following the Kuwait war.) Nothing substantial came of the reported Tamir talks.[1]

MISSILES, "SUPERGUNS," AND PROFITS

During this period, Israeli and Western intelligence analysts worried about Saddam's efforts to buy and develop superguns and long-range missiles. Iraqi work with Canadian, Argentine, German, and other foreign technicians to develop and construct these weapons had largely failed. However, the Soviet Union had supplied Iraq with several hundred Scud missiles, used against Iran during the Iran–Iraq war. In May 1987, the United States destroyer *Stark* had been struck and severely damaged in the Gulf at night by two "accidentally" fired missiles, probably French Exocets, from an Iraqi jet. This was the period when the U.S. Navy, to help Iraq, was escorting Kuwaiti ships with cargoes vital to the Iraqi war effort and was subject to frequent attack by Iranian aircraft or fast missile boats. Thirty-seven U.S. seamen had been killed and dozens of others injured on the *Stark*.[2] The destroyer was eventually repaired, and mourning families of the U.S. Navy victims eventually prevailed on the Reagan administration to obtain an apology from Iraq for its "error," as well as some financial compensation.

While the United States wrestled with its new, late twentieth century role as primary sea power in the Persian Gulf, Israel's intelligence services focused on Iraq's real and prospective WMDs. In 1987 Hussein Kamel, Saddam's son-in-law, then largely in charge of armaments, and his smooth, cultured deputy, senior Iraqi scientist Amir al-Saadi, whose fluent English and amiable manner became familiar to millions of Western TV viewers during the run-up to the 2003 war, approached Canadian tycoon Gerald Bull. They knew of his genius in fields like ballistic missiles, re-entry vehicles for space programs, and other branches of weapons technology in which Bull had served not only his own Canada but also the U.S. Pentagon and South Africa. Bull was also a lecturer to Israel's military on high-tech weaponry.

After discussions in Iraq about improving the range of Saddam's Scud missiles and design of a three-stage space rocket to launch satellites, Bull told his Iraqi hosts that for about $3 million he could make a "super-gun" that would dwarf designs being considered by the Pentagon and that could launch satellites for Iraq and other Arab states. Saddam had already invested over $200 million in Saad 16, his missile project. U.S. companies supplied some of the equipment for it. France, Italy, Japan, and Britain had chipped in too. A German–Austrian company, Gilde-meister, was reportedly the main builder. However, in April 1987 the United States, Canada, France, West Germany, Italy, Japan, and Britain signed the Missile Technology Control agreement, which banned the export of most missiles and their components. Amir al-Saadi apparently convinced Bull that Israel, not included in the agreement, now enjoyed an unfair advantage over the Arabs. Under Bull's general supervision, Iraq placed orders abroad through intermediaries for the 350-mile range Supergun parts, and assembly work was begun. Israeli intelligence began to shadow Bull and his family. From 1988 to 1990, during the run-up to Iraq's invasion of Kuwait, other agencies cooperated with Israel in inter-cepting and "interdicting" Iraq's efforts to obtain WMDs. In March 1990, U.S. Customs agents impounded a shipment of nuclear bomb detonators called "krytrons" in an international sting operation. Two British companies were involved.

In April 1990, Bull's Supergun project was blocked when British, Ital-ian, Turkish, and Greek police seized shipments of huge steel tubes destined for its barrel. Executives in the British steel firms of Sheffield Forgemasters Ltd. and Walter Somers Ltd. were later charged in British courts with assisting in illegal arms exports to Iraq. After delivering several polite but pointed warnings to Bull to cease his work, several individuals—Mossad agents, according to European news reports widely copied in the Israeli media—sent one or more gunmen to his home in Belgium on March 22, 1990, where they murdered him with five bullets in his head, neck, and back.[3]

The failure of the expensive Iraqi missile program and the aborting of the Supergun project were serious setbacks for Saddam. But it was commonplace for Western media to assert that Iraq had the world's fourth-largest military, with about 800 combat aircraft and over 5,000 tanks. The USSR had sold Iraq around $10 billion worth of weapons since the 1960s. When the U.S.-led coalition went to war again with Iraq in 2003, Iraq still owed Russia for most of them. France had sold about

$5 billion in arms; Britain over $1 billion and American companies around $5 billion. German Foreign Minister Hans-Dietrich Genscher, without citing monetary values, was first to come clean. He acknowledged that German technicians had helped extend the range of Iraq's Scud missiles so that they could reach Israel (which they soon did, in February of 1991). Official investigations in Germany would eventually find that up to 110 German companies had violated UN restrictions on arms exports to Baghdad.[4]

SADDAM BREWS THE KUWAIT CRISIS

By the time the Kuwait crisis broke in 1990, Saddam, like the Babylonian ruler Belshazzar in the Old Testament, should have seen the handwriting on the wall: signals of determined opposition, first in Israel, then in the West. If he saw them, he did not heed them. At the start of 1990, Iraq began accusing Kuwait and Saudi Arabia of deliberately overproducing oil and so lowering the world price. Iraqi revenue was being cut by the amount needed to service the country's huge arms debt, about $7 billion each year. Such ominous data did not stop U.S. Assistant Secretary of State John Kelly from visiting Saddam in Baghdad on February 12, 1990, and assuring him that the George H. W. Bush administration considered him a "force for moderation" and wanted to improve relations. However, at an Arab conference in Amman on February 24, 1990, Saddam angrily called on the United States to remove its navy—which only two years earlier had been protecting and defending Iraq's maritime and commercial interests— from the Gulf. He denounced U.S. support for Israel and called on the Arab states to set up an action plan to create a pan-Arab power base that could confront the West and Israel. This speech was far less heeded in Washington than Saddam's April 2 threat to burn "half of Israel" with his chemical weapons if Israel struck at Iraq's "metallurgical plants" (read weapons industries and stockpiles).

The Bush administration was distracted by the German unification process then underway and by preparations for a Bush–Gorbachev summit meeting. On April 12, Senator Robert Dole of Kansas led a bipartisan Senate delegation to Baghdad. Dole expressed concern over Saddam's WMD programs, but reassured him that a Voice of America journalist who had written an editorial harshly criticizing Saddam had been fired. President George H. W. Bush and Secretary of State James Baker, both close to the U.S. oil industry, seem to have judged that there was no serious threat of war.[5]

At the end of June, ABC News' *Prime Time Live* program, largely through my personal intervention with King Hussein, who often talked with Saddam and who knew that a serious crisis was brewing, obtained an interview with Saddam. The King phoned someone at the top in Baghdad (probably either Saddam himself or Tarik Azziz) and set it up. This was almost the first time Saddam had been interviewed on American TV since 1979. ABC News sent Diane Sawyer, one of its star commentators, with a huge entourage including three full camera crews, a director, engineers, and field producers to Baghdad. I traveled with them and was allowed to watch, but was not able to take part, nor was I consulted in the editing of the finished program. In 1987 I had met Vice-President Taha Yassine Ramdan who complained bitterly that the United States and Israel were two-timing Iraq with their covert aid to Iran in the war, but I had never before met with Saddam. When our ABC team shook hands with him before a festive luncheon table, then had to stand in a big group photo with Saddam in the middle, I felt cold chills at Saddam's ironic smile and baleful stare. It seemed to go right through you, and yet was focused somewhere in a void far beyond.

Saddam, with his interpreter beside him, responded to Diane Sawyer's questions on camera for over two hours, with only two brief pauses. The *Prime Time Live* staff had researched the questions carefully. Saddam answered everything, without referring to briefing notes or to senior advisers present. To brutally candid questions, such as "Is it true that you have killed former friends and associates with your own hands," he answered crisply. (That question he answered with a curt "no," which was of course a lie. He caused a ripple of grim though muted amusement among us when asked, "Why do you execute Ba'athists who leave the party?"; he responded, "We only execute the military ones".)

Crucial questions about his bitter quarrel with Kuwait, including Iraq's old territorial claim, complaints about oil prices and accusations that Kuwait was "stealing" Iraqi oil by horizontal drilling under the frontier into Iraq's part of the border-straddling Rumaila oilfield, he answered carefully and often in detail. When the interview was over and we had to pack up and head for the airport (our welcome ran out with completion of the interview), I left with the chilly conviction that Saddam fully intended to make war on Kuwait. I returned to my London base and the piece was edited down in New York to a program of no more than about 20 minutes. The questions about Saddam's personal actions, such as executing friends, were used in the program that was aired about a week later. However, many of his responses about substantive issues with Kuwait and others were omitted. This deprived viewers of a pretty clear idea of what he intended. As we flew out of Baghdad, I was distressed because we were not being allowed to see U.S. Ambassador April Glaspie, an old friend of mine, who desperately wanted and needed briefing on the meeting with Saddam. Her frustration was heightened because, when she went into her well-publicized meeting with Saddam on July 25, ABC News had refused to provide the crucial cuts from the interview on substantive war-and-peace issues. It was the network's firm policy never to release the "out-takes" or cuts from a program to anyone. As April told me later in Jerusalem, where her eclipse from favor in Washington had landed her a temporary job running UNWRA, the UN's relief agency for Palestinian refugees, in her July 25 meeting with Saddam she had to simply follow instructions cabled by James Baker.

Months later, when the State Department allowed April to break her long, officially imposed silence, causing her to be blamed for giving Saddam a "green light" to invade Kuwait, she appeared before the Senate Foreign Relations Committee. The Iraqi transcript of the July 25 meeting, she said, was edited by the Iraqis before release, deleting references to warnings she had given Saddam against using violence to resolve problems with Kuwait. During their conversation Saddam had received a phone call from Egyptian President Hosni Mubarak. Saddam promised Mubarak not to attack Kuwait. This, too, was cut from the Iraqi transcript.[6]

ISRAEL AND "DESERT STORM"

The diplomatic background to the war and the neglected intelligence warnings that foretold it have been amply related elsewhere. What must concern us here is the Israeli role (and in certain respects, the Israeli non-role) in the six-month run-up to Operation Desert Storm and during the war itself, January–March 1991.

From the beginning of the crisis, Saddam had tried to draw Israel into his confrontation with Kuwait. In Baghdad on August 9, 1990, a week after the invasion, Yassir Arafat and Abu Iyad (Salah Khalaf) of the PLO tried vainly to persuade Saddam to attend a summit of 20 Arab heads of state in Cairo on the next day. Saddam blustered that if the Arabs pressured him to withdraw from Kuwait, he would draw Israel into the war and so split the Arab coalition. "From the moment I am attacked," he said, "I will attack Israel. ... This aggression against Iraq will then be perceived as an American–Zionist plot." Saddam did not attend. The summit polarized the tension. The meeting, which this reporter covered, was so vitriolic that at lunch Taha Yassine Ramadan of Iraq threw a plate at Crown Prince Saad of Kuwait, narrowly missing him. In angry but less lethal exchanges, other delegates threw bread at each other and one Kuwaiti minister fainted with shock. The final resolution, calling for Saddam to withdraw his troops from Kuwait, was, some delegates charged, drafted by the Americans in English at the U.S. Embassy and hastily translated into somewhat awkward Arabic.[7]

Throughout the run-up to war, Saddam Hussein insisted publicly that he was linking the Kuwait problem to the Arab–Israeli conflict, and that its solution was tied to the continuing Israeli occupation of Palestinian land. He demanded the lifting of the newly-imposed UN sanctions and embargoes on Iraq, and that pan-Arab forces should replace the U.S. troops now pouring into Saudi Arabia. In Israel, Prime Minister Yitzhak Shamir denounced Saddam's linkage talk as a "maneuver to weaken the international alliance against him [Saddam]." In October, Saddam tried to exploit new violence that had erupted in Jerusalem when Israeli police fired on rioting Arabs at the Temple Mount, sacred to both Arabs and Jews. In a speech Saddam claimed Iraq possessed a missile he called al-Hajira (the stone). This referred to the stones Palestinian demonstrators in the first *intifada* or uprising against the occupation were throwing at Israeli security forces. He repeated warnings that he would hit Israel if he were attacked.

Israel now found itself in an uncomfortable position vis-à-vis its ally, the United States, and its old enemy, Iraq. President Bush and Secretary of State Baker had been angered by Israeli settlement policies in the occupied territories. Israel felt itself seriously threatened by Saddam's Scuds. Israeli schoolchildren had begun the 1990–91 year with chemical-warfare drills and gas-mask instruction. Since January 1990, General Danny Rothschild, deputy director of military intelligence, had been following closely the movement of Scud missile launchers into the "H-2" and "H-3" base areas of Western Iraq, from where the Scuds could reach Haifa, Jerusalem, and Tel Aviv. General Dan Shomron, the IDF Chief of Staff, said he believed that if the Israeli air force flew strike missions against the Scud launchers in western Iraq, Saddam—unlike after the Osirak attack in 1989—would retaliate. However, if Israel did not hit the Scuds, Shomron told the mass-circulation newspaper *Yediot Aharanot* after Saddam's speech, Iraq was less likely to attack Israel. Washington heard and appreciated Shomron's remark, and April Glaspie passed it on to Tarik Azziz.

Bush–Shamir political relations, as well as Israeli–American military ties, were difficult at the time. At one meeting in April 1990, the

American side blamed the Israelis for "overestimating" the Iraqi threat. David Ivri, who as a pilot had led the Osirak operation and was now director-general of the Israeli Defense Ministry, warned his Pentagon colleagues to pay closer attention to Iraq. On July 19, Defense Minister Moshe Arens met his counterpart, Defense Secretary Dick Cheney, in Washington. Arens showed Cheney what he said was evidence of Saddam's progress since the Osirak attack in enriching uranium to weapons-grade level. Cheney became an advocate of stronger cooperation with Israel. In August 1990, Ivri reportedly asked Cheney, in effect, to "forgive and forget" the savage Israeli attack on the U.S. intelligence ship *Liberty* off the Sinai coast during the June 1967 war, which Israel has always insisted was a "mistake." Ivri asked Cheney to start providing Israel with "real-time" data from U.S. spy satellites and an exchange of the two countries' aircraft identification, or IFF ("identification friend or foe") codes, to avoid tragic misunderstandings or accidents during combat or other periods of stress. Cheney apparently did not agree to either request.

The Temple Mount violence in Jerusalem in October and the tough Israeli response, which U.S. Ambassador to the UN Thomas Pickering on October 8 joined the other members of the Security Council in condemning, further muddied Israeli–U.S. waters. Sensing this, Saddam continued his anti-Israel rhetoric and threats. In December 1990, shortly before Christmas, he temporarily recalled his ambassadors from Washington, Tokyo, and major capitals in Europe and elsewhere. On December 28, he declared himself ready for "serious and constructive dialogue," but continued to link any discussions about his withdrawal from Kuwait to negotiations over Israeli withdrawal from the West Bank and Gaza.

On a Saturday evening at Christmastime, Deputy Secretary of State Lawrence Eagleburger, viewed favorably by Shamir's advisers, visited the Israeli prime minister at his Jerusalem home to impress upon him Bush's urgent wish that Israel, despite its strategic and defensive concerns, not initiate a preemptive strike on Iraq. In return, Eagleburger said, Washington would consider any Iraqi attack on Israel as a *casus belli* and reply in kind. To show serious U.S. concern, two Patriot advanced anti-missile or anti-aircraft batteries would be urgently shipped to Israel. "Hammer Rick," the code name for a secret communications link between Defense Secretary Cheney and Israeli Defense Minister Arens would be installed. U.S. Army Major General Mack Armstrong would be the new liaison with Israeli Chief of Staff General Avihu Bin-Nun, replacing a Central Command air force officer. Some Israelis believed the U.S. Central Command, based in Tampa, Florida, was less responsive to

Israeli needs than officers from Washington or the European Command, with whom Israel ordinarily liased on military matters.[8]

At about 2:04 a.m. Baghdad time (7:04 p.m. Eastern time in the United States) on January 16, the initial air phase of Operation Desert Storm was launched against Iraq. Waves of U.S. and British planes, and cruise missiles fired from U.S. and Allied warships in the Gulf thundered down on Baghdad and Iraq's other main cities and defense installations. Few Iraqi planes managed to get off the ground to challenge the attackers. Saddam chose to respond early on the next day, January 17, as he had promised, with an attack against Israel—but with missiles, not planes. Seven Scud missiles landed in Tel Aviv and Haifa. Another hit near Dhahran, Saudi Arabia. In Israel, air raid sirens wailed. Israeli radio directed families to put on gas masks and get into shelters they had prepared by sealing rooms with plastic sheets against poison gas. It was seriously believed that Saddam would keep his promise of chemical attack. After all, had he not already done so repeatedly against Iranian troops and had he not killed over 5,000 Kurds at Halabja and other places in Iraqi Kurdistan? During the first week of the air war in January 1990, Saddam's Scuds killed four and injured over 120 people.

The Pentagon rushed several batteries of the 17-foot long Patriot missiles with their launchers and U.S. crews to Israel. Although there had been plenty of U.S. military and naval maneuvers with Israel since the 1950s, this was the first time American GIs had directly defended Israeli territory. The Patriots, as Israel's veteran military historian, Ze'ev Schiff, recalled to me in February 2004, were hardly a brilliant success. Fragments of a few of the total of 39 Scuds fired at Israel that the Patriots did intercept caused ground damage and casualties. Some of the Scud warheads separated from the missiles in the air, and either caused ground damage or, if unexploded, had to be destroyed by ordnance crews. Near Dhahran, Saudi Arabia, two Patriots launched themselves, damaging buildings. Another, while chasing an incoming Scud, damaged an insurance agency in Riyad.

Defense Minister Moshe Arens promised on January 18 that Israel "will react, certainly." President Bush sent Eagleburger to Israel again, and by January 21 he confirmed Israel had promised to work with the United States and consult Washington before taking any unilateral action. On January 22 Israeli Foreign Minister David Levy said the United States would give Israel battle reports, logistical data, and, finally, "real time" satellite reconnaissance data coordinated by a "joint apparatus." Israeli Finance Minister Yitzhak Modai told Eagleburger that Israel wanted no less than $13 billion more than the annual $3 billion it was already getting in U.S. economic and military aid to meet Gulf war losses, including property destroyed and over 100 Israelis wounded up to mid-February 1991, and, to help absorb the waves of Jewish immigrants taking advantage of Mikhail Gorbachev's policies of *glasnost* and *perestroika* to come to the Jewish state.[9]

During the early Scud attacks, Defense Secretary Dick Cheney phoned Arens, as well as Prime Minister Shamir. Cheney told Shamir by phone that the United States could not give the Israeli air force the IFF codes used by the Allied air forces based in Saudi Arabia, which Israel wanted in case it responded to Iraqi attack. (If it had the codes it would not shoot down U.S. and Allied planes, not would its own aircraft be shot down by them.) If Washington would not provide Israel with the codes, Arens asked, would the Bush administration permit the Israelis to use a safe air corridor across Jordan where they would not risk hostile encounters with Allied planes? Eagleburger assured Shamir that the Allied coalition would take out the Scud missiles and launchers in western Iraq without need for Israeli action. While the Arens–Shamir talks were underway, General Bin-Nun had ordered Israeli fighter aircraft to scramble in a defensive mode to protect Jerusalem. Bin-Nun believed that Saddam would use his best Sukhoi-14 jets to hit Jerusalem, but would not risk firing Scuds at the city as that risked hitting Arab East Jerusalem or its holy Al-Aqsa Mosque. (Although no Scuds did hit Jerusalem, there were eyewitness reports of Arabs in East Jerusalem and in Ramallah, Nablus, and elsewhere in the occupied territories cheering at the westbound tracks of the incoming Scuds in the night skies.)

A few minutes after the Cheney–Arens conversation, President Bush phoned Prime Minister Shamir, who had informed Cheney that the Scud attack on south Tel Aviv was not chemical. Bush repeated his urgent request not to retaliate against Iraq, because that was what Saddam was hoping for. Shamir listened without comment. Hours later, General Bin-Nun argued for retaliation. Arguing against were Chief of Staff Shomron, and Shomron's deputy, Ehud Barak (who would later succeed him as chief and then become prime minister in the later 1990s, only to fail to conclude a comprehensive peace with Yassir Arafat during President Bill Clinton's second term). After hearing all the arguments for and against retaliation, Shamir ruled against it. He told his colleagues that what Saddam wanted was to transform Desert Storm into a war between Israel and all of the Arabs. The U.S.-led coalition was about to defeat or perhaps even destroy one of Israel's most dangerous enemies. Why, he argued, spoil that by bringing about a bloody Arab–Israel confrontation, which might also destroy the useful monarchy in Jordan?[10]

Shamir's decision became final and binding: no Israeli retaliation. It was up to the Americans—as it would be later to the Americans of the George W. Bush administration in 2003—to take care of knocking out Saddam and his war machine.

TARGET: SADDAM HUSSEIN

The personal targeting and assassination of Saddam did cross the minds of some of the American planners as an American war aim in 1991—as it did again in 2003, until the Americans, with help from Kurdish allies finally captured Saddam alive in a hole in the ground in his native Tikriti region in December of that year. As far back as September 1990, former U.S. Air Force Chief of Staff General Michael J. Dugan explicitly suggested that Saddam Hussein should be killed. Defense Secretary Dick Cheney immediately dismissed Dugan. As a reason Cheney cited an executive order prohibiting assassination (or even the planning of assassination) of foreign leaders—an order which had aimed at halting CIA involvement in plots to assassinate adversarial foreign leaders like Cuba's Fidel Castro on numerous occasions or the Congo's Patrice Lumumba in the 1960s.[11]

KUWAIT FREED: SADDAM SPARED

Desert Storm, in its ground phase, lasted just 100 hours. Kuwait was freed, though devastated and covered by billowing black smoke from hundreds of oil wells set afire on Saddam's orders by the retreating Iraqis. This was an environmental disaster from which Kuwait and surrounding Gulf regions have never completely recovered. The war had cost around 150 Allied dead and several hundred wounded, and many thousands of Iraqi military dead along with hundreds of civilian. Israeli planners, as well as many Western observers, were frustrated by President George H. W. Bush's failure to order Desert Storm's supreme commander, General Norman Schwarzkopf Jr., to destroy the Iraqi armed forces once they had evacuated Kuwait, or to march on Baghdad and kill, capture, or otherwise neutralize Saddam Hussein.

Instead, Bush senior and his men had made statements and broadcasts encouraging the Kurdish and Shia populations of Iraq to revolt. In March, however, they failed to help them against Saddam's once demoralized, but now regrouped loyalist forces. In the ceasefire that ended the war, the Iraqis had been allowed to keep their surviving military helicopters, nominally for "transportation" only. As gunships, the choppers became an instrument of merciless repression that killed hundreds of the unsuccessful Shia rebels in the south and Kurdish insurgents in the north. Thousands of refugees flooded into Turkey, Syria, and Iran. The United States and Britain, assisted for a short period by France (which as part of the Bush coalition had sent in ground troops in the final hours of the war), set up "no-fly zones" in northern and southern Iraq, initially to protect the populations from Saddam's vengeance, and forbade his aircraft to use these regions. Later, Iraqi ground defenses and many other targets were hit, sometimes on an almost daily basis throughout the 1990s, softening up the already gravely wounded Iraqi military establishment for what was to be its ultimate destruction in March and April of 2003 by the U.S.–British invasion.

Israel's planners, however, resented the fact that President George H. W. Bush had saved Saddam Hussein by not pursuing the war all the way to Baghdad and by not supporting the Iraqi insurgents (among whom were military officers and some entire units). Above all, the Israelis reasoned, as long as Saddam himself survived, and could command the loyalty of his family, the Tikriti clan, and several divisions of surviving Republican Guards and other loyalist troops, Iraq was still a potential, if diminished, strategic threat to Israel, just as it had been ever since 1948.

So, in 1991, right after the Kuwait war, during the watch of Yitzhak Rabin—destined to be briefly hailed in 1983, before his assassination by a Jewish extremist, as the "peace partner" (with Shimon Peres) of Arafat after the Oslo accords—secret planning began in Israel to assassinate Saddam Hussein, using Israel's elite army commando forces.

Several Israeli journalists, notably Ze'ev Schiff, the chronicler of Mossad's exploits, Uri Dan, and Leslie Susser of *The Jerusalem Report*, reconstructed the story once strict Israeli censorship on it had been lifted. In April 1991 Defense Minister Moshe Arens, "furious," as Susser wrote, at what he bitterly described as the U.S. failure to "finish the job," appointed General Ehud Barak as army Chief of Staff. Barak had the idea, Schiff and others assert, to kill Saddam. Some sources say that this was to be done with "plausible deniability" so that Israel could not be directly blamed. To succeed, the murder project required top-grade intelligence on Saddam's movements and whereabouts. This would have had to come from Saddam's inner circle. Ground troops of the elite Sayaret Metkal, commandos armed with short-range missiles, would have to be flown into an area, most likely western Iraq, which Saddam was known to frequent.

There was an immediate precedent. Israel's leadership has never been inhibited by the same kind of legislation or orders forbidding assassinations of enemy leaders that restricted U.S. forces until the catastrophic terrorist attacks of 9/11 by Osama bin Laden's Al-Qaeda. On February 15, 1992, Barak got Arens' approval for assassination of the Hizbollah official Abbas Musawi in southern Lebanon. Musawi was killed the next day in his car by an Israeli air strike—the method that would be used with lethal effect against Palestinian Hamas leader Sheikh Ahmed Yassine in Gaza on March 23, 2004, and against many other Arab enemies. Barak thought such a strike on Saddam might work. But Rabin was not so sure. Ze'ev Schiff is not certain that the more cautious and hesitant Rabin would have given his final approval to execute the operation. However, he did approve the planning and training.

It was apparently decided to use an Israeli-made missile with a miniature camera fitted to its nose that visually guides the missile to its target. The plan was to airlift the Sayaret Metkal unit to the near vicinity of Saddam's hometown of Tikrit. Saddam was expected to attend the funeral there of his father-in-law, who was dying from complications of diabetes. Before Rabin could finally approve or disapprove, there was a fatal accident at the desert training base of Tze'elim on November 5, 1992, in Barak's presence and during what was probably a final rehearsal of what could have been a potential suicide mission for the Israeli soldiers involved. A "guided" missile went off course, killing five of the Sayaret soldiers. Journalist Dan Baron of the Jewish Telegraph Agency says that it was reported that Barak left the scene as medics arrived. An investigation cleared Barak of any criminal culpability, since his command responsibilities were required elsewhere, but the memory, Baron claims, constantly haunted him afterward. Ironically, one of the survivors of the botched rehearsal was Eyal Katvan, the soldier "playing" Saddam. He was hospitalized with serious injuries. Uri Dan believes that "it was natural" for Rabin to inform President George H. W. Bush about the plan to kill Saddam before the November 1991 presidential election, which Bush lost to Bill Clinton. The weapons inspections in Iraq by UN teams had already begun, and accusations (justified at the time) were being made that Saddam was concealing his leftover weapons.[12]

This author has found no record of any further direct Israeli attempts on Saddam's life. And even as Rabin, Shimon Peres, and later Ehud Barak, under the auspices of two Clinton administrations, tried to reach either an interim or final peace settlement with the Palestinians, it was Washington's turn to use the CIA and whatever indigenous Iraqis it could find to cooperate in efforts to destroy Saddam's regime—and the dictator himself.

CLINTON'S CONTAINMENT; THE CIA'S BUNGLES

Between 1992 and 1996, the Clinton administration failed to follow up the huge military and diplomatic leverage the victory in Desert Storm had given over Saddam's Iraq. It was a period of attempts to organize covert action, and of contingency military planning. Diplomatic and economic efforts, described by major Clinton administration players like Secretary of State Madeleine Albright as "containment" of Saddam or "keeping him in his box," were ineffectual and indecisive. Equally indecisive was wishful thinking that Iraq might somehow, at last, be brought in from the cold to join in the ultra-slow-motion Israeli–Palestine "peace process."

That peace process, beginning with the Madrid peace conference in October 1991, was launched by the Bush–Baker planners in Washington in order to work toward what was hoped would be a final settlement of the Israeli–Palestinian dispute. Saddam Hussein's propaganda was describing Iraq's crushing defeat in what Saddam had called "the mother of all battles" in Kuwait as a victory. Later, official Iraqi commentators in Baghdad media outlets like *Babil*, a newspaper owned by Saddam's son Uday and the Ba'ath's official *Al-Thawra*, recognized that Madrid and its aftermath were facilitated by Iraq's own defeat and at Iraq's expense. Government publications republished that phoney and scurrilous old anti-Semitic document, *The Protocols of the Elders of Zion*, linking them to President Bush senior's 1990 Desert Storm exhortation to found a "new world order." Uday Hussein published a series of articles finding support for the old Arab rejectionist challenge to Israel's right to exist in the Koran. Uday insisted that strategically, time favored the Arabs and that "extinction of the Zionist entity was a necessity dictated both by the will of God and the need to recover exclusive Arab rights in Palestine." The Iraqi media blasted the stage in the Oslo peace process called the Gaza–Jericho agreement of August 20, 1993, establishing partial Palestinian control in the occupied territories.

Oslo deprived Saddam of his old claims of pan-Arab leadership. It also raised fears among Saddam's entourage that the "autonomy" accorded to the Palestinian Authority might set an example for recognizing a similar Kurdish entity in northern Iraq. Saddam's media branded the whole Oslo process as a disaster for the Arabs even greater than what Sadat had brought about by his 1979 peace treaty with Menachem Begin. As a result, Saddam's mouthpieces added, Arafat the "traitor" should meet Sadat's fate: assassination. Economically, the Iraqi line was that Israeli–American plans called for a "new Middle Eastern market." Arab states would be turned into "economic and political colonies in a Greater Israel from the Euphrates to the Nile." Arab countries were seen to be trying to circumvent the post-Desert Storm economic and trade boycotts of Iraq imposed by the UN, while at the same time tolerating or encouraging continuing Saudi and Kuwaiti sanctions. Strategically, Arab League members were seen to be negotiating peace with Israel without insisting that Israel dismantle its own nuclear weapons, even as UN inspectors swarming over Iraq were systematically discovering and dismantling some of Iraq's arms, but were not finding WMDs. This process, it was argued, left Iraq sandwiched between a real nuclear power, Israel, and a potential one, Iran, without its own nuclear "defenses."

AN ISRAELI PEACE WITH SADDAM?

While Iraq emitted its belligerent rhetoric and played cat-and-mouse games with the UN inspectors, from 1993 onwards a series of leaks in the Israeli media talked of moves to set up a secret "peace channel" between Israel and Iraq, aimed at bringing Saddam into the Oslo process. One Israeli newspaper, *Shishi*, claimed that Deputy Prime Minister Tarik Azziz and Nizar Hamdoun, ambassador to the UN, had broached the idea to Saddam Hussein, who did not reject it outright.

There followed a flurry of media stories about contacts at the UN, in Europe, and in Morocco (still the home of a large and active Jewish community, and the arena for the Egyptian–Israeli talks that had led to Sadat's 1977 peace pilgrimage to Jerusalem and to the 1979 peace treaty). The PLO, Russia, France, and certain politicians and businessmen in Europe were said to be facilitating the contacts. Issues under discussion were said to include the perennial one of reopening (or rebuilding) the Kirkuk–Haifa oil pipeline; Iraqi absorption of the 400,000-odd Palestinian refugees, living in limbo and without rights in Lebanon; and the opening of an "interest section," a kind of sub-embassy, in Jerusalem and Baghdad.

The politicians concerned, reports Israeli analyst Ofra Bengio, included President Ezer Weizman, Housing Minister Benjamin Ben-Eliezer and Police Minister Moshe Shahal. When questioned, Prime Minister Rabin and other senior officials made flat denials, saying Israel would not move behind America's back. In Iraq, Tarik Azziz denied "any" contacts with the Jewish state and added that Iraq would never "raise the white flag" and recognize Israel. Bengio believes that the contacts, if they really did exist, were trial balloons by both sides. Israel's interest would have been to show that if it prevailed on the United States to lift the embargoes, Iraq would have to pay a price in terms of peace and recognition. It may also have hoped to encourage the Jordanian public toward peace. King Hussein was already involved in secret talks that would lead to the Jordan–Israel peace treaty signed in the presence of President Bill Clinton in October 1994. Subsequent denials by Rabin and others seemed designed to prove to Washington that Israel was stoutly behind America's growingly tough, though still hesitant, policy toward Saddam and was not considering bilateral peace contacts with Iraq.

At the same time, Iraq's publicists and propagandists continued to try to show the Arab governments and the "Arab street," in *New York Times* columnist Thomas Friedman's famous phrase, that Iraq was the only Arab country remaining loyal to pan-Arab principles. In the end, there was no change in Israeli–Iraqi relations.

In Washington, the changeover from Bush to Clinton in 1993 brought a new national security team into office. It called its policy toward Saddam "containment." This had four major points. First was a strong military presence, with "Operation Southern Watch," the Allied enforcement of the northern and southern no-fly zones. These were no longer simply to protect Iraqi Shias or Kurds, but also to safeguard Saudi Arabia and Kuwait. Second was keeping in force UN economic sanctions and the arms embargo, to prevent Saddam from rebuilding his armed forces and from restoring his former regional financial power. The third element was to lean hard on UN arms monitors to track and destroy Iraqi nuclear, chemical, and biological weapons and longer-range missiles. Fourth, the Iraqi opposition was to be supported and encouraged.

As veteran *Los Angeles Times* correspondent and author Robin Wright pointed out in a perceptive study in *The Washington Quarterly* in 1998, "containment" was a passive concept. It reflected contradictions between Washington's gradually emerging policy of eventual regime change and the short-term mandate of the UN to disarm Iraq. Until Iraq had complied with that mandate, the United States could not go beyond preventing Saddam from threatening neighbors or foreign oil consumers, as he had done before Desert Storm. Still, as senior presidential aides almost certainly recognized, only a new leadership in Baghdad could realize the Clinton administration's wider objectives.[13]

MISADVENTURES OF THE UN ARMS INSPECTORS

UNSCOM, the United Nations commission set up to inspect Iraqi weapons facilities after Desert Storm, began work in June 1991. From then until November 1997, when Saddam barred inspectors with American nationality, the inspectors visited over 1,000 sites and managed to destroy thousands of banned weapons despite Iraqi obstruction and harassment, sometimes involving life-threatening measures. A German reporter in November 1997 summed up some of them. "Strange figures" would prowl into UN inspectors' hotel rooms in Baghdad's Sheraton Hotel, then disappear. The police escorts accompanying inspections did nothing to prevent "spontaneous protests" by civilians. Cars marked with the UN logo were cut off from convoys and sometimes bumped or rammed. Inspectors were spat on and threatened with Kalashnikov assault rifles. German military pilots who flew the UN inspectors around Iraq were doused with gasoline in the street. Zealots hammered on UN jeeps with iron bars. Iraqi "observers" riding in UN helicopters were known to interfere with their navigation.

One occasion, typical of hundreds and hundreds of others, foreshadowed the determined armed resistance that the U.S. army of occupation would face in 2003 and 2004 in Fallujah, Ramadi, and elsewhere in the "Sunni triangle" west of Baghdad. A British nuclear scientist named Mike Baker with an inspection team neared a military area outside Fallujah. "Today is Friday [the Muslim day of prayer], you can't come in," Iraqi guards told them. Baker climbed a nearby water tower and noticed a column of trucks exiting the military compound. He radioed the team leader, David Kay (who in 2003, after being sent back to Iraq by the CIA with a team of 1,400 U.S. inspectors, returned to Washington to report no weapons of mass destruction found). When Kay sent two UN inspectors to photograph the trucks, Iraqi guards fired shots near the unarmed inspectors. "All too often," wrote the German reporter, "members of the inspection team are like greyhounds running after the electric hare—out of breath, making no apparent progress." Most of the inspectors, only 110 in November 1997, were young. They included a mixture of scientists, professional and amateur weapons experts, commando veterans, and agents for one or more intelligence agencies (certainly for the CIA and probably for Israel's Mossad).[14]

In August 1995 Saddam Hussein's son-in-law, Hussein Kamel al-Majid, defected to Jordan. He began telling the Jordanians, the CIA, and anyone else who would listen about Saddam's concealed WMDs, including bioweapons. King Hussein personally disclosed to me for ABC News that a shipment of Russian gyroscopes intended for the guidance systems of Iraqi missiles had been seized at Amman airport. Using information supplied by Hussein Kamel before he and his brother-in-law were lured back to Baghdad by Saddam and murdered, UN inspectors visited an

Iraqi poultry farm. There they found boxes stuffed with documents on the armaments program in Iraq. This elicited the unprecedented admission that Iraq's scientists were indeed working on bioweapons programs, which they later denied ever existed.

In response to Saddam's "cheat and retreat" evasions, the United States mounted a limited and sporadic military response. U.S. planes shot down an Iraqi MIG-25 when it violated a no-fly zone in 1992. In the following year, U.S. forces attacked missile sites and a suspected nuclear facility near Baghdad when Iraq deployed missiles in the Basra area. When Washington got wind of a plot by some Iraqi intelligence operatives, in league with a gang of whisky smugglers, to assassinate ex-president George H. W. Bush during a visit to Kuwait, President Clinton ordered the Pentagon to fire 23 cruise missiles at Iraqi intelligence headquarters in Baghdad. The attack took place at night when few personnel were on duty in the building. A stray missile killed Leilah Attar, one of Iraq's best woman artists.

CLINTON: "OUST SADDAM"

When Iraq began to move troops toward the Kuwaiti border in early October of 1994, the Clinton administration, with Israeli approval, also began to move forces. On October 10, senior officials met in the White House situation room and reaffirmed a secret directive by Clinton to the CIA in 1991 to oust Saddam. At that time, the agency had recruited Ahmed Chalabi, the exiled Iraqi millionaire who had once arranged my trip to Kurdistan. He was organizing an umbrella organization of mostly exiled opposition groups, the Iraqi National Congress (INC), funded (at first secretly) since 1992 by the CIA. The INC eventually used U.S. government funds to train in Hungary an armed militia for occupation duty in "liberated" Iraq. The INC launched its own anti-Saddam propaganda campaign. This was partly intended to counter the sympathy aroused abroad by the draconian economic sanctions, which were causing severe suffering among ordinary Iraqis, including sick children deprived of medicine, many foodstuffs, and hundreds of other essentials. This campaign was subcontracted to John Rendon, a Washington PR specialist.

Chalabi—who would later be wholeheartedly supported, for a time, by the Pentagon and the neoconservative advisers of George W. Bush's Defense Secretary, Donald Rumsfeld—presented an unexceptionable program for a post-Saddam Iraq: a democracy with a government representing all the country's ethnic, religious, and political groups. Chalabi set about building a power base in northern Iraq's Kurdistan, where he and his followers were protected by Allied military and air power. In November 1993, Chalabi flew to Washington and lobbied, in vain, for U.S. government support for a scheme to win over military defectors from the Iraqi armed forces, including the Republican Guards, and to foment an uprising to unseat, capture, or kill Saddam and his ruling Tikriti clan. The idea was to take advantage of conspiracies of the type already mounted (unsuccessfully) against Saddam by Sunni Muslim officers from influential tribes, like the Juburis and the Dulaimis. Chalabi could not win any commitment for military support from a Clinton administration that was skeptical of his chances and dubious about some aspects of his past, such as his conviction for massive bank fraud in Jordan during the 1980s.

A rival of the INC was the Iraqi National Accord (INA), led by another Iraqi exile, Iyad Allawi, who had a long record of working with Britain's MI-6, the Secret Intelligence Service, and who became the "sovereign" Iraqi prime minister in June 2004. Senior British officials urged their CIA colleagues to take note of Allawi's supposedly good Iraqi army connections and to listen sympathetically to his requests for money and logistic support.

CIA Director James Woolsey was a fan of both Chalabi and Allawi, and a confirmed hawk. He believed Saddam Hussein was behind acts of international terrorism, such as the February 1993 bombing of the World Trade Center in New York. Woolsey and other senior officials listened to the differing opinions of his senior operatives at the October 1994 White House meeting. It apparently left some latitude to the field officers and their protégés to work out whatever they could. But there was heated debate over the options. Secretary of State Madeleine Albright, exasperated at hearing of all the difficulties involved in destroying Saddam, reportedly said "Why are we here?"[15]

One apparent result in March 1995 was the start of a military campaign in Iraqi Kurdistan by Chalabi's INC militias, which was intended to have the help of the two main Kurdish factions, Talabani's PUK and Massoud Barzani's KDP. Chalabi's people hoped that Tehran-based Shia groups would join them. When Barzani balked at the last minute and refused to commit his forces, these groups also decided to remain aloof. Nevertheless, combined INC–PUK forces, with small contingents of Christian Assyrian and Turcoman dissidents, captured several towns and pushed back Saddam's troops, taking 700 loyalist prisoners. A defector, General Wafik al-Samarrai, former chief of Saddam's military intelligence tried to guide the effort. Barzani, however, fearing that his Kurdish rival Talabani would eclipse him and his clan if the revolt were successful, switched sides. He ordered the KDP forces to attack Talabani in the towns of Penjawin and Nalbrize, killed 200 PUK fighters and captured the towns. Washington called off military support, which the KDP leadership had evidently expected. Despite the defection of hundreds of loyalist soldiers to the insurgents, the effort failed and the Kurdish factions continued to fight each other.

In August 1996 Talabani's PUK succeeded in trapping Barzani's forces in a pocket. Barzani appealed to their arch-enemy Saddam Hussein for support. He got it. In early September, Saddam's Republican Guard and Special Republican Guard units of at least brigade strength routed the PUK guerrillas, then charged northeast toward the Iranian border and occupied the regional Kurdish capital of Erbil. This was a fiasco for the Iraqi opposition and for their CIA backers, who hurriedly fled. Saddam's men captured hundreds of INC troops who were under direct CIA control, and thousands of documents revealing the CIA/opposition plans. Many of the Iraqi captives were executed. The United States, working in liaison with the Turks across the frontier, saved other hundreds and flew them to exile in the United States. U.S. Defense Secretary William Perry announced that the United States would not intervene. Later, official U.S. spokesmen blamed Saddam, without mentioning that the traditional ally of the United States and Israel, the KDP, had asked for Saddam's help. There was also little discussion of the fact that since 1995 Turkey had been sending incursions of some 20–40,000 troops into northern Iraq in pursuit of Turkey's own dissident Kurds, the Marxist Turkish Workers' Party (PKK), led by Abdallah Ocalan who fought openly for Kurdish independence, listed as terrorists by the United States and Britain. Following the fall of Erbil and the rout of the CIA operation based there, the Clinton administration fired another cruise missile at Baghdad. With the British, it extended the northern no-fly zone to the 32nd parallel, just north of Baghdad and asked the UN to suspend the humanitarian oil-for-food program.

The French officially ended their patrols in the no-fly zones. Only Israel and Kuwait supported the cruise missile attack and extension of the interdicted zone. Saddam's forces evacuated Erbil, taking with them prisoners and documents compromising the PUK and the INC. Saddam's propagandists proclaimed victory. Although the Kurds had involuntarily handed Saddam his victory, the Shi'ite Dawa (Islamic Call) party reacted. On December 12, 1996, several Dawa gunmen attacked Uday Hussein as he drove amid a convoy of Mercedes cars in central Baghdad, killing his driver and paralyzing Uday from the waist down. Surgeons from Iraq and Europe saved his life, but he never walked properly again.

In July 1997, the Swedish UNSCOM chief Rolf Ekeus, who had tried to keep the arms inspections impartial and independent of the hardliners in Washington and Israel, retired to become Swedish ambassador in Washington. His replacement, the Australian diplomat Richard Butler, took a much tougher public line toward the Iraqis. He kept ordering surprise inspections on sites signaled to UNSCOM (as the last chief inspector Hans Blix would later confirm) by allied intelligence services, including Israel's. Since 1992, inspector David Kay and probably others had at times submitted Iraqi documents to the United States before giving them to UN superiors. Iraq claimed that some inspectors, such as U.S. Marine Major Scott Ritter (who by 2002 would be expressing extreme skepticism about Saddam's supposed possession of WMDs), were reporting to Western or Israeli intelligence. Butler answered evasively and confronted the Iraqis with demands to inspect Saddam's scores of sumptuous palaces for hidden arms. The end of UN Secretary-General Boutros Boutros-Ghali's term and his replacement by the gifted and skillful Ghanaian diplomat, Kofi Annan led to compromises in 1998. These greatly increased Iraq's oil-for-food revenues and permitted "courteous" inspection of the palaces.[16]

During the later 1990s, the most senior members of the Clinton administration began to talk openly in terms which, while not openly advocating forcible "regime change," implied that this might some day become an option. At the same time, there was a more hidden sea change beginning in Washington, not without prompting from its allies in Jerusalem, with the assent of the basically concurring "New Labour" government of Prime Minister Tony Blair in the United Kingdom. In the United States, an assortment of neoconservative career officials and academics, who would later come to power in 2001 with the unilateralist and anti-UN George W. Bush Republicans in the disputed presidential election of November 2000, were already mapping this sea change. They were able to set it in motion after the cataclysmic Al-Qaeda terrorist attacks on the United States of September 11, 2001. The new policy planned for regime change; even, implicitly, for preemptive or preventive wars. Targets included Iraq (first on the priority list), then Iran, Syria, and other areas standing in the way of U.S. (and, in the Middle East, Israeli) objectives. In Afghanistan, the post-9/11 war against Al-Qaeda and its former Taliban hosts was taken as a more or less permanent U.S. commitment, and so did not need to be the central focus of this grandiose scheme. The strategy was cloaked in a mantle of sincere determination to bring "Western-style democracy" to benighted states around the world, especially those with Islamic societies or regimes.

U.S. POLICY SHIFTS

The beginning of the open or overt phase of this fundamental shift in U.S. policy, in the instance directed against Saddam Hussein's Iraq, has I believe rightly been identified as the appointment of Madeleine Albright to replace Warren Christopher as U.S. Secretary of State amid the crisis events in Iraq in early 1997. As UN ambassador, she had led the U.S. campaign to pressure Saddam Hussein. In her new job, she instantly continued it. In her first foreign policy speech, at Georgetown University in March 1997, Albright delivered a broadside at Saddam for his dismal record on human rights, UN arms inspections, embargo evasions, and failure to return assets looted during his occupation of Kuwait. The United States could not permit "the scorpion that bit us once to bite us again. That would be a folly impossible to explain to our children or to the veterans of Desert Storm." The United States would hold Saddam to account "as long as it takes" to force him to comply. She hinted at eventual "regime change" by declaring that Iraq could count on major Western help to rebuild once a "successor regime" had emerged.[17]

The new Clinton–Albright policy toward Iraq was contrary to those of the United States' former partners. Italy, Spain, and Greece reopened embassies in Baghdad. France staffed its interest section here for the first time since 1990. Delegations of European parliamentarians and businessmen flattered Saddam and closed new trade deals. Egypt led other Arab states in pressing to ease sanctions. Iran looked the other way as Iraq sent embargo-busting oil shipments through its coastal waters to the United Arab Emirates. Russian, Chinese, and French oil companies negotiated post-embargo production-sharing agreements with the Iraq National Oil Company for known but still undeveloped fields in southern Iraq, provoking the envy of U.S., British, Dutch, and German multinationals who were constrained by the embargoes. More and more countries, weary of the arms inspections crises and the unpopular and (for Iraqi society) destructive sanctions, and the resulting smuggling and other black operations that were enriching Saddam and his clique while impoverishing further the long-suffering Iraqi people, lobbied the United States and the UN to ease or lift the sanctions.

Secretary Albright, National Security Adviser Samuel Berger, and Defense Secretary William Cohen met a public forum at Ohio State

University in February 1998. When they tried to explain why the United States might have to launch a new and major military operation against Iraq, anti-war students heckled them and questioned about why the United States was headed into another Vietnam-type confrontation.[18]

THE "NEOCONS" AT WORK

By the time this book sees the presses, much has been published describing how the "neoconservative" advisers who entered the White House, the Pentagon, and even the State Department with the inauguration of President George W. Bush steered the United States into that confrontation. The most important of these and their positions of power are quickly listed: Paul Wolfowitz, deputy to Defense Secretary Donald Rumsfeld and a principal architect of the Bush war policy on Iraq; Richard Perle, a member (and former chairman) of the backstage but highly influential Defense Policy Board; James Woolsey, senior bureaucrat during four presidencies, CIA director for President Clinton, and now with the Booz Allen Hamilton management consulting firm; Kenneth Adelman, a veteran official of the Republican administrations of Ford and Reagan; Douglas Feith, deputy secretary and Number Three man in the Pentagon, in charge of "reconstruction" and democratization of Iraq beyond the June 30, 2004, date when sovereignty was supposed to pass from the U.S.-led occupation forces to a presumably docile Iraqi government; and J. Lewis ('scooter") Libby, chief of staff to Vice-President Dick Cheney.

In the State Department, Secretary Colin Powell and his staff of professional career diplomats and analysts were generally far less eager to go to war. Powell, however, publicly defended the largely fictional intelligence about Saddam Hussein's supposed WMDs before the UN and elsewhere, weeks before the U.S.-led attack in March 2003. A year later, he had to admit that the data he so dramatically presented had been wrong. Within State, the "neocons" had a powerful ally: John Bolton, Undersecretary of State for arms control. In the White House, with National Security Adviser Condoleezza Rice, a former Kremlinologist and senior academic with little or no Middle Eastern experience, was Stephen Hadley, her hawkish deputy.[19]

Most Washington observers agree that Wolfowitz, "Wolfie" to some of his friends and colleagues, who taught international politics at Johns Hopkins University in Baltimore and Washington, is the most intellectual of this group, most of them former "Cold Warriors." He is often credited with influencing President Reagan's conception of the Soviet

Union as the "Empire of Evil": a Republican Party ideologist's precursor of George W. Bush's concept of the "Axis of Evil" (Iraq, Iran, and North Korea), and of waging preventive or preemptive wars where necessary to maintain U.S. leadership or supremacy. Like many of the other neoconservatives, Wolfowitz is Jewish and, also like others, has shown strong affinities and links with Prime Minister Ariel Sharon and his ideas in Israel. A German author, Claus Lutterbeck, has pointed to Wolfowitz, whose parents were Jewish refugees from the Nazis in Poland and who lost many family members in the Holocaust, as a man driven by "the spirit of Munich," the 1938 betrayal of Czechoslovakia when British Prime Minister Neville Chamberlain, to ward off threatening war in Europe, agreed to Adolf Hitler's seizure of the Czech Sudetenland. Lutterbeck writes that:

> the Bush administration is secretly convinced that "old Europe" [a contemptuous reference by Donald Rumsfeld to France, Germany, and others who rejected the U.S.-led war in Iraq] hasn't learned from the shame [of Munich] and will always kowtow to dictators [like Saddam], sometimes for pacifist and sometimes for economic reasons, but always out of fear. So Wolfowitz pleads that, "it's better to fight small wars immediately than big ones later." Today the world faces a question of destiny. Therefore Saddam must be overthrown before he gives atomic weapons to terrorists.[20]

Wolfowitz, Perle, and Woolsey are disciples of the late Albert Wohlstetter, a University of Chicago professor who during the Cold War argued that passive nuclear deterrence was not enough, and that the underrated military power of the USSR should be neutralized by actually fighting a nuclear war against it. Wohlstetter supervised Wolfowitz's PhD degree and later invited Perle to work with Wolfowitz on a paper about the proposed Anti-Ballistic Missile (ABM) Treaty which Wohlstetter opposed and which the George W. Bush administration abandoned, as it did a number of other international treaties. Wohlstetter brought Perle to meet Senator Henry ("Scoop") Jackson, a confirmed Cold Warrior and advocate of Israel's interests. He also introduced Perle to Ahmed Chalabi, who hoped (in vain) to become president of the new Iraq after Saddam Hussein's fall. Perle in general supports Ariel Sharon and the views of the Likkud Party in Israel, and served at one time on the board of the strongly right-wing and pro-Sharon *Jerusalem Post*. Perle has had relations with many defense contractors who work closely with Israel as consulting clients.

He is a resident fellow at the conservative think tank, the American Enterprise Institute (AEI). At annual conferences at Beaver Creek, Colorado, co-sponsored by the AEI and ex-president Gerald Ford, Chalabi, Cheney, Rumsfeld, and Wolfowitz were all able to meet with Perle and with each other.[21]

In mid-1996 an Israeli think tank, the Institute for Advanced Strategic and Political Studies, sponsored a ground-breaking study that was meant to guide the new Israeli Prime Minister Netanyahu, a prominent Likud hawk, in his Middle Eastern ventures and adventures. Its authors included Richard Perle, Douglas Feith, and David Wurmser (who in early 2004 was given a White House job connected with pressuring Syria to bow to Washington's and Jerusalem's wishes to cease supporting Hizbollah in Lebanon, evacuate its troops from that country, and in general comply with the "new realities" created by the massive American presence in nearby Iraq). All three were serving policymakers or advisers in the George W. Bush administration. The paper bore the grandiose title of "Clean Break: A New Strategy for Securing the Realm" (which realm, Israel's or America's, or a confluence of both, was not exactly clear). The document was a sweeping recipe for re-making the entire Middle East to suit the common aims of Israel and the United States. It trashed the already faltering Oslo peace accords which President Clinton had managed to seal on the White House lawn in 1993 with Rabin, Shimon Peres, and Arafat. It urged Israel to reserve the right to invade the Palestinian Authority's areas of control in the West Bank and Gaza whenever Israel believes it necessary. It advocated removal of Saddam Hussein from power, by force, as would probably be necessary, and the overthrow or "destabilization" of the governments of Syria, Lebanon, Saudi Arabia, and Iran. It would re-establish and solemnize a policy of preemptive strikes.

The conservative *Washington Times*, quoting the report with approval, commented "Israel would transcend its foes" by "re-establishing the principle of pre-emption, rather than retaliation [for Arab violence] alone, and by ceasing to absorb blows to the nation without response." It proposed strengthening and formalizing an alliance between Israel, Turkey, and Jordan (leaving the "rogue regimes" of Syria and Lebanon out in the cold). It suggested that once Saddam Hussein had been overthrown, the old pre-1958 monarchy of the Hashemites might be restored in Iraq: "since Iraq's future could affect the strategic balance in the Middle East profoundly, it would be understandable that Israel has an interest in supporting the Hashemites in their efforts to redefine Iraq."[22]

In one of numerous interviews with conservative media, Richard Perle told Washington's *National Journal* in May 2003, two months into the American invasion of Iraq, that he had first called for Saddam's ousting in 1987, shortly after he had left the Pentagon and long before Iraq invaded Kuwait. His view, Perle said, was formed by "the nature of the regime and Saddam's ambitions, which became evident when he invaded Kuwait." Although Saddam was not seen then as directly threatening the United States, his views had hardened throughout the decade of the 1990s. "The terrorist connections [of Saddam's regime] are substantial," he added, but there was a political dimension too. By [the attacks of] 9/11, it was clear that American policy toward Iraq was collapsing." Sanctions against Iraq were ineffective and were making Saddam into "a hero in the whole Arab world, clinging to weapons of mass destruction, hostile and aggressive, and tied to terrorism. People forget where this was headed."[23]

The younger George Bush became President in January 2001, following a contested election decided by conservative judges in Florida and in the U.S. Supreme Court. It was soon evident that Bush and his newly appointed neoconservative advisers were intent on their crusade to remove Saddam by force and to make over the Middle East if they could. How all this tied in with Israeli plans for the area, what misfired in the realm of intelligence, and what resulted for the United States, Iraq, Israel, and the world, are our final subjects.

11
Endgame: Iraq Democratized or Dismembered?

*My home policy? I wage war. My foreign policy? I wage war.
Always, everywhere, I wage war ... And I shall continue to wage war
until the very last moment.*

(Georges Clemenceau, March 8, 1918)

"God's Punishment," in bold, black Arabic characters, was the way the
Iraqi state-owned newspaper *Al-Iktisadi* characterized the deadly
airborne attacks on New York and Washington of September 11, 2001,
on their first anniversary in September 2002.

A day later, President George W. Bush addressed the UN General
Assembly. He voiced impatience with the UN's inability to enforce any
of the resolutions it had passed during the 1990s to disarm Iraq:

All the world now faces a test, and the United Nations a difficult and
defining moment. Are Security Council resolutions to be honored
and enforced, or cast aside without consequence? Will the United
Nations serve the purpose of its founders or will it be irrelevant?

The UN now had the chance to enforce its will on Saddam Hussein. If it
did not, Bush made it clear that the United States and its associates—
later called by Defense Secretary Donald Rumsfeld "a coalition of the
willing"—would go to war against Iraq.[1]

The 9/11 attacks, which many senior Americans in Washington
thought might well be the start of World War III had caused the Pentagon to go on a global alert, DEFCON 3, for the first time since the 1973
Arab–Israel war. About 3,000 people had been killed in New York,
Washington, and Pennsylvania. Saddam was already beginning to be
associated (falsely) in American minds with the Al-Qaeda atrocities at
New York's World Trade Center and the Pentagon. On Wednesday morning, September 12, according to Richard A. Clarke, counter-terrorism
chief for President Clinton and now for President Bush, Rumsfeld and
his deputy Paul Wolfowitz began to talk about "getting Iraq." Clarke
recalled that Wolfowitz was insisting that Al-Qaeda could not have done

9/11 alone and that a state—namely Iraq—had helped. Clarke also remembered that in April 2001, at a deputy secretary-level administration meeting, Wolfowitz had said the same thing about the February 1993 bombing of the World Trade Center, possibly the first Al-Qaeda attack inside the United States. Wolfowitz, neoconservative colleagues, and such supporters as scholar and author Laurie Mylroie were again urging that Iraq was a principal suspect.

Secretary of State Colin Powell and his assistant, Richard Armitage, did not share the mindset of the neocons at the September 12 meeting. They argued that Al-Qaeda and its Taliban allies in Afghanistan, not Iraq, should continue to be the priority targets for the American counterattack. Nevertheless, Rumsfeld repeated that Iraq deserved punishment and presented "better targets" than Afghanistan. President Bush, writes Clarke, did not totally reject the idea of attacking Iraq, but said there was a need to change its regime and not just hit it again with cruise missiles. General Hugh Shelton, Chairman of the Joint Chiefs of Staff, reacted cautiously. He thought that only invasion of Iraq with a large force could finish off Saddam's regime, and that would take months to prepare. On that evening, says Clarke, Bush called him and several others into a small conference room and insisted that they "go back over everything, everything. See if Saddam did this. See if he's linked in any way." By the end of deliberations on September 13, there was a consensus that Al-Qaeda and Afghanistan were indeed to have priority, but that this was only a first stage in the "war on terror."[2]

"GET SADDAM"

At a National Security Council (NSC) meeting on February 1, 2002, Secretary of the Treasury Paul H. O'Neill arrived in the White House Situation Room to find briefing materials for a meeting dealing with Iraq. They concerned not only the economic sanctions regime, but also a "Political-Military Plan for Post-Saddam Iraq Crisis," classified Secret. During the discussion of improved, "targeted" sanctions that would be kinder to Iraq's civilian population, Rumsfeld, said Clarke, interrupted with "Sanctions are fine. But what we really want to think about is going after Saddam." O'Neill realized that the Bush administration's fundamental concern in the Middle East had in fact become removing Saddam's Iraq as a threat to U.S. power in the Middle East, and that such removal would serve as an example to others who might challenge this power.[3]

Bob Woodward's best-selling book, *Plan of Attack*, based on hundreds of interviews with principals, including President Bush, greatly bolstered the evidence of the Bush administration's relentless drive toward Saddam's ousting and the remaking of Iraq in some new, allegedly democratic image. Part of the Bush rationale was a belief in Laurie Mylroie's theory that Saddam was tied to the 1993 World Trade Center bombing, following which Paul Wolfowitz had sent neoconservative and former CIA director James Woolsey to Britain to gather evidence for this theory. Richard Clarke insists that no one would have been happier than he to find an excuse to go after Saddam Hussein's regime (he was furious when Saddam's elite troops and Saddam himself were spared after the 1991 Gulf War). However, all the reliable intelligence, and apparently the CIA's estimates, pointed toward Al-Qaeda and Osama bin Laden.[4] Clarke darkly quipped that the succession of Al-Qaeda related plots since 1993 in the Middle East, Africa, Asia, and America have so spread bin Laden's brand of terrorism and its associated doctrines that it was as though Osama bin Laden, in his hiding place, "were to find that a preemptive war against Iraq was being planned" (long before President Bush and Prime Minister Tony Blair were continuously repeating the mantra that "there's been no decision to go to war yet").[5]

War planning in the Pentagon went on throughout 2002. On August 26, the media carried stories that White House lawyers had ruled that ousting Saddam was legal under international law as he had violated the armistice accords ending the 1991 Gulf War. On the same day, Cheney in a speech in Nashville, Tennessee warned that unless it acted soon, the United States might find itself at the mercy of a nuclear-armed Iraq.[6]

THE PALESTINIAN DISCONNECTION

Many of the war planners seemed to believe that there was little or no connection with the Israel–Palestine issues: that the two problems, Iraq and Israel–Palestine, were in two separate boxes, so to speak. President Bush's first meeting with the principals of his NSC was set to deal with "Middle East Policy." President Bill Clinton's team had pushed hard for a lasting and comprehensive settlement between Israeli Prime Minister Ehud Barak and Yassir Arafat, elected President of the Palestinian Authority in the West Bank and Gaza. In meetings in 1999, first at Camp David, Maryland, and later at Taba, Egypt, with President Clinton practically breathing over the shoulders of the negotiators at Camp David, the two sides came close to agreement. The Israeli team hypothetically recognized many of the Palestinian territorial claims, including divisions in Jerusalem. Israel was to get binding security guarantees for its final, UN-patrolled frontiers and $32 billion more in international, mostly U.S., aid. The difficult and fundamental Palestinian claim of the "right of return" for the hundreds of thousands of Arabs who had fled or been driven out by the new Jewish state in 1948 was finessed. But both Barak and Arafat were in weakened political positions due to pressures from the radical elements in their constituencies. The Camp David talks failed after Arafat, apparently feeling his Palestinian constituency would not support the agreement he was being asked to sign, left the table. At Taba, the devil of failure appeared in the details. The negotiations ended.

After the new Bush NSC had reviewed the impasse and the resumption of large-scale violence in a new Palestinian *intifada*, Bush announced that he wanted to correct "imbalances" of the Clintonites on the Middle East conflict and that "We're going to tilt it back toward Israel. ... If the two sides don't want peace, there's no way we can force them." Bush then announced that he was going to try to work out a "relationship" with Ariel Sharon, the newly-elected Israeli prime minister, and that he thought it was time for the United States to disengage. [7] It soon became clear to all concerned that Bush's advisers had persuaded him to put Palestine "on the back burner," and to see what Sharon could do about it. It was also soon clear that Iraq had top priority from now on. In April 2004 Sharon visited Bush, who endorsed his project to leave Gaza, but keep many West Bank settlements, without consulting or negotiating with the Palestinians.

Karen Kwiatowski, a retired U.S. Air Force lieutenant-colonel who became a Pentagon intelligence analyst in May 2002, has clearly traced Bush's tilt toward Israel and toward war in Iraq. Her assignment was in the office of retired navy Captain Bill Luti, who under Bush became a deputy undersecretary of defense. She saw how other key personnel in this supposedly neutral "political" section of the Pentagon were being replaced by people with ideological mind-sets, most from outside the government. Her office mate, a career civil servant specializing in U.S. military-political relations with Egypt, warned her that if she wanted to succeed, "don't say anything positive about the Palestinians." One of Luti's temporary assistants was an Egyptian-American naval officer, Lt. Cdr. Youssef Aboul-Enein. Part of his job, she discovered, was to "peruse Arabic-language media for quotations or events which could be used to demonize Saddam Hussein or link him to nastiness beyond his own borders and with unsavory characters," in other words, terrorists. From mid-May through mid-July 2002, Kwiatowski found, "news in the daily briefing was based on war planning for the Iraq invasion."

THE CABAL IN ACTION

In late summer of 2002, Kwiatowski and others noted the establishment on the fifth floor of the Pentagon a new "Office of Special Plans" (OSP). They were cautioned not to comment on this or discuss it with anyone outside. All desk officers were instructed to use briefing materials from the OSP in preparation of their background reports.[8]

The distinguished investigative reporter Seymour Hersh explained in May 2003 the workings of the "Cabal," as the Office's incumbents "self-mockingly" called themselves. Hersh described how they produced their own intelligence reports, independent of the CIA, DIA, or other agencies (though they often incorporated information from them), to influence public opinion and government policy in favor of war with Iraq. Much of their information, later shown to be mainly false, came from Chalabi and other Iraqi exiles. The OSP's director was Abram Shulsky, a scholar who closely followed the radical ideas about bringing "democracy" to the Middle East, and who was a disciple of the political philosopher Leo Strauss, one of whose principles was to rely on intuition as much as on fact. Shulsky's associates included Douglas Feith, Bill Luti, and Paul Wolfowitz. They insisted that American policymakers and the U.S. public, were being wrongly told by CIA, DIA, and published reports that that there was little or no connection between Saddam Hussein and Al-Qaeda terrorism. They brushed aside the news that WMDs were simply not being found by the UN inspectors in Iraq, sent back there before Bush took office under the cool-headed Swedish chief inspector, Hans Blix. The neocon thesis was that Saddam Hussein did have close links with Osama bin Laden's men and that Iraq, in Hersh's words, "had an enormous arsenal of chemical, biological, and possibly even nuclear weapons that threatened the region and, potentially, the United States." Before the 9/11 attacks, Richard Perle had told a Senate Foreign Relations subcommittee hearings in March 2001 that "We know [Saddam] has" chemical and biological weapons. He "guessed" there were nuclear weapons in Saddam's arsenals as well.[9]

Kwiatowski observed that visiting Israeli generals and others were sometimes admitted to the Pentagon without having to show their IDs or to sign in, as authorized by Douglas Feith. Washington insiders were aware that the OSP was rewriting intelligence, or "bending" it, for the eyes of the senior decision-makers. Vice-President Cheney visited CIA headquarters at Langley several times to urge CIA analysts to look harder for incriminating evidence about Iraq. The OSP had an Israeli counterpart in Prime Minister Sharon's office in Jerusalem. It was an office depending neither on Mossad nor on Aman, the military intelligence organization. Its reports were written in English, not Hebrew, and sent directly to Washington.

MECHANICS OF AN ALLIANCE

As the most important and powerful Israel lobby organization in the United States, the America–Israel Public Affairs Committee (AIPAC) proudly recalled in a background paper in October 2003, the two governments work closely together on "combating terrorism and the threat of weapons proliferation." Israel is a formal (and the only non-NATO) member of the five-nation, U.S.-led Technical Support Working Group on counter-terrorism. AIPAC says that in 1997, Washington and Jerusalem agreed to share intelligence on early detection of missile launches. "Vital information" about Iran's ballistic missile and nuclear-weapons programs, which were causing the United States and the UN's IAEA much concern by 2004, came from Israel. So did intelligence on the activities of Hizbollah in Lebanon and other Middle Eastern terrorist groups. U.S. satellites have provided "near real-time intelligence" to Israel on impending missile or air attacks. Crucially, says AIPAC, "Israel provided intelligence to UN weapons inspections teams in Iraq after the [first] Gulf War," allowing them to find documents, data, and hidden facilities. AIPAC may provide a hint to the functioning of the two OSPs in Jerusalem and Washington: The Strategic Policy Planning Group, it reports, "meets to discuss ways to improve and strengthen the strategic relationship between the United States and Israel" on "missile defense, stopping rogue states from acquiring weapons of mass destruction, and early-warning procedures." An average of 300 U.S. Pentagon and military personnel visit Israel every month. Senior Israeli military commanders visit the United States and tour American facilities. Reciprocal visits to Israel are made by senior uniformed commanders from the Army, Navy, Air Force, and Coastguard "for exchanges with the IDF leadership."

A defense hotline operates between the U.S. Secretary of Defense and the Israeli Defense Ministry in Tel Aviv. Two formal top-level joint groups existed long before the Bush administration and its OSP. One is the Joint Political-Military Group, created in 1983 (when U.S. Marines were first sent to Lebanon, then withdrew from it after terrorist strikes on the U.S. Embassy and U.S. Marine base). This group meets twice yearly. Another is the Joint Secretary Assistance Planning Group. The second body, composed of Israel's Ministries of Defense and Finance and the U.S. Defense and State Departments, is supposed to meet annually, says AIPAC, "to discuss Israel's increasing requirements for U.S. military aid and its decreasing need for economic aid."[10]

The August 7, 1998, Al-Qaeda attack on the U.S. embassies in Kenya and Tanzania, killed nearly 300 people and wounded about 5,000, mostly Africans. When the U.S. Air Force had logistical problems sending help quickly, Israel immediately dispatched a special aircraft loaded with equipment and an expert search-and-rescue team aboard. It was first to arrive on the scene.[11]

Unfavorable publicity about the OSP in Washington—many felt that information for the President was being bent or falsified by data obtained from Iraqi defectors and elsewhere—led to its dissolution by the fall of 2003. But the damage which ideological mindsets had done to U.S. intelligence credibility had already been done. Hans Blix, in his memoirs, *Disarming Iraq* (New York, Pantheon Books, 2004), recalls that Vice-President Cheney once threatened to Blix that he would "discredit inspections in favor of disarmament" if Blix's inspection results did not suit the Bush administration. Blix asserts that every important claim made by its top officials about Iraq's WMD program turned out to be false: aluminum tubes supposedly for centrifuges to reprocess uranium; *soi-disant* yellowcake uranium ore imports to Iraq described in crudely-forged documents; mobile laboratories,[12] claimed solemnly by Colin Powell before the UN in February 2003 to be bioweapons labs, which Powell had publicly to acknowledge a year later was wrong. Blix reported that not a single intelligence lead given him had led to major WMD discoveries in Iraq.

One of Israel's staunchest supporters in Washington, Michael Ledeen, responded to an op-ed article in the *Wall Street Journal* by Brent Scowcroft, a former National Security Adviser critical of the neoconservative campaign for war with Iraq. Ledeen noted that Scowcroft feared that if we attack Iraq, "'I think we could have an explosion in the Middle East. It could turn the whole region into a cauldron and destroy [Bush's] War On Terror.' One can only hope that we turn the region into a cauldron, and faster, please. *If ever there were a region that richly deserved being cauldronized, it is the Middle East today.* If we wage the war effectively, we will bring down the terror regimes in Iraq, Iran, and Syria, and either bring down the Saudi monarchy or force it to abandon its global assembly line to indoctrinate young terrorists. *That's our mission in the war against terror,*" Ledeen concluded.[13]

ISRAELI INTELLIGENCE INPUT

One reason why Washington put such high value on Israeli intelligence on Iraq is apparent from Richard Clarke's record of his work in counterterrorism in several U.S. administrations. Before the 1991 Gulf War, Israeli intelligence reported that Saddam Hussein's scientists and engineers were nearing creation of a nuclear weapon. The CIA was skeptical. However, after the war, U.S. intelligence received a report that the Iraqis had hidden program documents in the Agricultural Ministry in Baghdad. A surprise raid and search led by U.S. arms expert Robert Gallucci hit pay dirt and found the documents. Iraqi security units surrounded the inspectors to prevent them from removing the evidence. After a standoff, Gallucci's team, including Arabic translators, succeeded in dictating the crucial data to Washington by satellite phone. Clarke believes that this showed that Israel had been right.[14]

Israeli academic analysts, including retired intelligence officers, produce papers that are highly influential in Israel's (and America's) policy and defense establishments. These analysts were unanimous about the benefits for Israel of a U.S. attack to remove Saddam Hussein and, once and for all, the strategic threat of Iraq's army on its eastern front. Shai Feldman heads the Jaffee Center for Strategic Studies (JCSS) at Tel Aviv University. When I met him there in February 2004, he provided me with a useful file of JCSS reports. In February 2003, when considering problems facing the new Ariel Sharon government that would emerge from the January 2003 Israeli general election, Feldman wrote that:

> Israel's security interests are served by the evolving U.S.-led confrontation with Iraq almost regardless of how it ends. This is because Saddam can only avoid a military confrontation by leaving the country or by surrendering the ... WMD in his possession, their delivery systems, and the capacity to produce such weaponry. ... [Israel would benefit] not only through the immediate disarmament but by reducing if not completely eliminating an additional grave danger—the possibility that Iraq may acquire nuclear weapons.[15]

Israeli military officers also predicted "beneficial" outcomes for Israel of a U.S. war against Iraq, including a possible demoralizing effect on the Palestinians. In October 2002, Major General Amos Gilad wrote that "A U.S.–Iraq war that topples Saddam Hussein ... would create dramatic change in the Middle East because Saddam is a leading symbol to tyrants like Arafat and others." Gilad also reflected that the immediate problem for Israel was terrorism, the second *intifada* then in progress in the Palestinian territories. He ruefully commented that:

> Monetarily, terrorism] is a good investment for poor families, who automatically receive [money] when a child [suicide bomber] blows himself up. They get $25,000 from Iraq, $5,000 from

Saudi Arabia, and $5,000 from the Palestinian Authority, and are publicly lauded as "heroes" in the Palestinian national pantheon. Compare this to sum to an average monthly family income of $400 a month.[16]

After the fall of Saddam and his capital Baghdad in April 2003, Major General Ya'akov Amidror recalled that Israel had helped America pave the way for its announced goal of democratization of the Middle East by "halting Iraq's nuclear plans in 1981, a demonstration of strategic cooperation between Israel and the U.S.." Israel has long feared the prospect of a Syrian–Iraqi coalition. "In 1973, the last-minute entrance of Iraqi forces almost saved the Golan Heights for the Syrians. Removing the threat of an eastern coalition alters the entire Israeli position regarding a war from the east."

The real reason for the new Iraq war, Amidror added, was:

> not purely to disarm Saddam Hussein and eradicate his stockpile of weapons. ... The subsequent stage is the stabilization of Iraq—a formidable task, given the frictions inside the society and the country as a whole. Absent the stabilization of Iraq, the consequences of the war could be disruptive for the entire area.

Prophetic words, as it turned out.

Iraq, Amidror went on, almost as though reading from an American neoconservative script, is only a step toward the "ultimate goal": "the Middle East, the Arab world, and the Muslim world." The administration of Bush the younger is far from being a new edition of that of the elder George Bush:

> rather it is the continuation of the ideologically motivated Reagan administration, reflected in its battle against the "axis of evil" [Bush's formulation for Iraq, Iran and North Korea] and support for democratization of the entire region. Its models are Japan and Germany following the Second World War and Eastern Europe ... after the collapse of the USSR. ... [T]he Americans know that ultimately if they win, and the Middle East begins a process of democratization, then nobody will remember the European criticism; history will judge them by the results.[17]

The diplomatic run-up to the massive U.S.-led attack on Iraq of March 19, 2003, is too familiar to need retelling. In the UN Security Council, which began its final reconsideration of Iraq's disarmament in January, France, Russia, and China all opposed any planned U.S. military strike. Germany was also opposed, and (unlike France and Russia) had no major oil interests in Iraq. Supporting the United States was Prime Minister Tony Blair's Britain, Iraq's former colonial master, and Spain, Belgium, Poland, and others whose governments (unlike most of their people) wished for various reasons to follow. Secretary-General Kofi Annan failed to play an important role in the debates. As the final countdown to war began in March, the UN as a body appeared paralyzed and unable to keep alive any meaningful diplomatic process that could have staved off the conflict.

Israel was one of the few countries where most people approved. Some Western and Arab observers were surprised by the amount of support from the Arab Gulf states and Jordan, support which Muslim media decried. In Iran and Syria, in particular, there was widespread concern about whether the Bush advisers pushing their dream of remodeling the Middle East would launch new military campaigns to subdue their regimes too, or even occupy their countries.

A (MILITARILY) WELL-PLANNED CAMPAIGN

The military campaign began with the Bush–Rumsfeld attempt at "regime decapitation" on March 20. U.S. cruise missiles and guided missiles launched by F-117 Stealth jets hit a Baghdad building, tipped in last-minute intelligence reports as sheltering Saddam. He was not hit. Strikes followed by aircraft and missiles from three U.S. carrier battle groups in the Gulf and two in the Mediterranean. Land-based aircraft and U.S. and British submarines armed with Tomahawk missiles joined the battering of Iraq's air defenses, long ago eroded by persistent pinprick raids. There followed weeks of massive "shock and awe" attacks, as Pentagon doctrine called them, on military objectives and cities that killed and wounded unnumbered thousands of Iraqis, civilian and military. An Anglo-American peace group, the Iraq Body Count Project, estimated between 7,784 and 9,596 Iraqi civilians killed and three times those numbers wounded in the initial air campaign. Land action began on March 21, when Britain's Royal Marines repeated World War I history, landing on the Fao peninsula under covering fire from U.S., British, and Australian warships. By the next day, British and U.S. Marines had secured Iraq's southern oilfields, avoiding mass sabotage like that Saddam Hussein inflicted on Kuwait's oil installations during his 1991 retreat. By March 25, allied

forces had begun mine clearance around Iraq's short southern coast-
line. After some fighting Um Kasr became the main seaport of entry
for the allied forces and their supplies.

Despite sandstorms the U.S. V Corps, led by the 3rd Infantry Division
on the left flank and the 1st Marine Expeditionary Force on the right,
drove so rapidly into southern Iraq that their lines of communication
became extended. The Iraqis attacked one American logistics convoy,
partially destroying it. Urban areas like Basra, Najaf, Karbala, and Kut
put up stiffer resistance in some cases than expected, because the regular Iraqi army tended to retreat into the cities. Resistance by the so-called
Saddam fedayeen and Ba'ath party militiamen foreshadowed the later
heavy fighting against the American occupation forces by thousands of
both Sunni and Shia guerrilla insurgents, Iraqi and foreign.

By April 5, U.S. forces had approached the capital and captured Baghdad International Airport, not without some sporadic but fierce resistance. U.S. heavy and light armored units and infantry entered and
secured most of the city on April 9, following heavy raids by tank units
with close air support. Saddam, after a last televised street appearance
to a few cheering supporters, disappeared. He would not be captured by
U.S. forces until December 16, 2003, five months after both sons, Uday
and Qusay, had been killed in a gun-battle with besieging American
troops on July 22. A U.S. Army engineering vehicle helped to topple
Saddam's statute in Ferdowsi (Paradise) Square, a symbolic event carefully staged for the television cameras.

Allied planners had not planned to make Basra a priority target.
However, local uprisings supported by some allied Special Forces failed
to end Ba'ath party control or prevent Iraqi counterattacks by regular
and guerrilla forces from the city. British commanders therefore decided
to occupy the city. The UK's 1st Armored Division, including an
armored, an air assault, and a commando brigade, began attack forays
into Basra, which was under effective British control by April 8.

In the north, the main Kurdish groups, the PDK and the PUK, had
over the past ten years of allied air protection and cooperation with
allied land forces, prepared the terrain well. The U.S. 173rd Air Assault
Brigade airdropped onto Bashur airfield. The plan to send the 4th U.S.
Infantry Division through Turkey into Iraqi Kurdistan had been rejected
by a narrow vote of the Turkish parliament in Ankara. "Plan B" was to
drop the 173rd and move the 4th by sea all the way from the Mediterranean through the Suez Canal to the Gulf and into Iraq from Kuwait.
A combined Kurdish Pesh Merga force captured Kirkuk on April 11.
American forces at first secured the nearby oilfields, pipelines, and other

installations, but these were continually damaged and crippled by sabo-teurs throughout the occupation, making it impossible during the early months to export oil through to Turkey's Mediterranean tanker termi-nals. U.S. troops operating in western Iraq near the Syrian border enforced the closing of the Iraq–Syria pipeline that had earlier pumped millions of barrels of oil into Syria in violation of the UN- and U.S.-imposed sanctions. Most of the organized major fighting in Iraq ended by April 14, well before President Bush, dressed in a flight suit, theatri-cally, and, as it turned out, very prematurely, declared an end to major combat on the deck of the aircraft carrier *Abraham Lincoln* just off the California coast on May 1.[18]

THE UNPLANNED OCCUPATION

With the regime's collapse, Baghdad was plunged into a nightmare of looting. The invaders, despite numerous warnings from diplomats and others, failed to foresee or prevent the pillage, providing guards only for the Iraqi Oil Ministry. This led commentators around the world to repeat their earlier claims that the war was fought mainly to seize Iraq's oil. The looters targeted banks, shops, offices, government buildings, and museums. Parts of entire buildings were dismantled. Priceless treas-ures of art and archaeology, from the Babylonian period up through the Islamic centuries, were stolen from the National Museum, apparently in part by its employees or well-organized gangs working for antiquities dealers abroad. "One tank or APC and a couple of soldiers at the entrances would have prevented this," said a Museum official. Senior U.S. and British officials up to the level of Defense Secretary Rumsfeld, were either silent, or when pressed, declared that the invasion had freed the Iraqi people and that "in war, bad things happen."

A document of Saddam's intelligence service found after the war called for a campaign of economic sabotage and armed resistance in case of the regime being overthrown. The killing of Saddam's sons Uday and Qusay near Mosul on July 22 did not demoralize the increasing numbers of guerrilla fighters and terrorists or reduce the attacks. Instead, they increased, and began to enflame religious tensions. On August 29 a car bomb exploded outside the holiest Shia shrine in Najaf, killing over 100 people including Ayatollah Muhammad Bakr al-Sadr. He had been one of Saddam's most courageous surviving opponents and had been coop-erating with the coalition forces.

The August 19 bombing of the UN compound in Baghdad was disas-trous for hopes that the United Nations, so scorned and bypassed by the

Bush administration before the war, could play an expanded and politically healing role in the post-war period. This killed the highly popular special UN envoy, Sergio Vieira de Mello, veteran and successful peacemaker and crisis manager, and two dozen of his staff. The shock waves were lasting. In April 2004, UN Secretary-General Kofi Annan was still replying cautiously to newsmens' queries about an expanded UN role. Algerian diplomat Lakhdar Brahimi, as a UN envoy, was to plan and in some aspects manage the "handover of sovereignty" in June 2004 to a new Iraqi government body, prior to national elections supposed to take place by January 2005.

In autumn of 2003 the insurgency became intense, killing an average of about one U.S. or allied soldier every day. Insurgents proclaimed November 1 as "guerrilla warfare day." The Baghdad streets emptied and heavily armed U.S. Marines and soldiers patrolled, but could not prevent the shooting down of a helicopter at Falluja, west of Baghdad. Later, in March and April of 2004, Falluja became a city where an armed civilian population was virtually mobilized to fight against the besieging American Marines and Special Forces. Simultaneously, a young Shia cleric, Muqtada al-Sadr, appeared at the head of an insurrection sweeping through and around the central cities of Najaf, Kerbala, and Kut, where rebels forced the occupying Ukrainian troops of the coalition to withdraw. American reconstruction efforts proceeded for the most part slowly, particularly in restoring water and electricity services, lack of which so added to Iraqi hardships, although many new schools were built and other public services restored despite the fighting and insecurity.[19]

As the campaign for the November 2004 presidential elections moved into high gear, the Democratic challenger to President George W. Bush, Massachusetts Senator John Kerry, emphasized the huge mistakes being committed in Iraq—such as the decision immediately after the fall of Baghdad to disband the entire pre-war Iraqi armed forces of about 389,000 (not counting reserves), without disarming them or providing them with useful employment. In April 2004 Bremer backtracked and announced that senior ex-Ba'athist officers would be put back on active duty. This was partly an attempt to counter the growing refusals of newly trained Iraqi security officials to fight for the Americans against their own people.

INTELLIGENCE FIASCOS

The hue and cry in the United States and Europe over the patently false intelligence reports about Saddam's supposed weapons of mass destruction began to reach a crescendo after an interim report in late December by David Kay, the former UN inspector chosen by the Bush administration to lead a new and expensive search for arms, using 1,400 inspectors. Kay reported that his team had found no unconventional weapons at all, but that the search would continue. When Kay resigned and returned to the United States, to be replaced in March 2004 by another former UN expert, Charles Duelfer, Kay publicly admitted that "We were all wrong, probably" about the weapons. By July 2004, a long, bi-partisan Senate intelligence committee report in the United States and a UK inquiry into British intelligence failures had basically reached the same conclusions, and Bush's CIA director George Tenet had resigned "for personal reasons." All this was of course new fuel for Kerry's presidential campaign and put the Bush White House increasingly on the defensive.

In Britain, prior to the Butler report, controversy over a British intelligence dossier and conversations of a BBC correspondent with British bioweapons expert David Kelly badly damaged Bush's wartime ally, Prime Minister Tony Blair. A formal inquiry after Kelly's July 18 suicide, following his identification as a source for a BBC report that the Blair government had exaggerated the WMD threat from Saddam Hussein, blamed the BBC more than it did the government. But the damage to Blair and his leadership of the ruling New Labor Party was done.

Controversy, punctuated by periodic opinion polls in the United States and Britain that indicated declining confidence in both Bush and Blair because of the war, nearly drowned out some significant news from Israel. The Jewish state's role in the war has never been publicly clarified, although Prime Minister Ariel Sharon's critics in Israel, as well as many politically neutral military and academic figures, sought clarity behind closed doors.

In September 2003, Ephraim Halevy, a career intelligence specialist who from 1998 to 2002 had served as director of Mossad, then for a year as head of Israel's National Security Council, announced he was quitting government service for good. The American CIA had given Halevy a medal for his decades of cooperation, and he had received signed photos of appreciation from two dead leaders, Yitzhak Rabin and King Hussein of Jordan. Halevy had been appointed to replace former Mossad chief Danny Yatom in 2002, after Yatom had run, for Prime Minister Benjamin Netanyahu, a failed and tragic–comic "Keystone Cops" operation to kill Hamas leader Khalid Mashal in Amman. Mossad agents had entered Jordan with purloined Canadian passports and sprayed poison into Mashal's ear on an Amman street. Jordanian city policemen caught the two actual perpetrators; others took refuge in the Israeli Embassy. An enraged King Hussein threatened to close the Embassy and break off relations unless Netanyahu and Yatom promptly sent an antidote, which would save Mashal's life. They apologized and sent the antidote. The Israeli settlement with Jordan included release from Israeli prison of quadriplegic Hamas spiritual leader Sheikh Ahmed Yassine—whom the Israeli army finally liquidated in a "targeted killing" at morning prayers outside a mosque in Gaza in March 2004.

The Mashal episode, hardly Mossad's finest hour, left Halevy in charge. His Israeli admirers praised his career after he retired, and said he had expressed misgivings about the course Sharon was steering, away from a realistic settlement with the Palestinians.[20] Sharon replaced Halevy with Meir Dagan, an old and close friend of Sharon, who announced that he would make fighting terrorism his top priority—in line with the Bush administration's concerns in Washington. Sharon's most powerful deputy was now being identified as national security adviser Dov Weissglass, who probably supervised Iraq war intelligence and the OSP while it lasted.[21]

The damning Senate intelligence committee report in July 2004, as we saw, concluded that the administration had gone to war with Iraq on the basis of wrong intelligence, both about Iraq's supposed WMDs and about the imagined operational links between Saddam and Al-Qaeda. A second report was to follow on how the administration used and/or manipulated the phoney intelligence to make the case for war.

In Israel, retired Brigadier General Shlomo Brom sounded an alarm about Israel's own intelligence reporting on Iraq. In a study for the Jaffee Center in Tel Aviv, Brom, whom I visited at his office at Tel Aviv University in February 2004, published a wake-up call for the intelligence establishments of Israel and its allies. Israeli intelligence, he said, had seriously miscalculated the threat posed by Saddam Hussein. This contributed to the "false" picture he said was painted by U.S. and British services. Brom wrote and repeated in interviews that:

Israeli intelligence was a full partner with the U.S. and Britain in developing a false picture of Saddam Hussein's weapons of mass destruction capability. It badly overestimated the Iraqi threat to Israel and reinforced the American and British belief that the weapons existed.

Leftist opposition politician and Knesset member Yossi Sarid, as quoted by Israel Radio, commented, "From now on, when we present serious data on other countries, like Iran for example, who will treat us seriously?"[22]

Brom's report struck raw nerves in Israel. It should have done so in Washington and London as well. In December 1997, there had been another major intelligence failure during Danny Yatom's watch. A 63-year-old veteran Mossad agent, Yehuda Gil, was arrested, tried, and soon convicted to a five-year prison sentence (later reduced to three years) for falsifying data about Syria's supposed intentions to attack Israel. Gil, the prosecution showed, had collected cash fees which he said he had been passing on to an apparently non-existent Syrian 'source." Some of Gil's fabricated intelligence about supposed (and non-existent) Syrian troop movements that might presage an attack on the Golan Heights caused the Rabin government to move troops and make unneeded preparations for an imaginary emergency. Gil's misinformation led to ominous government statements about Syria, and torpedoed some prospective peace talks. Ze'ev Schiff commented, "strategic, diplomatic and political decisions were taken based on these false assessments."[23]

ISRAEL'S STEINITZ INQUIRY

As early as September 2003, the foreign affairs and intelligence subcommittee of the Knesset, under its chairman Yuval Steinitz, began hearings that lasted until March of 2004, on Israeli intelligence failures. Scores of politicians, intelligence officials, journalists, military men, and academics, including Shlomo Brom, Ze'ev Schiff, and top staff officers gave testimony behind closed doors. An open, 81-page report submitted to Israeli President Moshe Katsav on March 28, 2004, was followed by a later detailed, classified version. In the open version the Steinitz Commission castigated Israeli intelligence services for exaggerating the risk of an Iraqi attack before and during the U.S.-led invasion of Iraq. It blamed them equally for apparently neglecting the threat posed by Libyan nuclear projects. After months of secret negotiations with the United States, Libyan leader Colonel Muammar Qaddafi publicly renounced and physically surrendered his nuclear equipment to U.S. and UN inspection officials in early 2004.

The Steinitz Report called for a thorough shakeup and reorganization of the Israeli services. A key passage put the Bush and Blair governments on notice that Israeli information on Iraq had been no better than theirs. When I spoke with General Brom before the report's release, he acknowledged that "probably" some of the misinformation received by all three governments had come from the same or parallel sources, especially Iraqi exiles. Although Brom named no names, critics of the war in the United States placed Ahmed Chalabi and his INC high on the list of probables. In Haaretz, Ze'ev Schiff remarked that in the open report, there was no hint of what happened to the WMD and some missiles that had earlier been in Saddam Hussein's possession. Schiff advanced alternative theories, investigated, he said by Military Intelligence chief General Aharon Ze'evi-Farkash (and perhaps elucidated in the classified version): that there had not been any WMDs for some time before the war; that they were destroyed just before it began; that they had been too well-hidden to be found, even by the thousands of inspections; or that they had been moved to Syria (a theory eagerly propounded by some of the hawks in Washington). Since none of these theories had so far been substantiated, Schiff concluded, "It is not the intelligence evaluation that should be the cause of concern ... but rather that Israeli intelligence did not have sufficient information at its disposal, and that Israel's human intelligence ('humint') system is apparently not good enough."[24]

SHARED WEAPONS, SHARED TRAINING

Israel's actual role in Iraq, though it rarely made headlines, was manifold: war testing of jointly-developed weapons; Israeli classroom and field training of U.S. Special Forces in the same rough tactics that the IDF has been using for years to keep the Palestinians in the West Bank and Gaza subdued, and in the parallel task of fighting terrorism; solid support on the propaganda and psy-war fronts (as reflected in Israeli media, especially the foreign-language news broadcasts of Israel Radio).

One of the most successful weapons the U.S. Army used in the war turned out to be Hunter drones, unmanned aerial vehicles developed in part by Israel Military Industries (IMI) and produced by Northrop Grumman Corporation of the United States. It was disclosed in July 2003 that the U.S. Army was seeking to purchase more. The U.S. Army sent a request to Northrop Grumman for up to 24 drone systems, costing an estimated $60 to $70 million. IMI developed the drones early in the 1990s in cooperation with the American company TRW, at U.S. Army request. The Hunters, supposed to become the Army's main tactical unmanned vehicle (UAV) at a cost of about $1 billion, were found to have "bugs" when first tested in 1996 and could not do active combat service. However, new tests proved they were valuable collectors of intelligence and battlefield surveillance platforms. After Northrop Grumman took over TRW and bought the rights for the Hunters, it went to work with IMI to upgrade the drones. The Pentagon's Undersecretary for Intelligence Kevin Meiers reported that the United States operated 100

UAVs of nine different types, 16 of which were Hunters. They flew 190 sorties in the Iraq war, twice as many as the CIA's Predator drone. During the main fighting before May 1, 2003, the United States lost three Hunters; two to enemy fire and one in an accident; three Predators; one Pioneer (another Israeli weapon) and two British-made drones. At last reports the Hunters were being equipped for firing air-to-ground missiles, as well as intelligence gathering.[25]

By September 2003, an Israeli military software program to teach U.S. soldiers in Iraq how and how not to behave as occupiers was being shown to American junior commanders. The program's developer was Lieu-tenant-Colonel Moshe Guiora, an Israeli military lawyer. It was used to indoctrinate IDF soldiers in "humane behavior" toward the Palestinians, using film clips, animations, photographs, and true-or-false quizzes. One section opened with a scene from the Oliver Stone movie about the Viet-nam war, *Platoon*, showing U.S. soldiers torching huts in a Vietnamese village, tossing hand grenades down wells, and leading away villagers trussed at the neck. Next, the animation shows how mistreating civilians turns them into enemies[26]—lessons evidently not totally absorbed by all of the "coalition" forces in Iraq, as the subsequent Abu Ghraib prisoner abuse scandals showed (of which more below).

One aspect of Israeli–U.S. military and intelligence relations not welcome in Washington was the reported arrival there in the summer of 2003 of the alleged Israeli recruiter of the convicted American spy, Jonathan Pollard. According to a UPI report, this was retired General Rafael "Rafi" Eitan, a veteran Israeli clandestine operator. Eitan had taken part in the successful Israeli kidnapping of the former Nazi holo-caust supervisor Adolf Eichmann and other covert operations. Pollard in 2004 was still serving a life sentence in U.S. federal prison for giving hundreds, if not thousands, of highly-classified U.S. documents to his handlers in the Israeli Embassy in Washington in the early 1980s.

Eitan, once a close friend of Ariel Sharon, ran an Office of Special Tasks called LAKEM in the Israeli Defense Ministry (Sharon was then Defense Minister), tasked with collecting technical and scientific, includ-ing nuclear, intelligence. Pollard's main handler in the United States became Aviem Sella, a key player in the raid on Iraq's Osirak reactor in 1981 and the Israeli Air Force's top gun in matters of nuclear targeting and delivery of airborne nuclear weapons. The recruitment of Pollard in September 1981 came at a time when Sharon and Prime Minister Menchaem Begin were at odds with the Carter administration, which did not want to finance a KH-11 satellite intelligence downlink for Israel in Tel Aviv. White House advisor Richard Allen told Sharon this was impossible (it became possible, as we saw, a decade later when Iraqi missiles were hitting Israel during Operation Desert Storm). Sharon went home angry, calling the U.S.–Israel strategic relationship all "band aids and mustard plasters." Pollard was recruited soon afterward. The FBI was reportedly investigating why Eitan had been regularly entering the United States with an Israeli passport but using a false name.[27]

Despite contretemps like the Pollard–Eitan affair, the Bush administration, and especially Secretary Rumsfeld's Pentagon, gained crucial support from Israeli advisers. Israeli instructors in 2003 began training U.S. forces in the kind of aggressive counter-insurgency tactics with which Israel enforces its own nearly 40-year-old occupation of the Palestinian territories. As early as September 2002, Martin van Creveld, military historian and strategist at Hebrew University, briefed U.S. Marine officers at Camp Lejeune, North Carolina. He found his auditors to be "interested in what it would be like fighting a guerrilla war, especially urban warfare of the kind we were conducting in Jenin," on the West Bank. In early 2004, Palestinian friends in Ramallah told me that eyewitnesses had seen "English-speaking foreigners," probably Americans, with the IDF in Jenin, observing the Israeli house-to-house tactics. At Camp Lejeune, and later at Fort Bragg, Marine and Army officers, already trained in Guam and southern California on lessons from previous American combat in Somalia and Russian fighting against insurgents in Chechnya, showed strong interest in Israeli techniques for subduing a city. One was firing specially armed tank rounds to punch holes in buildings without totally collapsing them, as in Jenin. There, the IDF also used bulldozers and wire-guided missiles fired from helicopters to crush about 200 gunmen barricaded inside the refugee city. U.S. troops later began using these techniques in Iraq, as in the siege of Falluja in the spring of 2004.

Van Creveld warned his audience of "moral and ethnical problems sure to come from fighting among civilians," and noted that Israel used helicopters in Jenin only because the Palestinians had no effective weapons, other than small arms, because "helicopters are very vulnerable."[28] This was another lesson the American forces had to re-learn in Iraq. There the guerrillas, well armed from thousands of abandoned Iraqi army arsenals, fired machine guns, RPGs, and various missiles, bringing down about a dozen helicopters and killing some of their crews by May 2004.

By late 2003, the Pentagon had assembled Task Force 121, composed of Army Delta Force members, Navy Seal commandos, and CIA paramilitary operatives, and Rumsfeld ordered that they should undertake "manhunts" to kill targeted insurgent leaders. Israeli commando and intelligence personnel traveled to Fort Bragg to instruct at the Special Forces training base there. Seymour Hersh reported in the *New Yorker* magazine that two sources told him that Israeli "consultants" had also visited coalition forces in Iraq. (Ze'ev Schiff vehemently denied to me in February 2004 that any Israeli personnel had gone to Iraq.) Hersh found U.S. officials who were skeptical about "manhunts" and targeted assassinations. They recalled the Phoenix Program during the Vietnam war. Special Forces teams were sent to capture or kill Vietnamese thought to be working with or even sympathizing with the Vietcong. The choice of targets depended largely on information supplied by South Vietnamese army officers and village chiefs, often false or highly unreliable. Between in 1968 and 1972, Phoenix killed over 41,000 or around 20,000 victims, depending on whether you believed the higher Vietnamese or the lower American figures. Hersh wrote in some detail of how Iraqis, including former Saddam loyalists like Farouk Hijazi, who had directed foreign operations for the old Iraqi Mukhabarat (intelligence service), were being recruited by the Americans.

Colonel Yoni Fighel, who served in intelligence in Israel's Lebanon invasion in 1982 and later as a West Bank military governor, noted that Iraqi insurgents appeared to have studied Israeli and Palestinian tactics. Suicide bombings and guerrilla warfare, he told a U.S. reporter, are "an excellent tool to build a fence" between coalition soldiers and Iraqi civilians. Like the Israelis in the occupied territories, and the U.S. forces in Vietnam, U.S. and British forces in Iraq have tried to rely on intelligence gleaned from collaborators and prisoners to raid suspects' homes, seek weapons, and extract more intelligence. They use Israeli tactics in bulldozing trees, farmland, and houses to open lines of fire. This has led news media in both Israel and the Arab world to publish comparable images of guerrilla and anti-guerrilla tactics used in Palestine and Iraq.[29]

THE ABU GHRAIB NIGHTMARE

In the spring of 2004, CBS television news and the enterprising investigative journalist Seymour Hersh in the *New Yorker* magazine first publicly exposed U.S. use of another technique, often attributed to Israel in the past, but now a seemingly purely American operation legitimized by the Pentagon: interrogation of Arab prisoners under extremely abusive conditions, characterized by an outraged International Committee of the Red Cross as "tantamount to torture." The most-publicized cases happened at the notorious Abu Ghraib prison, which had been used by the pre-1958, British-protected monarchy and by subsequent

Iraqi regimes. The worst atrocities against prisoners there were perpetrated by Saddam Hussein's torturers. But American personnel, civilian
security contractuals, and possibly CIA interrogators continued the
tradition. As of the late summer of 2004, despite multiple investigations
which the Bush administration ordered at various levels of the military
hierarchy, from local commanders up to the Pentagon level, only "a few
bad apples"—as the Pentagon termed the handful of U.S. soldiers and
non-commissioned officers, male and female, who had been charged or
brought to trial by then—were getting official blame. The episodes,
which both local military commands and Secretary Donald Rumsfeld
and the highest-echelon generals did their best to conceal or hush up
once the initial revelations were made, undoubtedly did more to demol-
ish American moral authority in the world community than any of the
other egregious events of the Iraq war.

The pictures and reports graphically depicted coercion, sexual humiliation, and degradation of Iraqi prisoners. These were being "prepared"
for interrogation by U.S. Army military policemen (and policewomen) at
the request of military intelligence officers. The purpose was to extract
information about terrorism, the spreading guerrilla insurgency, and the
medium and long-term plans of the insurgents. This was apparently part
of Rumsfeld's wish, as Hersh wrote, "to wrest control of America's clandestine and paramilitary operations from the CIA" of George Tenet,
who resigned as CIA director in July of 2004 just before the cascade of
damning reports about CIA intelligence failures before and after 9/11,
especially in Afghanistan and Iraq.

In their rush to extract "operational" intelligence, Rumsfeld and his
aides authorized severe interrogations of prisoners and detainees in
secret prisons and detention centers. These ranged from Guantanamo
Bay in Cuba to "The Pit," a nightmarish prison near Kabul,
Afghanistan, a remote desert jail in Qatar, a hanger near Baghdad International Airport, Abu Ghraib, and about 13 other secret military prisons in Iraq. Following the nominal June 28, 2004, "handover" of
sovereignty to the Iraqi administration, units of the over 130,000 U.S.
troops remaining in Iraq after that date kept control of the secret jails
and interrogation centers. A *Washington Post* investigation found that
the prisons, ranging in size from shipping containers to the vast Guantanamo Bay complex, were part of "an elaborate CIA and military infrastructure whose purpose is to hold suspected terrorists or insurgents for
interrogation and safekeeping while avoiding U.S. or international court
systems, where proceedings and evidence against the accused would be
aired in public." The global network of centers where human rights

charters and the Geneva Conventions on treatment of war prisoners are unknown or ignored also included small CIA-run facilities for top Al-Qaeda and other suspects, and the interrogation centers of "friendly" foreign intelligence services, many with well-documented records of torture. A number of suspects have been "rendered" to these countries, including Syria and Jordan, where the rights of habeas corpus or freedom from physical abuse are observed more in their absence than in practice.

What contributed more than anything else to the global scandal provoked by the torture disclosures was the global dissemination of disks containing hundreds of digital photographs taken by the accused soldiers at Abu Ghraib. They show the soldiers using snarling dogs in attack positions near naked prisoners, human pyramids of naked prisoners with grinning GIs watching them, an accused female soldier holding a prostrate Iraqi prisoner on a dog leash, and other unmentionable scenes of which the photographers or those who instigated the photographs, or both, appeared to have been proud. In a long report prepared by the ICRC on Red Cross visits to coalition jails and internment sites between March and November 2003, similar abuses are detailed at a British-run center in Basra and other parts of the British occupation zone, including forcing hooded, handcuffed, and bound prisoners to sit or kneel on burning hot surfaces, causing unconsciousness and serious burns. Abu Ghraib photographs released later on included pornographic images of some of the American soldiers having sex with each other. There were rumors—although to my knowledge not confirmed by any of the released images—that there were also photos of the sexual abuse of Iraqi women prisoners.

After days of hesitation, President Bush, facing the worldwide reactions of shock, horror, and disgust, on May 6, standing beside visiting King Abdallah of Jordan, said he was "sorry for the humiliation suffered by the Iraqi prisoners and the humiliation suffered by their families." Bush added that he was "equally sorry that people seeing these pictures didn't understand the true nature and heart of America."

The top American commanders in Iraq ordered a halt to torture and abuse. However, international pressure from the UK and elsewhere not withstanding, no such written orders were made public by late summer of 2004, relative to Afghanistan, Guantanamo, or elsewhere, despite court actions by detainees' families.

Israeli commentators reacted vigorously to a charge by retired U.S. Middle East diplomat Eugene Bird, broadcast by the Canadian Broadcasting Corporation (CBC), that Israeli intelligence personnel had been operating in Iraq, including in the interrogations, since the war began. CBC quickly issued a clarification that it had no evidence for Bird's claims. Allegations about Israeli involvement, repeated by Brigadier General Janice Karpinski, the U.S. officer in charge of Abu Ghraib who was suspended from her command after the revelations, seemed to stem from several circumstances. A long report written by U.S. Major General Antonio Taguba, an official investigator, mentions "third-party nationals" (names and nationalities not given) at Abu Ghraib. One of the seven suspects initially arrested (but later released and not charged or tried at the time of writing) was a civilian named John Israel. He was apparently a contract worker with Titan, a company providing services to the U.S. military in Iraq. One of its board members is former CIA chief James Woolsey, a strong supporter of Israel and the "neocons" in Washington, Titan claimed it did not employ John Israel directly, but through an undisclosed subcontractor. Some media reports mentioned California Analysis Center Inc. (CACI) as a firm employing two of the Abu Ghraib suspects. CACI has Pentagon contacts in intelligence and information systems. Its founder and president, Dr. Jack London visited Israel in late 2003 or early 2004. Israeli media reported that he had received an Albert Einstein Technology Award at a special ceremony attended by Iraqi-born Defense Minister Shaul Mofaz.

All of these circumstances proved nothing, of course. They produced emphatic denials in Israel, including some by human rights advocates. However, critics of Israel, many of them Jewish, recall that in 1987 the judicial Landau Report, named after former Israeli Supreme Court judge Moshe Landau, revealed details of how Shin Bet (internal security) interrogators had extracted confessions from prisoners under duress and "unacceptable" physical and psychological pressure, and had lied in court about it under orders from their superiors. Following this, the Knesset enacted strict laws forbidding torture of suspected Palestinian terrorists and others, but permitting "moderate physical pressure." How well these guidelines have been followed is a subject of controversy in Israel. (Much more egregious claims were made about a prison maintained in occupied south Lebanon before the Israeli withdrawal in May 2000, where Lebanese mercenaries of the Israeli occupation forces allegedly used extreme torture techniques.)

The non-profit National Security Archives, a Washington think tank, released CIA manuals from 1963 and the 1980s. In one, a section called "The Coercive Counterintelligence Interrogation of Resistant Sources" approves use of "threats and fear," "pain," and "debility." Another of manuals says that in CIA interrogations intended to get information, the interrogator "is able to manipulate the subject's environment." There is also a recommendation "to create unpleasant or intolerable situations, to disrupt patterns of time, space, and sensory perception."

A former senior officer in the Shin Bet's interrogations branch told *Haaretz* and Israeli TV reporter Yossi Melman: "When one reads all the American documents and reports, it is clear that the Americans did not need us to conduct interrogations. The reports and the pictures of the torture, abuse, and humiliation from the prison in Iraq portray a reality compared to which the interrogations of the Palestinians by us are really child's play."[30]

ISRAEL, TURKEY, AND THE IRAQI KURDS

The *New Yorker*'s intrepid and well-informed Seymour Hersh in early summer of 2004 discovered what was certain to become a serious, if not fatal barrier to the Bush administration's avowed purpose of unifying and democratizing a "new" Iraq. He uncovered what appeared to be a concerted Israeli effort—to the intense chagrin of Turkey, the ally of both Israel and America—to renew the old Israeli covert ties with the Kurds of northern Iraq. Not the least of Jerusalem's purposes in sending its intelligence and military operatives back to Iraqi Kurdistan, whose history we reviewed in Chapter 5, was to use the Kurds as instruments against what Israel viewed as its next and biggest strategic enemy—a (possibly nuclear) rearmed Iran, which in 2003–04 responded evasively to increasingly anxious United Nations (IAEA), American, and European queries, and limited IAEA inspections.

The Ankara government was alarmed, as always, about Kurdish separatism in Iraq as a possible stepping stone to an "independent" Kurdistan which could act as a magnet for Turkey's Kurds. This would threaten the unity of Turkey as well as of Iraq. That Turkey's good military ally Israel lukewarmly denied Seymour Hersh's reports was mild encouragement for Ankara: Turkish Prime Minister Recep Tayyip Erdogan said he "wanted" to believe the Israeli denials. At the same time, as the authoritative Middle East Economic Survey (MEES) reported on July 13, 2004, Turkey quietly but emphatically warned the U.S.-installed Iraqi interim government of Prime Minster Ahmed Allawi that it wanted Kurdish separatism in Iraq curbed, and that Kirkuk and its regional oilfields in particular should not come under exclusive or extremist Kurdish control. According to Hersh, Mossad and Israeli military operatives, some posing as businessmen, were training Kurdish commandos and "most important in Israel's view, running covert operations inside Kurdish areas of Iran and Syria."

Hersh said he had been told by a former senior Israeli intelligence official that an Israeli concern, following the nominal coalition handover of power to the Allawi government on June 28, was to build and strengthen Kurdish commando units. These would balance the Shi'ite militias in southern Iraq of Imam Muqtada al-Sadr and others fighting the coalition. The Israeli idea, Hersh's source told him, was to make the Kurds as effective in this deadly work as Israel's "most secretive commando units," the Mistaravim. This would enable them to go further than the Americans had been able to do to "penetrate, gather intelligence on, and then kill off the leadership of the Shi'ite and Sunni insurgencies in Iraq." However, Hersh's informant acknowledged, the Turks were upset "no end" because they feared the same Kurdish commandos, once trained, "could infiltrate and attack in Turkey."

Israel's Washington Embassy denied the story. Neither the Iraqi Kurds nor the U.S. State Department would comment on it. However, Hersh insisted that a senior CIA official confirmed to him that the Israelis were indeed operating in Kurdistan and that this was widely known in the American intelligence community.[31]

Of all of the possible signals or precursors of civil war, and possibly cross-border wars in post-Saddam Hussein Iraq, this looked to be one of the direst.

NATION-BUILDING—OR DISSOLUTION?

In the spring of 2004 the U.S. presidential election campaign began to heat up, with the conduct of affairs in Iraq a central issue between President George W. Bush and his Democratic challenger, Senator John Kerry. The London-based International Institute for Strategic Studies (IISS) took its customary distance from the often sensational reporting of daily mayhem and the coalition's frustration in Iraq. In its annual *Strategic Survey* the IISS undertook a prescient analysis of the progress and the multiple mistakes of American policy. It took into account the manifest linkage— largely ignored by the senior Bushites in Washington—between Iraq and the Israel–Palestine question. A timid Bush administration (under strong influence of AIPAC and the other Israeli lobby organizations and of the Pentagon's neocon war hawks) had more or less given the Sharon government in Jerusalem a blank check to act as it pleased. However, the IISS study failed to consider any Israeli involvement, direct and indirect, in the war and occupation in Iraq. It also barely did justice to Washington's disastrous decision to disband the entire Iraqi army, and to start from scratch retraining new Iraqi security and police forces. Many of these, after hasty training, left their posts when asked, before the June 28 handover, to fight their fellow Iraqis, insurgents in towns like Falluja and Najaf.

Quite correctly, the IISS survey did point out the total failure of the Americans—as in Somalia and other places where their troops faced insurgencies—to disarm the Iraqi population after Saddam fell and major conventional combat ceased. This encouraged the Iraqi insurgents, terrorists, and foreign jihadists of Al-Qaeda and other organizations, who crossed Iraq's (at first) largely unguarded borders and joined, or in many cases directed, the rebel action. The IISS wrote that a combination of the Iraqi provisional authority's "inability to guarantee personal safety and its inconsistent and biased application of disarmament edicts—for instance, allowing Kurdish militias to retain their arms while demanding that certain Shi'ite ones relinquish them" encouraged the insurgents' attacks.

Wavering and uncertain U.S. plans for Iraqi reconstruction, the IISS found, passed through four stages. Initially, ex-U.S. Army General Jay Garner and a team of senior civilians from various other services including the CIA followed on the tracks of the liberators of Baghdad. Garner, without any coherent Pentagon plans to prevent looting or restore water, electricity, and other essentials for the population, lasted only a short time. Garner's replacement, career Foreign Service officer L. Paul Bremer III, went in with an apparent mandate to buffer disagreements between Pentagon neocons supposedly supervising reconstruction and Secretary Colin Powell's State Department, whose elaborate and thoughtful paper planning for occupation and reconstruction had been dismissed by Rumsfeld.

On the political front, Bremer at first delayed passing power to an Iraqi leadership council, composed mainly of returned former exiles, including of course Ahmed Chalabi's INC. Attempts during the first weeks of the occupation, on Garner's watch, to constitute some kind of embryonic representative assembly had foundered, in large part because the huge unpopularity of the U.S. occupation forces and the belief that their presence might be temporary caused Iraqis to play "wait and see what's going to happen" before committing themselves to involvement in any new political process.

In July 2003 Bremer created the Iraqi Governing Council (IGC). Its members, handpicked by him and his advisers after many negotiations with seven main exiled groups, had 13 members including Shi'ites, five Sunnis, one Turcoman, and one Christian. Chalabi, accused of serious though unproven malfeasance including passing information on U.S.

code-breaking to Iran, was excluded, after his $340,00 monthly Pentagon subsidy had been stopped. As insurgent violence mounted in November 2003, the coalition recognized the IGC's flaws. Even Rumsfeld's Pentagon hawks (and one or two media commentators in Israel) recognized that Washington's "go it alone" strategy was not working. Washington and London (where Prime Minister Tony Blair suffered rising unpopularity with a population overwhelmingly opposed to the war) decided it would be better, after all, to bring European allies and the UN, leery of involvement after its popular emissary Vieira de Mello's murder, into the picture.

It was also recognized, though not admitted in public by Bush administration spokespeople, that the occupation and the resistance against it were acting as a magnet for all manner of Al-Qaeda and other foreign terrorist adventurers, who were pouring into Iraq[32] and bringing with them some new and sophisticated terrorist techniques: multiple car bombs, roadside bombs, mortar, rocket, and sniping attacks which took an almost daily toll of coalition troops, and even more so of Iraqi civilians and newly recruited policemen.

Washington felt compelled to pledge the handover of power to the Iraqis by June 30, 2004. On November 15, 2003, the ICG endorsed a U.S. scheme for drafting of a quasi-constitution, a "fundamental law," to be followed by the creation of a transitional assembly of 200 to 300 delegates. This would choose a cabinet and leader and was supposed to guide Iraq toward democratic elections, tentatively set for January 2005. After months of wrangling in which several deadlines could not be met, the interim constitution, known as the Transitional Administrative Law (TAL) was agreed on March 7, 2004. By the end of 2005, a new permanent constitution and government were supposed to be in place. It was also expected that Saddam Hussein and eleven of his imprisoned top aides, notified to their faces in early July of the sweeping charges of war crimes and crimes against humanity that would be brought against them, would be tried and judged by Iraqis, backed up by international advisers, sometime in 2005.

After an initial lull following the June 28 handover of power, major terrorist attacks resumed during the summer weeks. The new interim prime minister was Iyad Allawi, a tough former Ba'athist and leader of the exiled Iraqi National Accord (INA). He had been chosen in effect by Bremer, after lengthy political consultations by the UN's indefatigable veteran diplomat, Lakhdar Brahimi, throughout Iraq. In July Allawi formally asked NATO, the North Atlantic Treaty Organization, to help lift Iraq out of it morass of violence and lagging reconstruction.

Immediately after Bremer's departure on June 28, the Bush administration sent John Negroponte, U.S. Ambassador to the UN, to take over the huge new American Embassy, which replaced Bremer's occupation authority and occupied the same heavily fortified "Green Zone" amid Saddam's former palaces in central Baghdad. Negroponte, a career diplomat, had acquired a reputation as a ruthless Cold Warrior in Central America, and as a skilled and highly capable ambassador at the United Nations. Prime Minister Allawi, with Negroponte behind him, decreed emergency powers that amounted to martial law and promised a merciless crackdown on the insurgents. Everyone knew he needed American troops, along with the nascent Iraqi security forces, to accomplish this. This seemed to preclude any American pullout for the foreseeable future. And indeed, the Pentagon began recalling thousands of the "ready reserves," Army veterans who had already served their full terms, and launching campaigns to persuade men leaving the downsized U.S. Navy and Air Force to join the Army.

Chosen to be head of the nominally sovereign Iraqi state was President Ghazi al-Yawar. He was an unusual combination of tribal sheikh—heading the 3-million strong and very influential Shamar tribe and wearing flowing white robes and a gold-rimmed cape at his inauguration—but at the same time a practical and experienced businessman. Senior NATO officials flew from a NATO summit in Istanbul to Baghdad to meet with Allawi, but especially with U.S. Army General David Petraeus, who headed the U.S. mission training the new Iraqi security forces.

Although some NATO allies, including the Netherlands, new NATO member Poland (which sent over 12,000 troops, the third largest coalition contingent), and Italy were prepared to pitch in and help, other members of what Rumsfeld had once termed "the coalition of the willing" turned out to be highly unwilling. Spain, had already withdrawn its large contingent after the horrendous terrorist attack in Madrid in May and the closely-following Spanish election defeat of Prime Minister Asnar's conservative government by the Socialists, who had made a campaign promise to leave Iraq. Fellow Hispanics, Salvador and the Dominican Republic, pulled out their token forces. Thailand withdrew its soldiers. A series of kidnappings and taking of hostages (similar to several insurgent attacks in Saudi Arabia) and the barbarous beheading of foreign civilians taken hostage threatened to make Bulgaria, the Philippines, and other coalition partners reconsider their alignment with Washington and London and pull their troops out. President Gloria Aroyo of the Philippines ordered the 51-man Filipino force to leave several weeks before their mandate expired in

August, yielding to popular pressure to secure a Filipino hostage's release.

Basically, as historian William Pfaff pointed out, there remained crucial and divergent views about the future of NATO, and the strategic future of the expanded European Union. Should they get involved in nation-building, once anathema to the Bush administration in Washington, or in trying to reshape the larger world beyond? The Bush administration gradually realized how much they needed European and, if obtainable, Arab help in rebuilding Iraq.

However, the basic split between America and Europe over Iraq persisted. The Bush program, which might remain on Washington's agenda even after the end of a first or even a second (and final) Bush term, was to replace "axis of evil" governments in the Middle East, with U.S.-sponsored Muslim "democracies," (which the neocons hoped against hope might thaw their frigid hostility toward Israel). The Europeans, especially in France and Germany, considered that bringing democracy to the Arab and Muslim worlds might well be an unrealistic, even impossible, dream, especially when, as in Iraq (and projected by some neocons for Iran, Syria, and others), it was brought about by crushing military force.

Europeans and others almost universally opposed the Bush policy of unqualified support for the Sharon government in the Israel–Palestine struggle (though there was some approval of Sharon's determination to evacuate Gaza while retaining most West Bank settlements), a position which Democratic presidential contender Senator John Kerry was also supporting verbally by the summer of 2004. The European NATO members in general preferred to return to the multilateral peace negotiations of the Clinton era, following conclusion of the (failed) 1993 Oslo accords between Israel and the Palestinians. The United States, anxious to seek company in misery, worked frantically to get NATO, once scorned along with the UN by Washington, involved in Iraqi peacekeeping and reconstruction, but at first had only gotten half-hearted pledges from several NATO members to help train Iraqi security forces.[33]

AN ENDGAME BEGINS; AN ALLIANCE HOLDS FIRM

The American-led war and occupation, which began in March 2003, accomplished some of its purely military objectives. It destroyed the military institutions and much of the infrastructure of Saddam's tyrannical Ba'ath-ruled state, and ousted him from power. But by summer of 2004, despite the nominal transfer of sovereignty, it had failed dismally to restore a viable state or to bring about economic and social well-being for Iraqis. A kind of huge American protectorate has been implanted in the center of the Arab world. Nominal Iraqi sovereignty was supposed to have been restored in the handover of June 28, 2004. But the UN and/or NATO supervision which, in desperation, the Bush administration had to request when guerrilla insurgency and political chaos seemed to be getting out of hand, were lacking The disorder and license which raged through post-war Iraqi society had, in fact also provided freedoms of speech, press, and assembly rarely if ever enjoyed under Iraq's past Arab, Turkish, or British rulers. Israel's cherished objective of removing the Iraqi armed forces as a formidable foe on its "Eastern Front" and ally of the stubborn Palestinian resistance movement had been accomplished, largely without loss of either Israeli blood or treasure. The former close Israeli–American partnership had to all intents and purposes become a firm and even a formal political, economic, and military alliance. Israel could count on U.S. congressional and administration support for almost any move the Sharon and post-Sharon Israeli leaderships in Jerusalem chose to make, and the protection of an almost automatically guaranteed U.S. veto in the UN Security Council to prevent pressure against Israel by the rest of the international community.

One downside of the occupation of Iraq was that corruption appeared to be rife among the firms hand-picked by the Pentagon to work in reconstruction. Ironically, in February 2004, following the admission by the U.S. giant firm of Halliburton (Vice-President Dick Cheney's former company) that it had overcharged the U.S. military in Iraq for fuel by passing on inflated prices from Kuwaiti suppliers, the U.S. Army, according to Israeli media reports, awarded Israel's Sonol gasoline company and its foreign partner Morgantown International a tender worth $70–80 million to pump fuel to the U.S. forces in Iraq. Israel has seen its dream of restoring the old pre-1948 Iraq-to-Haifa oil pipeline evaporate, and still imports its fuel by sea. The Sonol fuel, refined in Israel, was being shipped from the Beersheba area by land through Jordan to Iraq. Israeli businesses and businessmen have shown interest in getting pieces of the action, even as Israeli intelligence and covert military forces appear to have returned to Iraqi Kurdistan.

What the war and occupation in Iraq have not accomplished is, quite simply, peace and the national unity of Iraq's three main regional ethnicities: the Sunni center and west, the Shia south, and the Kurdish north. Indeed, there have been published editorials urging that Iraq be dismembered and left back in its Ottoman or pre-Ottoman status as three separate entities. Some Israeli commentators and at least one American (Leslie Gelb, former head of the Council on Foreign Relations) have contended that this would be desirable because they would be so weak that they could not threaten anyone, except each other.

I strongly disagree. The centripetal and trans-national forces of these three main ethnic groups and some of their satellite minorities would in the event of Iraq's division seriously threaten stability and unity in neighbors like Turkey, Jordan, Iran, and Syria. In the long run Israel, with or without its 1967 territorial conquests, would suffer too, as it would be drawn directly or indirectly into new regional conflicts. By summer of 2004 its seemingly permanent military alliance with Turkey was under great strain, due to Turkish fears about growing U.S. or Israeli-backed Kurdish strength in Iraq, and Turkish disapproval of Sharon's iron methods against the Palestinians.

Even, in some cases, before they acceded to power in 2001, President George W. Bush and his advisors were bent on radical "regime change" and reform in the larger Muslim world. American force, they made clear, should be used to bring this about—even at the cost of a mounting and already astronomical U.S. budget deficit, never equaled before, of at least $400 billion. Until the 1990s, few serious commentators had believed that the United States would fight again in either Iraq or the Gulf, at least before the older and more fundamental conflict over Palestine was resolved. The U.S. neoconservatives' response has been that the road to war on Iraq does not lie through an Israel–Palestine peace, but rather that the road to Israel–Palestine peace lies through Baghdad. By invading Iraq, the United States not only adopted Israel's old methods—initiative, offence, and pre-emption—but also made Israel's foes its own; especially since the Bush policymakers believed that two neighboring members of the Bush "Axis of Evil"—Iraq and Iran—were arming themselves with WMDs. In March 2003, when the war began, Ariel Sharon told *The Times* of London that the United States and Britain, once Iraq had been "pacified," should turn to Iran. Well over a decade earlier, senior Israelis like former minister Moshe Sneh were insisting that if the Western states did not "do their duty" and block Iran's nuclear ambitions, "Israel will find itself forced to act alone, and will accomplish its task by any [i.e. including nuclear] means." A Washington Cassandra, analyst John Pike, predicted in 2003 that "either the U.S. or Israelis are going to attack [Iranian nuclear sites] or acquiesce in Iran being a nuclear state."[34] After President George W. Bush's re-election in November 2004, Iran risked further hostile attention by the U.S. and Israel.

In the end, I can only repeat my deep conviction, even deeper now than when I first published it during my first years in the region in the 1960s and 1970s: none of the Middle Eastern conflicts, including those affecting what was once Mesopotamia, will ever be peacefully resolved until there is a fair settlement between Israel and the Palestinian Arabs. As a distinguished Israeli general and intelligence analyst and highly cerebral author, the late General Yehosafat Harkaby, told me once in 1969, "Our problem is not what happened in 1948, 1967, or what catastrophes may occur in the future. Our problem is existential: how are we to live in peace, now, side by side, with the Palestinians and with our other neighbors?"

The late President Anwar al-Sadat of Egypt, in his 1978 memoirs, *In Search of Identity*, had a cogent answer. It applies to the Middle East as a whole, and in particular to the lands running eastward from the Mediterranean's shores to the rivers Tigris and Euphrates. The United States and its Israeli ally, seemingly welded to the United States more firmly than ever in the crucible of their parallel adventures in Iraq, should keep in mind Sadat's reminder: "There can be hope only for a society which acts as one big family, and not as many separate ones."[35]

Notes

1 THE BABYLONIAN HERITAGE

1. Steven Bayme, "Iraq, Babylon and Baghdad in Jewish History and Thought," *American Jewish Committee*, June 1, 2003 (internet document), p. 1.
2. *The Hodder and Stoughton Illustrated Bible Dictionary*, Herbert Lockyer Sr. (ed.) (Thomas Nelson, Nashville, Ky., 1986), pp. 208–9.
3. Neil MacFarquhar, "Outdoing Nebuchadnezzar," *International Herald Tribune*, p. 5, August 20, 2003; Gavin Young, *Iraq: Land of Two Rivers*, Photos by Nik Wheeler (London, Collins, 1980), pp. 17–18. "Ancient Babylon," The History of the Ancient Near East, Electronic Compendium, undated, pp. 1–2 online.
4. Rudolph Fischer, *Babylon, Entdeckungsreisen in die Vergangenheit* (Thienemann, Edition Erdmann, place and date of publication unspecified), p. 35.
5. James Wellard, *By the Waters of Babylon* (London, Hutchinson, 1972), pp. 18–19.
6. A. J. Arberry (ed.), *Religion in the Middle East: Three Religions in Concord and Conflict* (Cambridge University Press, 1969), Vol. I, *Judaism and Christianity*, pp. 136–7, p. 192.
7. Melissa Block, NPR's "All Things Considered," August 6, 2003, online transcript.
8. Arberry, op. cit., p. 192.
9. Stephen Bayme, op. cit., pp. 1–2.
10. Sandra Mackey, *The Reckoning: Iraq and the Legacy of Saddam Hussein* (New York, Norton, 2002), pp. 96–7.
11. Hanna Batatu, *The Old Social Classes and the Revolutionary Movements of Iraq* (Princeton University Press, 1978), p. 286.
12. Batatu, op. cit., pp. 287–8.
13. Batatu, op. cit., pp. 290–1.
14. Mackey, op. cit., pp. 89–90.

2 THE OTTOMAN EMPIRE DIVIDED

1. Mackey, op. cit., pp. 100–1.
2. Peter Mansfield, *A History of the Middle East*, Second Edition, revised and updated by Nicolas Pelham (London, Penguin Books, 2003), pp. 151–7.
3. Mackey, op. cit., pp. 105–9.
4. "Behind the War in Iraq," *Monthly Review*, May 1, 2003, p. 3, online.
5. *New York Times*, July 18, 2003.
6. Mansfield, op. cit., pp. 197–9.
7. Marion Farouk-Sluglett and Peter Sluglett, *Iraq Since 1958: From Revolution to Dictatorship* (London and New York, I. B. Tauris), p. 8.

8.   Mansfield, op. cit., p. 214.
9.   David Fromkin, *A Peace to End All Peace: The Fall of the Ottoman Empire and the Creation of the Modern Middle East* (New York, Henry Holt, 1989), p. 29.
10. Fromkin, op. cit., p. 501.
11. Fromkin, op. cit., pp. 502–3.
12. Joseph Heller, *The Birth of Israel: 1945–1949, Ben-Gurion and His Critics* (Gainsville, University Press of Florida, 2000), p. 2. Remarks in parentheses are mine.
13. Fromkin, op. cit., pp. 519–20.

3 "OPERATION EZRA AND NEHEMIAH": BITTERSWEET FLIGHT TO ZION

1.   Raise Marcus, "Flight from Babylon," *Jerusalem Post*, August 23, 1996, online.
2.   Batatu, op. cit., p. 19.
3.   Batatu, op. cit., pp. 247–8.
4.   Batatu, op. cit., p. 312.
5.   Batatu, op. cit., p. 19; Mackey, op. cit., pp. 142–7 and 168–70.
6.   Sraya Shapiro, "Bye-bye Baghdad," *Jerusalem Post*, November 12, 1998, online; Shlomo Hillel, *Operation Babylon, Jewish Clandestine Activity in the Middle East 1946–51* (Glasgow, Fontana/Collins 1985), p. 22.
7.   Hillel, op. cit., pp. 13–30 and 145–70, passim; Ian Black and Benny Morris, *Israel's Secret Wars: A History of Israel's Intelligence Services* (New York, Grove Press, 1991), pp. 87–9.
8.   "The Jews of Iraq," in *The Link*, published by Americans for Middle East Understanding, Inc., Vol. 31, Issue 2, April–May 1998, pp. 1–5.
9.   Dalia Karpel, "It Could have been Paradise Here," *Haaretz*, English online edition, October 29, 2003.
10. Mordechai Ben-Porat, *To Baghdad and Back: The Miraculous 2,000 Year Homecoming of the Iraqi Jews* (Jerusalem and New York, Gefen, 1998), p. 178.
11. *The Link*, p. 7.
12. *The Link*, pp. 7–8.
13. David Hirst, *The Gun and the Olive Branch: The Roots of Violence in the Middle East* (New edition, London, Faber and Faber, 2003), p. 280. Hirst cites original Israeli sources.
14. Hirst, op. cit., pp. 280–1; Ben-Porat, op. cit., pp. 179–81.
15. Hirst, op. cit., pp. 281–2; *The Link*, passim.

4 IRAQ ENTERS THE PALESTINE ARENA

1.   Black and Morris, op. cit., pp. 8–10.
2.   Heller, op. cit., p. 10.
3.   Black and Morris, op. cit., pp. 18–34.
4.   Hirst, op. cit., pp. 233–4.
5.   Heller, op. cit., pp. 85–93.
6.   Farouk-Sluglett and Sluglett, op. cit., pp. 38–41.
7.   (Pakistani) Brig. Gen. (Ret.) Syed Ali El-Edroos, *The Hashemite Arab Army 1908–1979: An Appreciation and Analysis of Military Operations* (Amman, Jordan, Publishing Committee, 1980), pp. 243–5.

8. El-Edroos, op. cit., pp. 246–7; p. 256.
9. El-Edroos, op. cit., pp. 258–63; p. 268; Heller, op. cit., pp. 302–3.
10. Michael B. Oren, *Six Days of War: June 1967 and the Making of the Modern Middle East* (New York Ballantine Books, 2002, 2003), pp. 4–5.
11. Oren, op. cit., p. 5.; El-Edroos, op. cit., p. 271.
12. See John K. Cooley, "The U.S. Pushes 'Regime Change' at its Peril," *International Herald Tribune*, November 18, 2003, p. 6. A personal account of the CIA's role in Syria in 1949 by an involved former CIA operative appears in Miles Copeland, *The Game of Nations: The Amorality of Power Politics* (London, Weidenfeld and Nicolson, 1969–70), pp. 28–49.
13. El-Edroos, op. cit., pp. 271–2.
14. Quoted in El-Edroos, op. cit., p. 272.
15. Heller, op. cit., p. 303. Although he disagrees with historian Avi Shlaim's dovish interpretations, Heller, like some other mainstream Jewish and Israeli historians, cites Shlaim's two volumes, *Collusion across the Jordan: King Abdallah, the Zionist Movement and the Partition of Palestine, 1921–1951* (Oxford, Clarendon, 1988) and *The Politics of Partition: King Abdallah, the Zionist Movement, the Zionists and Palestine, 1921–1951* (Oxford, Oxford University Press, 1990).

5 *MÉNAGE À QUATRE*: THE U.S., ISRAEL, IRAN, AND THE IRAQI KURDS

1. AFP dispatch, Maseef Salahadin, Iraq, April 29, 2003.
2. Ezer Weizman, *The Battle for Peace* (New York, Bantam, 1981), p. 91.
3. See "U.S. 'Plans to Keep Bases in Iraq,'" *Guardian Weekly*, April 24–30, 2003, page 1.
4. Fromkin, op. cit., pp. 404–5.
5. Fromkin, op. cit., pp. 398–9.
6. Gordon Thomas, *Gideon's Spies: The Secret History of the Mossad* (New York, Thomas Dunne Books of St. Martin's Press, 1999), p. 42.
7. Black and Morris, op. cit., pp. 183–4.
8. David McDowall, *A Modern History of the Kurds* (London and New York, I. B. Tauris, 1996), p. 314.
9. Marion Woolfson, *Prophets in Babylon: Jews in the Arab World* (London and Boston, Faber and Faber, 1980), p. 218.
10. Yediot Aharonot, May 10, 1978, extracts quoted in Woolfson, op. cit., pp. 221–2; conversations with author's private sources.
11. Edmund Ghareeb, *The Kurdish Question in Iraq* (Syracuse University Press, 1981), pp. 142–3.
12. Lee Dinsmore, "The Forgotten Kurds," *The Progressive*, April 1977, p. 39.
13. Kevin Alan Brook, "The Genetic Bonds Between Kurds and Jews," untitled online newsletter found at www.barzan.com, undated. The article also contains references to genetic and anthropological studies by researchers at the Hebrew University of Jerusalem and elsewhere, and a bibliography of other articles and books supporting the supposed genetic affinity of Kurds and Jews.
14. G. H. Sedan, "Consulate Attack Marks Low Point in Israeli–Kurdish Relations," *Jewish Telegraph Agency*, published by *Jewish News of Greater Phoenix*, February 26, 1999, p. 2.

15. Ghareeb, op. cit., pp. 138–9, quoting what may have been the original source, the newspaper *Al-Ahad*, Beirut, August 10, 1969. I have confirmed most of these details in various conversations over the years with U.S. and other officials involved.
16. Henry Kissinger, *Years of Renewal* (New York, Simon and Schuster, 1999), pp. 576–87.
17. Private memorandum, November 2003.
18. Author's reporting notes for the *Christian Science Monitor*, April 1975.

6 HOW THE CIA GAVE SADDAM A LEG UP

1. Al-Ahram, September 27, 1963, quoted in Batatu, op. cit., p. 986.
2. Tariq Ali, *Bush in Babylon* (London and New York, Verso, 2003), pp. 77–86.
3. "James H. Critchfield, Colonel, United States Army, Central Intelligence Agency Official," obituary, Arlington National Cemetery Website, April 23, 200, online.
4. Batatu, op. cit., pp. 685–6.
5. Batatu, op. cit., pp. 983–5; "How West Helped Saddam Gain Power and Decimate the Iraqi Elite," by Mohamoud A. Shaikh, Muslimedia August 16–31, 1997, online.
6. Critchfield obituary; Andrew and Patrick Cockburn, *Out of the Ashes: The Resurrection of Saddam Hussein* (London, Verso, 2000), quoted online in a blog by Tim Buckley, December 26, 2000.
7. Stephen Dorril, MI-6, *Inside the Covert World of Her Majesty's Secret Intelligence Service* (New York and London, Simon and Schuster, 2000), pp. 681, 689.
8. Critchfield obituary.
9. Con Coughlin, *Saddam: The Secret Life* (London, Pan Macmillan, 2002), pp. 41–2.
10. Quoted by Coughlin, op. cit., p. 43.
11. Farouk-Sluglett and Sluglett, op. cit., pp. 97–8.
12. Aburish, Said, *Saddam Hussein: The politics of Revenge* (London, Trafalgar, 2000), pp. 60–4.
13. The foregoing is drawn from "The Influence of the Peripheral Arab States on Arab–Israeli Wars," by Israeli analyst Dov Tamari, published by the Jaffee Center for Strategic Studies, Tel Aviv University, undated; my own personal notes from the period and from the excellent book of the Israeli historian Michael B. Oren, *Six Days of War: June 1967 and the Making of the Modern Middle East* (New York, Ballantine, 2003), pp. 1–127, passim, especially p. 2 (the Aref–Nasser meeting in February 1967).
14. Oren, op. cit., p. 321.
15. Farouk-Sluglett and Sluglett, op. cit., pp. 99–101.

7 SADDAM'S REIGN (I): BUSINESS WITH THE U.S.; WARFARE WITH ISRAEL

1. Oren, op. cit., p. 10.
2. Aburish, op. cit., pp. 73–4.
3. Aburish, op. cit., pp. 76–8; Sluglett and Sluglett, op. cit., pp. 113–15.
4. Farouk-Sluglett and Sluglett, op. cit., pp. 119–23.
5. Biographic sketch of Saddam Hussein by British Embassy in Baghdad, November 15, 1969, Public Record Office, London, FCO 17/871, summarized by National

Security Archive (NSA), Washington, DC, online, December 20, 2003.

6. Jackob Nimrodi (English spelling on title page), *My Life's Journey* (in Hebrew), (Or Yehuda, Israel, Ma'ariv Book Guild, 2003), in two volumes. The first volume basically recites his earlier military career in Etzel and the Palmach during the War of Independence, and his adventures as a Jewish Agency and Mossad representative unofficially accredited to the Shah's court in Tehran; the second, his business coups and successes, especially in the arms trade and in development projects inside and outside Israel. Nimrodi claims that the Israeli military censor held up the book's publication for a long period due to the sensitive nature of many of his disclosures. As of this writing in early 2004, the memoirs had not been published in English.

7. Samuel Segev, *The Iranian Triangle: The Untold Story of Israel's Role In The Iran–Contra Affair* (New York, Macmillan, Free Press, 1988), pp. 2–3; Black and Morris, op. cit., p. 328; Nimodi, op. cit., Vol. I, passim.

8. Black and Morris, op. cit., pp. 206–9.

9. Coughlin, op. cit., pp. 79–82.

10. Black and Morris, pp. 255–6. For extensive background to the events of "Black September" 1970, see John K. Cooley, *Green March, Black September: The Story of the Palestinian Arabs* (London, Frank Cass, 1973).

11. Cooley, op. cit., pp. 110–14.

12. El-Edroos, op. cit., pp. 445–6, 450–1, 452–6; Cooley, op. cit., pp. 112–21. The Washington sequences are drawn from personal interviews and from Walter Isaacson, *Kissinger: A Biography* (New York, Simon and Schuster, 1992), pp. 292–9.

13. Aburish, op. cit., pp. 90–1.

8 SADDAM'S REIGN (II): POWER PLAYS AND WAR, 1970–80

1. Ofra Bengio, "Crossing the Rubicon? Iraq and the Arab–Israeli Peace Process," in *MERIA* journal, Tel Aviv, Vol. 2, No. 1, March 1998, hereinafter referred to as Bengio.

2. Andrew and Leslie Cockburn, *Dangerous Liaison: the Inside Story of the U.S.–Israeli Covert Relationship* (New York, Harper Perennial, HarperCollins, 1992), pp. 169–70. The late Archibald Roosevelt expressed these thoughts in his memoirs, *For Lust of Knowing* (Boston, Little Brown, 1988), p. 448, and expanded on them in a personal interview with the author during a private presentation to invited guests at a London club in 1983.

3. El Edroos, op. cit., pp. 485–9.

4. El-Edroos, op. cit., p. 488.

5. Oren, op. cit., p. 315.

6. See Cooley in the *Monitor* and Hoagland in the *Post*, issues of July 5, 1973.

7. Black and Morris, op. cit., pp. 300–3. This quote is on p. 303.

8. Interview with Antoine Touma, ABC News representative in Damascus, 1980. Touma served at the time in an anti-aircraft unit of the Syrian army near Latakia, which came under fire during the engagement.

9. Black and Morris, op. cit., pp. 305–13.

10. Farouk-Sluglett and Sluglett, op. cit., pp. 172–3.

11. Aburish, op. cit., pp. 162–4; personal interviews in 1979 and 1980.

12. Aburish, op. cit., pp. 171–6.

13. Farouk-Sluglett and Sluglett, op. cit., pp. 151–2.
14. Aburish, op. cit., pp. 187–91; author's private interviews in Amman, Jordan, 1981–85 and 1995.

9 SADDAM'S REIGN (III): DEFEAT AND DEFIANCE, 1980–90

1. John K. Cooley, *Payback: America's Long War in the Middle East* (London and New York, Brassey's, 1991) foreword by Pierre Salinger.
2. National Security Archive Update, *The Saddam Hussein Sourcebook*, December 18, 2003, online, p. 3.
3. Segev, op. cit., pp. 4–6.
4. A photocopy of the letter appears on p. 424 of Nimrodi's memoirs, published in two volumes in Hebrew by Maariv Book Guild, Or Yehuda, Israel, vol. 1.
5. Segev, op. cit., pp. 7–11 and Nimrodi's memoirs, passim.
6. The scientist now lives in Britain. His brother, a prominent Arab editor, is my source. At the time of the attack, I was a temporary Senior Associate at the Carnegie Endowment for International Peace in Washington, and helped to prepare a disapproving report on the attack for the Arms Control Association.
7. Black and Morris, op. cit., pp. 332–4; Donald Neff, "Israel Bombs Iraq's Osirak Nuclear Research Facility," in *Washington Report On Middle East Affairs*, newsletter, June 1995, pp. 81–2.
8. Gerald Westerby, *In Hostile Territory: Business Secrets of a Mossad Combatant* (New York, Harper Business, 1998), pp. 25–32.
9. Neff, op. cit., pp. 81–2.
10. Alan Friedman, *Spider's Web: Bush, Saddam, Thatcher and the Decade of Deceit* (London and Boston, Faber and Faber, 1993), pp. 4–5.
11. National Security Archive (NSA) Update, NSSM 4–82, mention on p. 3.
12. NSA Update, NSDD 114, Documents 28, 32, 36, 44, 58, pp. 3–4; Friedman, pp. 27–8.
13. NSA Update, Documents 47, 48 and 61, p. 5; Friedman, op. cit., p. 29; author's interviews in London with senior oil company sources in 1984.
14. Friedman, op. cit., pp. 29–30
15. Cooley, *Payback*, pp. 115 and 119–21. For much more elaborate detail and the inside story from an Israeli viewpoint, see Samuel Segev, op. cit., passim, especially pp. 167–83.
16. NSA Update, Documents 44 and 58, p. 4.
17. Aburish, op. cit., pp. 24–241.
18. NSA Update, pp. 6–7.
19. Loretta Napoleoni, *Modern Jihad: Tracing the Dollars Behind the Terror Networks* (London and Sterling, Va., Pluto, 2003), p. 185.
20. Napoleoni, op. cit., pp. 55–6.
21. Bengio, op. cit., pp. 4–5, and a series of FBIS (Foreign Broadcast Information Service) transcripts, May–August 1989 and April 3 and May 8–9, 1990.

10 FROM JERUSALEM TO WASHINGTON: AN ALLIANCE STRENGTHENED AND CONFIRMED

1. Black and Morris, op. cit., pp. 519–21; author's interview with Jalal Talabani, head of the Patriotic Union of Kurdistan, London, April 1991.

2. See Cooley, *Payback*, p. 125, p. 229.

3. Black and Morris, op. cit., pp. 517–18.

4. Gemini News Service, London, "A Big Boost for Suppliers," undated, reprinted by World Press Review, Stanley Foundation, New York, April 1991 and 2003 (brochure), pp. 21–2.

5. Cooley, *Payback*, pp. 185–7.

6. Cooley, *Payback*, pp. 188–90, and private conversation with Glaspie in Jerusalem, March 1992 (subsequent to publication of *Payback*).

7. Author's own notes and reports to ABC Radio News from Cairo, August 10, 1990.

8. U.S. News and World Report, *Triumph Without Victory: The Unreported History of the Persian Gulf War* (New York, Times Books, Random House, 1992), pp. 131–5.

9. Cooley, *Payback*, pp. 216–18; conversation with Ze'ev Schiff, Tel Aviv, February 2004.

10. *U.S. News*, pp. 247–50.

11. Cooley, *Payback*, p. 215.

12. Uri Dan, "Saddam's Head," *Jerusalem Post*, March 18, 1999, online, pp. 1–2.; Leslie Susser, "Target: Saddam," The Jerusalem Report.com, December 17, 2003; pp. 1–2; Ze'ev Schiff, "The Assassination that never took place," *Haaretz*, December 17, 2003, online; Dan Baron, "Israel says 1992 accident came," *Jewish Telegraph Agency*, December 16, 2003.

13. Robin Wright, "America's Iraq Policy: How Did it Come to This?" *Washington Quarterly*, Summer 1998, online, p. 5; hereinafter as Robin Wright.

14. Hans Leyendecker, "In the Belly of the Beast," Sueddeutsche Zeitung, Munich, November 25, 1997, in *World Press Review*, February 1998, pp. 26–7.

15. Cockburn and Cockburn, *Out of the Ashes*, pp. 165–71.

16. Aburish, op. cit., pp. 340–9.

17. Quoted in Robin Wright, op. cit., pp. 9–10

18. Robin Wright, op. cit., p. 11, pp. 15–17.

19. My listing and characterization closely follows Elizabeth Drew, "The Neocons in Power," *New York Review of Books*, June 12, 2003, p. 1 of online text.

20. Quoted by Wilhelm Dietl, *Schwarzbuch Weisses Haus: Aussenpolitik mit dem Sturmgewehr* (The Black Book of the White House: Foreign Policy With An Assault Rifle), (Erfstadt, Germany, Area Verlag 2004), p. 31.

21. Drew, op. cit., pp. 2–3.

22. Quotations from the original document in Bill and Kathleen Christison, "Too many Smoking Guns to Ignore: Israel, American Jews and the War on Iraq," *Counterpunch* newsletter, January 25, 2003, p. 1 and passim; "U.S.–Israeli interests in Iraq," cooperative research.Org, pp. 19–20.

23. Julie Kosterlitz, "The Neoconservative Moment," *National Journal*, May 17, 2003, online, p. 3.

11 ENDGAME: IRAQ DEMOCRATIZED OR DISMEMBERED?

1. M. J. Cohen and John Major, *History in Quotations* (London, Cassell, 2004), p. 942.

2. Richard A. Clarke, *Against All Enemies: Inside America's War on Terror* (New York, Free Press, Simon and Schuster, 2004), pp. 30–2.

3. Ron Suskind, *The Price of Loyalty: George W. Bush, the White House, and the Education of Paul O'Neill* (New York, Simon and Schuster, 2004), pp. 82–6.
4. Clarke, op. cit., pp. 95–6, in part quoting a report by Jason Vest in the *Village Voice*, November 27, 2001.
5. Suskind, op. cit., p. 129.
6. Suskind, op. cit., p. 172.
7. Suskind, op. cit., p. 71.
8. Karen Kwiatkowski, "In Rumsfeld's Shop: A Senior Air Force Officer Watches as the Neocons Consolidate their Pentagon Coups," The *American Conservative*, p. 2, online.
9. Seymour M. Hersh, "Selective Intelligence," *New Yorker*, May 12, 2003, online, posted May 5, 2003, pp. 1–2.
10. "United Defense," AIPAC brief, October 24, 2003, pp. 1–2, online.
11. Clarke, op. cit., p. 183.
12. Fareed Zakaria, "'Disarming Iraq': Lack of Evidence," *New York Times* book review, April 11, 2004, online, pp. 1–2.
13. Bill and Kathleen Christison, op. cit., p. 18, online.
14. Clarke, op. cit., p. 67.
15. Shai Feldman, "Dilemmas Facing the Second Sharon Government," *JCSS Strategic Assessment*, Vol. 5, No. 4, pp. 1, 3.
16. Maj. Gen. Amos Gilad, "A New Palestinian Agenda After Iraq?" *Jerusalem Issue Brief*, Vol. 2, No. 10, October 29, 2002, pp. 1, 4.
17. Maj. Gen. Ya'akov Amidror, "Israel's Strategy After the Iraq War," *Jerusalem Issue Brief*, Vol. 2, No. 24, April 16, 2003, pp. 1, 2, 5.
18. International Institute for Strategic Studies, *The Military Balance 2003–2004* (London, Oxford University Press for the IISS, 2003), p. 98, and daily news reports.
19. Michael Gordon, "U.S. Forces Defeat Saddam, Then Face Guerilla Attacks," and Timothy L. O'Brien, "At the UN, Bitterness Persists After the War," *The New York Times Almanac 2004*, pp. 17–19; news reports and personal interviews, winter and spring, 2003–2004.
20. Ari Shavit, "The Waiting Game," *Haaretz*, September 4, 2003, online. The author covered the Mashal episode and aftermath for ABC News in Amman.
21. Ronen Bergman, "New Boy at Mossad," *Yediot Aharonot*, April 22, 2003, online: a long and detailed article about the internal politics of Mossad.
22. Shomo Brom, "An Intelligence Failure?" *JCSS Strategic Assessment*, Vol. 6, No. 3, November 2003, pp. 8–9; BBC News Report, online, December 12, 2003.
23. *Jerusalem Post*, December 7, 1997, online; *Jane's Foreign Report*, December 14, 1998, pp. 1–2; *Washington Post*, December 6, 1997, p. A22; *Washington Times*, December 7, 1997, p. A6.
24. Ze'ev Schiff, "The Lesson of Iraq," *Haaretz*, April 2, 2004, online.
25. Amnon Barzilal, "U.S. Army Wants to Buy more Israeli Hunter Drones," *Haaretz*, July 8, 2003, online.
26. Cameron W. Barr, "U.S. Eyes Israeli Software as Training Tool for Forces in Iraq," *Christian Science Monitor*, September 29, 2003, online.
27. Richard Sale, "Pollard Recruiter Resurfaces in U.S.," *United Press International*, July 11, 2003, online.
28. James Bennet, "U.S. Military Studied Israel's Experience in Close-Quarter Fighting in Refugee Camps," *New York Times*, April 1, 2003, online, pp. 1–2.

29. Bennet, op. cit., p.2; Seymour M. Hersh, "Moving Targets," *New Yorker*, December 15, 2003, online, pp. 1–8, passim, online; John Borger, "Israel Trains U.S. Assassination Squads in Iraq," *Guardian Unlimited*, December 9, 2003, pp. 1–3 online.

30. Seymour Hersh, "Torture at Abu Ghraib," May 10, 2004; "Chain of Command," May 17, 2004; "The Gray Zone," *New Yorker*, May 10, 17, and 24, 2004; Dana Priest and Joe Stevens, "Secret World of U.S. Interrogation," *Washington Post*, May 11, 2004; Helena Cobban, "A Matter of Culpability in Iraq," *Christian Science Monitor*, May 13, 2004, online; "La rapport du CICR sur le traitement des prisonniers Irakiens," *Le Monde*, May 13, 2004, online; Susan Sontag, "Regarding the Torture of Others," *New York Times Magazine*, May 23, 2004, online; Eitan Feiner, "The Painful Lesson Israel Learned About Torture," *International Herald Tribune*, June 1, 2004, online; Yossi Melman, "All Evidence Refutes Claims of Israeli Involvement in Iraqi Prison Affair," *Haaretz*, May 19, 2004, online.

31. Seymour Hersh, "Plan B," *New Yorker*, June 28, 2004, online; Mathew Gutman, "Israeli Intelligence Agents Infiltrating Iran—Report," *Jerusalem Post*, June 20, 2004, online; "Five Kurdish Rebels Killed, Turkish Soldier Wounded in Clash," AFP from Diyarbakir, June 21, 2004.

32. IISS, Strategic Survey 2003/4, *An Evaluation and Forecast of World Affairs* (Oxford University Press for the IISS 2004), pp. 165–70.

33. William Pfaff, "Europe Should Take its Own Mideast Stand," *International Herald Tribune*, July 12, 2004, op-ed page.

34. The quotes and some of these ideas I owe to an edited extract from an updated version of David Hirst's classic, *The Gun and the Olive Branch*, the first edition of which appeared 25 years ago. The extract appeared in the *Observer*, Sunday September 21, 2003, online.

35. Given to me in an interview with Sadat in Cairo, October 1974.

Selected Bibliography

BOOKS

Aburish, Said, *Saddam Hussein: The Politics of Revenge*, London, Trafalgar, 2001.

Ali El-Edroos, Brig. (ret.) Syed, *The Hashemite Arab Army 1908–1979: An Appreciation and Analysis of Military Operations*, Amman, Publishing Committee, 1980.

Ali, Tariq, *Bush in Babylon*, London and New York, Verso, 2003.

Batatu, Hanna, *The Old Social Classes and the Revolutionary Movements of Iraq*, Princeton University Press, 1978.

Black, Ian and Morris, Benny, *Israel's Secret Wars: A History of Israel's Intelligence Services*, New York, Grove Press, 1991.

Ben-Porat, Mordecai, *To Baghdad and Back: The Miraculous 2,000-Year Homecoming of the Iraqi Jews*, Jerusalem and New York, Gefen Publishing House, 1998.

Clarke, Richard A., *Against All Enemies: Inside America's War on Terror*, New York, Free Press, Simon and Schuster, 2004.

Cockburn, Andrew and Cockburn, Leslie, *Dangerous Liaison, the Inside Story of the U.S.–Israel Covert Relationship*, New York, Harper Perennial, Harper-Collins, 1992.

Cooley, John K., *Green March, Black September: The Story of the Palestinian Arabs*, London, Frank Cass, 1973.

—— *Payback: America's Long War in the Middle East*, London and New York, Brasseys, 1991.

—— *Unholy Wars: Afghanistan, America and International Terrorism*, London and Sterling, Va., Pluto, 1999, 2000 and 2003.

Copeland, Miles, *The Game of Nations: The Amorality of Power Politics*, London, Weidenfeld and Nicolson, 1969–70.

Coughlin, Con, *Saddam: The Secret Life*, London, Pan Macmillan, 2002.

Dietl, Wilhelm, *Schwarzbuch, Weisses Haus: Aussenpolitik mit dem Sturmgewehr* (The Black Book of the White House: Foreign Policy With an Assault Rifle), Erfstadt, Germany, Area Verlag, 2004.

Dorril, Stephen, *MI-6: Inside the Covert World of Her Majesty's Secret Intelligence Service*, New York and London, Simon and Schuster, 2000.

Fischer, Rudolph, *Babylon: Entdeckungsreisen in die Vergangenheit* (Babylon: Voyages of Discovery in the Past), Thienemann, Edition Erdmann, undated.

Friedman, Alan, *Spider's Web: Bush, Saddam, Thatcher and the Decade of Deceit*, Boston, Faber and Faber, 1993.

Fromkin, David, *A Peace to End All Peace: The Fall of the Ottoman Empire and the Creation of the Modern Middle East*, New York, Henry Holt, 1989.

Ghareeb, Edmund, *The Kurdish Question in Iraq*, Syracuse University Press, 1981.

Heller, Joseph, *The Birth of Israel 1945–1949: Ben-Gurion and His Critics*, Gainsville, University Press of Florida, 1975.

Hillel, Shlomo, *Operation Babylon: Jewish Clandestine Activity in the Middle East 1945–51*, Glasgow, Fontana/Collins, 1985.

Hirst, David, *The Gun and the Olive Branch: The Roots of Violence in the Middle East*, London, Faber and Faber, 2002.

IISS (International Institute of Strategic Studies), *The Military Balance 2001–2002* and *The Military Balance 2003–2004*, London, Oxford University Press, 2003 and 2004.

—— *Strategic Survey 2003–2004: An Evaluation and Forecast of World Affairs*, Oxford University Press, 2004).

Issacson, Walter, *Kissinger: A Biography*, New York, Simon and Schuster, 1992.

Kissinger, Henry, *Years of Renewal*, New York, Simon and Schuster, 1999.

Mackey, Sandra, *The Reckoning: Iraq and the Legacy of Saddam Hussein*, New York, Norton, 2002.

Mansfield, Peter, *A History of the Middle East*, Second Edition, revised and updated by Nicholas Pelham, London, Penguin Books, 2003.

Napoleoni, Loretta, *Modern Jihad: Tracing the Dollars Behind the Terror Networks*, London and Sterling, Va., Pluto, 2003.

Nimrodi, Jackob, (in Hebrew) *My Life's Journey*, Or Yehuda, Israel, Ma'ariv Book Guild, 2 vols., 2003.

Oren, Michael B., *Six Days of War: June 1967 and the Making of the Modern Middle East*, New York, Ballantine Books, 2002, 2003.

Segev, Samuel, *The Iranian Triangle: The Untold Story of Israel's Role in the Iran–Contra Affair*, New York, Macmillan, Free Press, 1988.

Shlaim, Avi, *Collusion Across the Jordan: King Abdallah and the Partition of Palestine, 1921–1951*, Oxford, Clarendon, 1998.

—— *The Politics of Partition: King Abdallah, the Zionist Movement, the Zionists and Palestine*, Oxford, Oxford University Press, 1990.

Farouk-Sluglett, Marion and Sluglett, Peter, *Iraq Since 1958: From Revolution to Dictatorship*, London and New York, I. B. Tauris, 1998.

Suskind, Ron, *The Price of Loyalty: George W. Bush and the Education of Paul O'Neill*, New York, Simon and Schuster, 2004.

Thomas, Gordon, *Gideon's Spies: the Secret History of the Mossad*, New York, St. Martin's Press, 1999.

Weizman, Ezer, *The Battle for Peace*, New York, Bantam, 1981.

Westerby, Gerald, *In Hostile Territory: Business Secrets of a Mossad Combatant*, New York, Harper Business, Harper Collins, 1998.

Woodward, Bob, *Plan of Attack*, New York, Simon and Schuster, 2004.

Woolfson, Marian, *Prophets in Babylon: Jews in the Arab World*, London and Boston, Faber and Faber, 1980.

Young, Gavin, *Iraq: Land of Two Rivers*, Photos by Nik Wheeler, London, Collins, 1980.

WORKS OF REFERENCE

Arberry, A. J. (ed.), *Religion in the Middle East*, Vol. I, *Judaism and Christianity*, Cambridge University Press, 1969.

Cohen, M. J. and Major, John, *History in Quotations*, London, Cassell, 2004.

Lockyer, Herbert (ed.), *The Hodder and Stoughton Illustrated Bible Dictionary*, Nashville, Ky., Thomas Nelson, 1986.

New York Times Almanac, 2004.

ARTICLES, EXTRACTS, AND TRANSCRIPTS

AIPAC Brief, "United Defense," America–Israel Public Affairs Committee, October 24, 2003

Amidror, Maj. Gen. Ya'akov, "Israel's Strategy After the Iraq War" *Jerusalem Issue Briefs*, Vol. 2, No. 24, April 16, 2003.

Anon., "Ancient Babylon," The History of the Ancient Near East, Electronic Compendium, online newsletter, undated.

Anon., "The Jews of Iraq," *The Link*, Americans for Middle East Understanding, Inc., Vol. 31, No. 2, April–May 1998.

Anon., "James H. Critchfield Obituary," Arlington National Cemetery website, April 23, 2000.

Anon., "U.S. Plans to Keep Bases in Iraq," *Guardian Weekly*, April 24–30, 2003.

Anon. "Behind the War in Iraq," *Monthly Review*, May 1, 2003.

Anon., "Five Kurdish Rebels Killed in Clash," AFP dispatch, Diyarbakir, June 21, 2004.

Barr, Cameron, "U.S. Eyes Israeli Software as Training Tool for Forces in Iraq," *Christian Science Monitor*, September 29, 2003, online.

Baron, Dan, "Israel Says 1992 Accident Came," Jewish Telegraph Agency, December 16, 2003.

Barzilal, Amnon, "U.S. Army Wants to Buy More Israeli Hunter Drones,"*Haaretz*, July 8, 2003.

Bayme, Steven, "Iraq, Babylon and Baghad in Jewish History and Thought," American Jewish Committee brief, June 1, 2003.

Bengio, Ofra, "Crossing the Rubicon? Iraq and the Arab–Israel Peace Process," *MERIA*, Tel Aviv University, Vol. 2, No. 4, March 1998.

Bennet, James, "U.S. Military Studied Israel's Experience in Close-Quarter Fighting in Refugee Camps," *New York Times*, April 1, 2003.

Bergman, Ronen, "New Boy at Mossad," *Yediot Aharanot*, April 22, 2003.

Block, Melissa, National Public Radio's "All Things Considered," transcript, August 6, 2003.

British Embassy in Baghdad, "Biographic Sketch of Saddam Hussein," November 15, 1969. Public Record Office, London, FCO 17/871, summarized by National Security Archive, Washington, DC, online, December 20, 2003.

Brom, Brig. Gen. (ret.) Shlomo, "An Intelligence Failure?" *JCSS Strategic Assessment*, Vol. 6, No. 3.

Brook, Kevin Alan, "The Genetic Bonds Between Kurds and Jews," undated, online at www.barzan.com.

Christison, Bill and Christison, Kathleen, "Too Many Smoking Guns to Ignore: Israel, American Jews and the War in Iraq," *Counterpunch* newsletter, January 25, 2003.

CICR, Geneva (International Committee of the Red Cross), "La rapport du CICR sur le traitement des prisonniers Irakiens," *Le Monde*, May 13, 2004 (extracts).

Cobban Helena, "A Matter of Culpability in Iraq," *Christian Science Monitor*, May 13, 2004.

Cooley, John K., "The U.S. Pushes "Regime Change" at its Peril," *International Herald Tribune*, November 18, 2003.

Dan, Uri, "Saddam's Head," *Jerusalem Post*, March 18, 1999.

Dinsmore, Lee, "The Forgotten Kurds," *The Progressive*, April 1977.

Drew, Elizabeth, "The Neocons in Power," *New York Review of Books*, June 12, 2003.

FBIS (Foreign Broadcast Information Service), Washington: transcripts, May–August 1989 and April 3 and May 8–9, 1990.

Feiner, Eitan, "The Painful Lesson Israel Learned About Torture," *International Herald Tribune*, June 1, 2004.

Feldman, Shai, "Dilemmas Facing the Second Sharon Government," *Strategic Assessments*, Vol. 5, No. 4, 2003.

Gemini News Service, London, "A Big Boost for Suppliers," undated, reprinted by *World Press Review*, Stanley Foundation, New York, April 1999 and 2003, brochure.

Gilad, Maj. Gen. Amos, "A New Palestinian Agenda After Iraq," *Jerusalem Issue Briefs*, Vol. 2, No. 10, April 16, 2003.

Gutman, Mathew, "Israeli Intelligence Agents Infiltrating Iran—Report," *Jerusalem Post*, June 20, 2004, online.

Hersh, Seymour, "Torture at Abu Ghraib," May 10, 2004; "Select Intelligence," May 12, 2004; "Chain of Command," May 17, 2004; "Plan B," June 28, 2004, *New Yorker*.

Karpel, Dalia, "It Could Have Been Paradise Here," *Haaretz*, Oct. 29, 2003.

Kosterlitz, Julie, "The Neoconservative Moment," *National Journal*, May 17, 2003.

Kwiatowski, Karen, "In Rumsfeld's Shop: A Senior Air Force Officer Watches as the Neocons Consolidate Their Pentagon Coups," *The American Conservative*, undated, online.

MacFarquhar, Neil, "Outdoing Nebuchadnezzar," *International Herald Tribune*, August 20, 2003.

Marcus, Raise, "Flight from Babylon," *Jerusalem Post*, August 23, 1996.

Melman, Yossi, "All Evidence Refutes Claims of Israeli Involvement in Iraqi Prison Affair," *Haaretz*, May 19, 2004.

National Security Archive updates, The Saddam Hussein Sourcebook, December 18, 2003; Docs. 44, 47, 48, 58, 62.

Neff, Donald, "Israel Bomb's Iraq's Osirak Nuclear Research Facility," *Washington Report On Middle East Affairs*, June 1995.

Pfaff, William, "Europe Should Take Its Own Mideast Stand," *International Herald Tribune*, July 12, 2004.

Priest, Dana and Stevens, Joe, "The Secret World of U.S. Interrogation," *Washington Post*, May 11, 2004.

Salahadin, Masseef, AFP dispatch from Kurdistan, April 29, 2003.

Sale, Richard, "Pollard Recruiter Resurfaces in U.S.," UPI dispatch, Washington, July 11, 2003.

Schiff, Ze'ev, "The Assassination that Never Took Place," December 17, 2003; "The Lesson of Iraq," April 2, 2004, *Haaretz*.

Sedan, G. H., "Consulate Attack Marks Low Point in Israeli–Kurdish Relations," Jewish Telegraph Agency dispatch in *Jewish News of Greater Phoenix* [Arizona], February 26, 1999, online.

Shapiro, Sraya, "Bye-Bye Baghdad," *Jerusalem Post*, November 12, 1998.

Shavit, Ari, "The Waiting Game," *Haaretz*, September 4, 2003.

Sontag, Susan, "Regarding the Torture of Others," *New York Times Magazine*, May 23, 2004.

Susser, Leslie, "Target, Saddam," *Jerusalem Post*, December 13, 2003, online.

Tamari, Dov, "The Influence of the Peripheral Arab States on Arab–Israel Wars," brief, Jaffee Center, Center for Strategic Studies, Tel Aviv University, undated.

Wright, Robin, "America's Iraq Policy: How Did it Come to This?" *Washington Quarterly*, Summer 1998.

Zakaria, Fareed, "Disarming Iraq: Lack of Evidence," *New York Times Book Review*, April 11, 2004.

Index